CultureShock!

A Survival Guide to Customs and Etiquette

Laos

Robert Cooper

Marshall Cavendish
Editions

This 2nd edition published in 2011 by:
Marshall Cavendish Corporation
99 White Plains Road
Tarrytown, NY 10591-9001
www.marshallcavendish.us

First published in 2008.

Other Marshall Cavendish Offices:
Marshall Cavendish International (Asia) Private Limited. 1 New Industrial Road, Singapore 536196 ■ Marshall Cavendish International. PO Box 65829, London EC1P 1NY, UK ■ Marshall Cavendish International (Thailand) Co Ltd. 253 Asoke, 12th Flr, Sukhumvit 21 Road, Klongtoey Nua, Wattana, Bangkok 10110, Thailand ■ Marshall Cavendish (Malaysia) Sdn Bhd, Times Subang, Lot 46, Subang Hi-Tech Industrial Park, Batu Tiga, 40000 Shah Alam, Selangor Darul Ehsan, Malaysia

Marshall Cavendish is a trademark of Times Publishing Limited

ISBN: 978-0-7614-5871-5

Please contact the publisher for the Library of Congress catalogue number

Printed in Singapore by Times Printing Pte Ltd

Photo Credits:
All black and white photos by the author. All colour photos from Photolibrary except pages a, f–g, l–m (Getty Images).
■ Cover photo: Photolibrary.

All illustrations by TRIGG

ABOUT THE SERIES

Culture shock is a state of disorientation that can come over anyone who has been thrust into unknown surroundings, away from one's comfort zone. *CultureShock!* is a series of trusted and reputed guides which has, for decades, been helping expatriates and long-term visitors to cushion the impact of culture shock whenever they move to a new country.

Written by people who have lived in the country and experienced culture shock themselves, the authors share all the information necessary for anyone to cope with these feelings of disorientation more effectively. The guides are written in a style that is easy to read and covers a range of topics that will arm readers with enough advice, hints and tips to make their lives as normal as possible again.

Each book is structured in the same manner. It begins with the first impressions that visitors will have of that city or country. To understand a culture, one must first understand the people—where they came from, who they are, the values and traditions they live by, as well as their customs and etiquette. This is covered in the first half of the book.

Then on with the practical aspects—how to settle in with the greatest of ease. Authors walk readers through topics such as how to find accommodation, get the utilities and telecommunications up and running, enrol the children in school and keep in the pink of health. But that's not all. Once the essentials are out of the way, venture out and try the food, enjoy more of the culture and travel to other areas. Then be immersed in the language of the country before discovering more about the business side of things.

To round off, snippets of basic information are offered before readers are 'tested' on customs and etiquette of the country. Useful words and phrases, a comprehensive resource guide and list of books for further research are also included for easy reference.

CONTENTS

Chapter 7
Enjoying the Culture 216

Chapter 8
Learning Lao 239

Chapter 9
Lao Business 249

Chapter 10
Fast Facts at Your Fingertips 268

FOREWORD

What is a Lao? Who are we talking about? In a way, this whole book is a definition of 'Lao'. I use 'Lao' in the broadest cultural sense to mean a species of Man sharing common attributes and a common self-identity and in the geo-political sense as an inhabitant or citizen of the country known, among other names, as Laos. When precision is necessary to differentiate between ethnic groups of Lao citizens, I provide it by adding a qualifier: Lao Loum (Lowland Lao), Lao Hmong, Lao Khmu, etc.

I use Laos to refer to the country where most Lao live or originated. The country's official name is The Lao PDR, which is itself short for The Lao People's Democratic Republic. I use the alternative 'Laos', as a convenient shorthand, to make things easier for the reader and the writer. I am aware that the Lao in daily conversation call their country 'Lao', with no 's', and I am aware that foreigners visiting Laos often refer to it in English as 'Lao' rather than 'Laos'. While the 's' was added by French colonialists, the word Laos, with a pronounced 's', avoids the possible confusion of referring to the country, people and language by a single word: Lao. The term Laos is also the term most often found in literature on the country written in English, and the term for the country used by all current guides to Laos. Nowhere in this book do I refer to a plurality of Lao by adding an 's' to the ethnic or political term.

As will become evident in the section on People, not all citizens of Laos are Lao in the sense of being Lao Loum, and not all Lao citizens speak Lao as their mother tongue or share many common attributes with the Lao Loum. This book makes occasional mention of Lao citizens of minority ethnicities and languages, who together make up perhaps 30–40 per cent of the population (depending how you count), but is concerned principally with the culture of the Lao Loum, and how the foreigner in Laos can best co-exist with that culture, and how s/he can best do certain things, and best not do certain things in Laos. 'Things' being actions that might have required very little thought in the visitor's country of origin, but could require a search for information and advice in Laos. This book provides that information and advice, but because not all Lao are the same and not all foreigners are the same, it cannot be exhaustive. It aims to set the foreigner in situations and enhance skills of interaction.

This book is at one and the same time a guide to the Lao and to those aspects of Laos of which a foreigner staying awhile should be aware. It is an advisory, not a Bible, and like all advisories will be updated from time to time as Lao and Laos change. It offers non-Lao a shortcut to understanding the Lao and a fast-track to functioning within slow-track Laos. It is not simply a list of do's and don'ts: the non-Lao visitor is a foreign guest and should first and foremost enjoy Laos and the Lao. The best way of doing that is to allow that the Lao are going to do many things differently to the way you are used to and avoid providing Lao with any reason not to respect you. At the same time, do not become overly-preoccupied with details of daily life that would not worry the Lao themselves.

Robert Cooper

NOTES

Any book written in English and dealing with Laos is going to use transliteration of Lao names and common words. Since there is no standard system in use, writers tend to pick and choose and make up depending on what they think best represents the sound as it would be made by a Lao. So do I.

I do not change transliterations of place names that have become established: thus I keep Vientiane, knowing that a reader is likely to pronounce it Vi-en-ti-arn, rather than Wien-jan, which is closer to a Lao pronunciation of the capital city. Similarly, I keep Luang Prabang, which probably was pronounced almost like that a few hundred years ago but is today pronounced Louang Pha-bang by most Lao. Where transliterations have changed, I use the new version which usually comes closest to actual pronunciation—thus Sanyabouli, not Xayaburi. I am aware that most English readers will mispronounce Lane Xang and that it would be better rendered Lan Sang, but I keep Lane Xang for the name of the Avenue and hotel in Vientiane and the original name of the country, because such forms are now institutionalised in the literature and place signs. I don't throw out all French-origin transliterations—'boun' is better than the usual English transliteration frequently used in Thailand (*bun*) because pronunciation of the word rhymes with 'moon' not 'sun'. Similarly, I use 'touk-touk' for the vehicles, not 'tuk-tuk' as it rhymes with look-look not f*ck-f*ck. I do not use 'k' when it is pronounced 'g'—so I do not write 'kin khaw' but 'gin khao'. I write Mekong, not Mekhong, Vieng Sai, not Vieng Xai, and keep the accepted That Luang, making the point here that every Lao word written with 'th' is pronounced with an aspirated 't'; the English 'th' does not exist in Lao. Also 'ph' is pronounced as an aspirated 'p', like the English Peter not the French Pierre, and not like the English 'phone' or the Vietnamese *pho*. Like other writers in English or French on Laos, I do not in the text attempt to include the tone of a word in transliteration—however, this is done in the Glossary at the end of the book; thus any reader learning Lao can refer to those pages.

A few words have been brought into Laos from Thailand, mostly by foreigners. Chief among these is 'falang' (*farang* in Thai). Many foreigners use the word in Laos as they would use it in Thailand, to mean any European-origin person, including South African, Australian, etc. This is a useful word in Thailand, since Thais use it with this meaning. Lao also use it, but with the meaning of 'French'. Since the word now has an ambiguity, I avoid it and stick to 'foreigner' or 'visitor' or 'expat'.

Some English translations of Lao words take on a meaning in Laos different to that in Europe. Where these are commonly used, I use them. Thus the English word 'village' in England means a small rural community. In the Laos sense, *baan* means both the rural community and an administrative section of a town. So Vientiane really is a collection of villages. If use of 'village' to mean rural community and urban quarter confuses you, just think how English uses the word 'country' in two senses which are really quite different. If you want to make it clear in Lao that you refer to a rural village, you can always say *mu-baan* (literally friend-locality not domestic pig —get the tone right), which is unambiguously rural.

Another translation that I keep is 'militia', which sounds a lot more military than *thamnuat baan* (literally: village police). Since these guys like to dress up in camouflage suits and carry much heavier armaments than the regular police, and look a lot more fierce, 'militia' is perhaps more appropriate than the far sweeter term 'village police', which conjures up an image of a cheerful bobby on a push-bike.

In time, 'standard' Lao will be more actively promoted—in fact this is already happening and evident in Lao TV news and most government speeches and newspapers. Once this process has completed and there is clearly a recognised and used standard Lao language, perhaps a better system of transliteration into English will follow. At the moment, however, a Lao word can be transliterated almost any way you want to write it. Which often means that a reader can understand it in any way he wants to understand or misunderstand it. In the end, I try my best and hope that my transliterations and translations help rather than confuse.

A WORD ON CULTURE SHOCK

Culture shock is not necessarily a negative condition. The term does imply a shock to the senses induced by a sudden meeting with a social environment very different to that which your body and mind is used to. Perhaps shock is too strong a word. Surprise might be a better word. But the phrase Culture Shock is now part of the English language and the name of a very successful series of books dealing with major cultures of the world, so I am not about to introduce a new concept-term—even if I could think of one more appropriate.

Having taught and written on culture shock for 25 years, I know it exists as both an acute and chronic condition. I am also aware that people respond to it differently, depending on many factors, not least their own personality and history. Thus no two individuals are going to experience 'exculturation' in precisely the same way even if they arrive in the same place at the same time. But all foreigners in a strange land will feel something of the disorientation known as culture shock, and all will find that learning about the new country and culture into which they are transplanted pays dividends in making their life in a new cultural world far less problematic and far more enjoyable.

Culture shock is not a linear experience. Most people go through several stages. They begin by being either enrapt and enchanted or discouraged and even disgusted, they pass through a state of confusion, and eventually most come to terms with their new situation: a foreigner functioning in a culture that is not his or her home culture. If you do not expect too much, learn to cope with failure and success, and above all, maintain or develop a sense of humour, you will have a good rather than a bad time.

MAP OF LAOS

CHINA

MYANMAR

VIETNAM

LAOS

GULF OF
TONKIN

● VIENTIANE

THAILAND

CAMBODIA

FIRST IMPRESSIONS

CHAPTER 1

'Keep your eyes and ears wide open,
keep your thoughts in your head,
and keep your elephants well fed.'
—Chao Anou, Lao king advising his army
during the Lao-Siam war that ended in 1828.

FOR THE PAST YEAR, I have been asking new arrivals to Laos who visit my book shop in central Vientiane, what they think of the country.

Beautiful country: beautiful people. This sums up most of the first impressions of visitors to Laos. And it's really not a bad standpoint from which to begin to explore the heart of Laos and the Lao. Keep repeating it, like a mantra, and the Lao will love you, and you have the makings of a self-fulfilling prophecy. Visitors feel welcome, have no great hassles, and interaction with Lao, if somewhat superficial and hampered by a language barrier, is overwhelmingly sympathetic. Laos is not the land of the hard sell, people smile much of the time, and you never hear the cry 'Hey, You.' Of course, first impressions are by nature superficial and do not delve beneath the surface to a more meaningful reality—if they did, you would not need this book.

For the past year, I have also been asking my Lao staff of the same bookshop for their impressions of the foreigners entering the shop. At first they were reluctant to have any impression at all. Then I began to interpret for them what the foreigners impression was of the Lao, and *khwam khit nay chay* ('thinking in the heart'—the nearest I can get to the Lao for 'impression') became a game between us: placing foreigners into different categories, just as the foreigners were placing the Lao. It wasn't a Lao game, but I learnt a lot about Lao, and the Lao for the first time were giving their impressions of foreigners to a foreigner. But it was only a game. I will come back to the subject of Lao first impressions of foreigners, but first, let's get your first impressions sorted out.

The most important thing about first impressions is that if these are bad, they often preclude the possibility of second or third impressions qualifying the picture. If, on the other hand, they are just a bit too rosy, they might lead on to disappointment, as if in some way people had set out to deceive you. If you recognize that there will be ups and downs in your perception of the Lao and their ways—and this is what culture shock is all about—the highs and lows won't flatten out completely, but your psyche may be easier for you and for the Lao to live with. Euphoria, Yes. Depression, No.

First impressions are only first if they come from first-timers. And Laos being the landlocked 'Land in Between', first impressions are as largely influenced by the country the visitor was just in as by comparison with the home country. First impressions cannot exist in a vacuum; they are always comparative.

First impressions of Laos are also almost entirely first impressions of Vientiane: over 90 per cent of visitors come into Vientiane as their point of arrival. Most of the remaining 10 per cent have been to Vietnam first and cross into Laos in the east. Comparatively few come up overland from Cambodia and down from China. All come knowing that Vientiane is the capital city, and almost all think or know that Laos is communist—although they don't know that Lao government documentation, in Lao or in English, never uses the word communist. First impressions of those who have never been here before therefore have a lot to do with preconceptions. So what we are talking about here is first impressions of Vientiane compared to some place outside Laos and the preconceptions of a 'communist state'.

By the time they have been to a few large cities in Southeast Asia (excluding Singapore), travellers are usually at the point where they expect any capital to be a *tour de force*: somewhere to grapple with the horrors of congestion and pollution, come to terms with the difficulty of getting around and signs they don't understand, learn to ignore the persistent touts on every corner and allow effort, money and time to settle in and do the simplest things. This is perhaps less 'culture' shock as 'third-world city' shock. Good news: this does not apply to Vientiane.

Whether they come from the airport and are in the centre of town in ten minutes or come across the land bridge from Thailand and travel 25 km to Vientiane, visitors are all pleasantly relieved to find the capital of Laos unlike the other cities they have seen. Those coming direct from Bangkok or Hanoi are genuinely delighted that they can do the simplest things of life—like cross the street—without making it a major expedition. They are also pleased at finding themselves in the town centre while still looking for it.

Sure, Vientiane can be so hot in April and May that anybody is going to complain about the weather, and even before then, in the beautiful 'winter' months, it can be dusty if the wind stirs. But the atmosphere is unpolluted and the pace is visibly suburban. Visitors love the fact that they can walk to most places, and that the must-sees are set in almost a straight line from the President's Palace on the Riverside, up the Lane Xang Boulevard to the 'Monument', with a tiny detour to take in Wat Sisaket and Wat Pa Keo, and eat a cheap and simple lunch at the Morning Market. All of that can be got out of the way without any rush at all and you can still fit in the National Museum and be back at the guest house or hotel in time for an afternoon siesta before having a sundowner by the river, and taking in Vientiane's restaurant scene and night life.

On the first day in town, the newly-arrived visitors have to have their eyes open as they can never be fully open again. So, what do they see? An observant visitor notes the crumbling beauty of a French colonial building, probably not knowing that he is looking at the National Library, marvels at a beautifully renovated piece of the same architecture, probably not knowing that he is looking at the Asian Development Bank, and wonders at the feeling of calm while walking through a beautiful and sleepy Buddhist temple, not dreaming that this is the Buddhist University of Laos. The visitor might experience the pleasure of contrast when popping out of the hot Lao sun into an air-conditioned bank where he is seen efficiently, and, if he has visa and ID card in order, opens accounts in three currencies while having coffee with the Thai manager, and emerges with bundles of unfamiliarly-fascinating kip. He might be exposed to just enough adventure by taking a jumbo or *touk-touk* back to temporary accommodation where he finds that a Laotian kip can, in the middle of a humid day, be very nicely divided into forty winks. And the visitor rapidly comes to terms with the fact that he is now a millionaire in the banknote-only, wallet-straining currency of the Lao People's Democratic Republic.

The cold-war images of No Entry, No Photograph, no going where you like, no fraternization with the locals, no food, no service; all are simply flickers from an old cold-war movie. The cold war years left behind the mother of all impressions, and while a whole generation has grown up out of the cold, nobody has put the same efforts into demolishing the impression as was put into carefully fabricating it over many years. Laos is certainly not the austere communist state some visitors were expecting to find; at the same time, the occasional hammer and sickle on the Party's red flag, when one can be found, provides a safely-sanitized reminder that the visitors are comfortably cocooned in an exotic side-line of world history.

So much for first impressions by foreigners. Laos scores highly, and the Lao don't have to lift a finger to get top marks. Now, what impression do the Lao have of these same foreigners?

They also use comparison in their judgment-impressions, and, subconsciously of course, they, just like the visitor, cannot detach their thoughts, feelings, and impressions, from the way they have been brought up to see the world.

The bookshop staff sees every day odd Lao walking up and down the street. Probably in most western countries all would be in an institution; here, they are an institution. Nothing dangerous about them. There is the woman, about forty, who went to Paris for a few years and came back a bit crazy. She walks the streets of the village (Vientiane is officially and appropriately divided into 'villages') dressed in her very finest and flamboyant traditional Lao clothes, all in red, with exaggerated make-up and swinging a handbag. She changes her clothes six times a day. She talks to no one. There is a 16-year old boy who walks a similar circuit, walks fast, dressed in a clean T-shirt, slacks and plastic shoes, eyes down to the road and talking to himself continuously. He talks to no one. There is another young man, early twenties, who wanders talking into an imaginary mobile phone, two fingers held up to an ear; he sometimes directs the traffic. He talks to no one. There is the woman dressed in dirty rags and barefoot, who carries a young baby on her shoulder. Her hair matted and unkempt, the baby crying in the hot sun or rain. She begs from everyone. All ignore her. She calls abuse at whoever goes by. There is a man who never wears a shirt or shoes and has long hair and a grim face, who talks to no one. Five people in one small street. Seen every day. No Lao would dream of interfering in their lives, not even for the baby's sake. But no Lao befriends them. They just exist in isolation; very 'un-Lao', yet very Lao. No one asks why.

Some of the foreign visitors to the bookshop, in fact probably half of them, come close to the image of the five lonely wanderers. Some of them go beyond that image. Some wear no shoes and dress in rags, their hair matted like Indian holy men. Their impression of the Lao might be good; the Lao impression of them is not good. Like the five wanderers, they live in a different world. Such foreigners inspire only fear in the Lao. They are strange and one should not get involved with them. If they want a book, it is sold to them. If they try to bargain, staff point at the fixed-prices sign. If they try to talk to any of the staff, the staff calls me to talk to the foreign devil. The Lao are confused about these people who obviously had enough money to come here but choose to walk barefoot and go unwashed and unkempt, and maybe order the cheapest tea and sit for hours. I must say I am equally confused about such people. They cause no trouble and they move on, so we do not get involved with them.

Not all bookshop customers are like this. Some come in with a smile and a hello in Lao. Some smell nice. Some even take off their shoes at the door in spite of supplications to keep them on. Some even buy books. These are the ones my Lao staff likes. These are the ones who get the free chocolate biscuit if they order coffee. And believe me, it is not simply a matter of being nice to those who have money—at least I don't think it is that simple.

First impressions, and probably second and third impressions, whether you are Lao or non-Lao, are based on what you see and hear around you. How people look, what they do and what they tell you, or choose to tell you.

Impressions contain some elements of truth, but can be very far from reality. If you are only passing through, never mind. Even then, it might not be long before you begin to wonder if you have really landed in paradise. And the fact of the matter is of course that you have not. If there is a paradise on earth, little landlocked Laos, with its life expectancy of some 57 years, is not the Shangri-la that so many people want it to be. Never mind. Once that illusion self-dissolves, you can get down to enjoying Laos for what it is.

AN OVERVIEW

CHAPTER 2

'Everybody gotta' be someplace.'
—Groucho Marx.

GEOGRAPHY

Laos is very much 'the land in between'. Surrounded on five sides by its neighbours, which from the North clockwise are: China, Vietnam, Cambodia, Thailand and Myanmar (Burma), Laos is landlocked and relies for trade on access to the ports of Thailand (Bangkok) and to a lesser extent, Danang in Vietnam. All five neighbours have been instrumental in the history and development of Laos as a nation. At times Laos, or parts of Laos, has been involved in wars with each neighbouring country and influences from its neighbours are evident in contemporary politics, ethnic make up, trade and industry, and international communications. The land in between is today an equal partner in ASEAN (Association of Southeast Asian Nations) and goes to lengths to live in productive peace with its neighbours.

Laos covers an area of 236,800 sq. km (91.429 sq. miles), which makes it a tad smaller than the United Kingdom and just under half the size of Thailand. Its land borders (which include those marked by the Mekong River) total 5,083 km (3.158 miles); 1,754 km (1,090 miles) with Thailand to the West, second only to Vietnam to the East, which has 2,130 km (1.324 miles) of common border with Laos.

A country of contrasting elevations, Laos has low altitudes of 70 m (230 ft) in the Lower Mekong region

Two Mekong-based cities: Vientiane above, dry season, Luang Prabang below, rainy season.

and highs up to Phu Bia's 2,817 m (9242 ft), in upland Xieng Khouang Province. Topographically, it is divided into the plain areas of Vientiane Province in the middle and Champassak Province in the south, both of which produce most of the country's rice, the high plateau areas in the northeast (the Plain of Jars in Xieng Khouang) and in the south (the coffee-growing Boloven Plateau), with most of the rest of the country taken by mountains and valleys. Arable land is estimated at around 4 per cent of the total surface area with irrigated land under 1 per cent of the total surface. For comparison, neighbouring Thailand has 30 per cent of its land designated as arable and 10 per cent of its surface area irrigated. Perhaps the most inaccessible part of the country is to be found in Khammuang Province, where a vast area of jagged limestone towers broken by deep, narrow gorges provides a helicopter experience that is as far out of this world as any planet surface known to Man.

Laos is comparatively sparsely populated, a factor which has encouraged migration from Vietnam, and the majority of its 6,993,767 citizens (2010 figures) live north of the median line which invisibly follows that part of the Mekong River through Vientiane. Laos may well be described as the land of hill farms and padi fields, with around 80 per cent of its population subsisting on some form of agriculture. Communications remain basic, with 4,590 km (2,852 miles) of paved road, which is about the same total length as all its waterways combined. The first passenger rail line was opened in 2009: three kilometres of line which crosses the First Friendship Bridge to the only railway station so far within Laos and makes possible a train journey from Bangkok into Laos.

The country's urban population is largely confined to Vientiane and smaller towns on the Mekong River, from North to South: Luang Prabang, Paksan, Savannakhet and Pakse. Smaller towns and larger villages are most often located on the banks of one of the many rivers in the country, some of which, like the Mekong itself, originate in a neighbouring country and almost all of which flow into the Mekong, which grows in volume until it floods a width of 14 km (8.7 miles) around the 'four thousand islands' area of Champassak and crosses into Cambodia.

> **The Mekong River**
> Known respectfully in Laos as the Mae Nam Kong, or simply as Mae Nam (Mother Water), the Mekong River has its source in the Tibetan Plateau in China. More of the River flows through Laos than any other Southeast Asian country. It is the habitat of the pa beuk, a fish which can grow up to three metres (10 ft) and weigh 300 kg (661 lbs), and of dolphins in the southern areas. The first Europeans to cross the Mekong included Marco Polo in the 13th century and the first bridge across the Mekong in Southeast Asia was the Thai-Lao Friendship Bridge completed in 1993. Long the major source of communication in Southeast Asia, the possibilities of blasting parts of the riverbed in Laos, to make it navigable all-year, is currently under consideration.

CLIMATE

The climate is tropical monsoonal, although some high parts of Laos are temperate or even cold for much of the year. The monsoon rains fall throughout May to October, which is the time of major crop cultivation. At the end of the rainy season, rivers are at their highest and most navigable, which is convenient for moving rice and other weighty loads, although most transportation now uses all-season roads that follow the Mekong and its major tributaries. Inland water within landlocked Laos is estimated at 6,000 sq km (2,317 sq. miles), almost three times that of Thailand, although there are significant seasonal variations in surface area as the country dries up during the short winter and the very hot months of February–April that precede the rainy season. Much of this water is to be found in reservoirs that feed the hydro-electricity dams. Flooding forests to create reservoirs is not without controversy, and if existing plans are completed on time, total inland water could double within the next five years, almost doubling exportation of electricity. How far this contributes to universal climate change is uncertain, on one hand large areas of forest land are harvested or destroyed, but on the other hand hydro-power is a lot cleaner than fossil fuels.

ENVIRONMENT

Dams and hydro-projects are not necessarily negative to the overall natural environment, but some sort of trade-off is usually required. It being not always possible to have one's cake and to eat it, longer-term economic goals and prosperity tend to take precedence over environmental problems that might result from development activity. The question for the Department of the Environment in the Prime Minister's Office is whether the inevitable trade-off serves a greater priority need. All responsible projects, even comparatively small ones seen as eco-tourism should now address the issue of environment in project documentation before project work begins. This is not always the case, but the situation in Laos is certainly not the worst in the world and the environment of Laos has in a sense benefited from comparatively late development. Indeed, some projects in Laos have been greatly assisted by reference to problems encountered in neighbouring countries, particularly Thailand. Laos is of course not a simple continuation of Thailand by another name, and models from outside the country require adaptation to Lao specifics.

The Chiang Rai Accord

In 1995, all of the six Mekong countries met in Chiang Rai, Thailand, to establish a means to settle disputes over exploitation of the Mekong River. Laos, Cambodia, Vietnam and Thailand signed the Chiang Rai Accord, China did not.

It is recognised that Cambodia and Vietnam, at the end of the River, have the most to lose. China, with plans to build over the next 20 years, 20 dams on the sections of Mekong and the Mekong's tributaries within its territory, now seems to be the key to the Mekong's future.

Some responsible examples exist in Laos of projects that have been preceded by years of environmental study and agreement on means to limit environmental damage and set aside part of profits for the monitoring and remedy of environmental problems.

While natural herds of wild elephants and free-roaming tigers stand to lose by large-scale deforestation and flooding of land, this is likely to enrage foreign environmentalists rather than affected villagers. Those villagers most affected by the recent construction of the Nam Theun 2 hydro-project cited roaming elephants and tigers as their biggest problem before construction on the project began and were happy to relocate to areas of good farmland, where they received some of the benefits of modernisation along with agreed compensation. On the other hand these same villagers stand to lose the 70 per cent of their food, which is hunted and gathered in the forests and 100 per cent of such income as they get from selling forest products.

The effects of blasting the Mekong, in Laos and in China (where it has already begun) may create problems or even bring to the edge of extinction the giant pa beuk cat fish, as the fishing nets used in Cambodia create similar problems for the Irrawaddy dolphin who cross the southern Mekong border into Laos. The Mekong has been the key to environmental balance throughout the long formation of Southeast Asia and this has been recognised by the creation of the Mekong River Commission, set up in 1957 by the UN, to coordinate the activities of the six bordering countries.

The eco-system of Laos, while currently of concern to environmental groups, is probably one of the most stable in the region. This is undoubtedly because of the comparative underdevelopment of Laos and the very low population within the country. There is, however, absolutely no basis for complacency. The continued existence in Laos of wildlife that has disappeared from other Asian countries makes Laos the target of a trade in wildlife for its curiosity value and the value of the parts of certain animals. The same availability of some plants that have disappeared from neighbouring countries threatens the continued existence in Laos of endangered plant species. Along with China and Thailand, Laos has more species of bamboo growing naturally than any other country in the world. It also has more species of snake!

Laos is faced with maintaining a balance between the benefits of conservation and the benefits of exploitation. While some caution is exercised in studying the effects of planned hydro-power projects, it is also sadly the case that even when these projects are delayed or called-off, it is sometimes too late to save the forest cover of the areas under threat of deliberate flooding, as logging companies quickly harvest the forests before final decisions shelve project plans. Timber is big money and corruption is everywhere a reality. On one hand the authorities of Laos are committed to sustaining a minimum of 40 per cent forest cover in the country as a whole, on the other hand national development and international demands for alternative renewable energy resources, qualify that commitment. At this time, about half of the surface area of Laos contains some form of forest cover, placing Laos 11th in the world in terms of percentage land area under forest. However, every new dam and every tree cut reduces this percentage.

National Protected Areas and National Park

Since 1993, 20 NPAs (National Protected Areas) have been created covering some 14 per cent of the land surface area of Laos. A further nine sites are being actively considered, and if added to plans, NPAs would cover some 20 per cent of the country. The harvesting of timber is not forbidden in all of these areas, but should be subject to controls aimed at sustainability. Hydro-electric projects are also not necessarily excluded, although compensatory action is expected from exploiters. Laos has only one National Park, Phu Khao Khuay, about 90 minutes north of Vientiane and open to the public in exchange for a small entrance fee.

Deforestation is a principal concern of environmental agencies and the Government of Laos. Quality hardwood timber is still found in Laos in sufficient quantities to tempt some corrupt Lao, in partnership with non-Lao, into breaking national laws on the destruction of forest cover. Much timber is taken by Chinese in northern areas bordering China; the same Chinese road makers providing benefits to Laos are sometimes involved. It has been suggested that the underpaid Lao army is responsible for much of the traffic in timber to Vietnam. Every time a new road is cut or a village is connected to the national electricity grid, initial action requires the cutting of a path through forest land; this path is often twice the width required for the task, and the timber felled disappears without accountability.

Deforestation in Laos, as in other developing countries, often goes hand in hand with economic development and modernisation. It is sometimes necessary to choose between maintaining the forests, and all this implies, and activities that might benefit the population, or at least a section of it. The eventual elimination of poverty is a goal of all development projects, but even in those that do not flood forest land or require any significant cutting of timber, pre-project studies sometimes suggest some surprising conclusions. Thus, plans to construct a large casino-hotel in Champassak next to the famous Khon Phapeng waterfalls initially inspired positive environmental comment: local villagers were cutting timber to make charcoal and over-fishing the Mekong River to the detriment of the dolphins in the area. The construction and subsequent tourism would have provided alternative livelihoods for these poor villagers. Plans were shelved (perhaps temporarily) when the World Bank finally published the results of an environmental study that concluded that increase of human activities in the area would lead to environmental degradation and that the negative ecological consequences of the project would outweigh any benefits.

> **Birds**
>
> Many foreign writers on Laos have noted the lack of bird life.
> This is certainly true in Vientiane, where small birds are regularly
> netted and those not bought and freed to make religious merit
> often end up in the frying pan. In spite of this urban situation,
> Laos as a country would seem to be a bird-watcher's paradise.
> In 1998, a British team of ornithologists recorded 437 species of
> bird in Laos, including eight globally threatened and a further 21
> on the danger list.

Swidden agriculture is also responsible for forest destruction. This has been practiced in Southeast Asia since the growth of its civilisations and small populations, such as that of Laos, posed no threat to the environment that can compare to that of large logging companies. The same farmers who practice swidden have an interest in maintaining the forests, which provide 'free' some 70 per cent of non-rice foodstuffs. Swidden (*het hai* in Lao) is an agricultural system in which fields are cleared within the forests and the timber largely burnt to provide space for crops to grow while enriching the soil enough to sustain a couple of annual rain-fed crops before usually being abandoned to natural renovation, which can take 10 to 50 years.

The trick is to farm the forests at a sustainable rate. Thus the nascent furniture industry of Laos needs regular supplies of timber, and regular supply requires sustained forests. Laos will not sustain its forests by providing timber to furniture industries in neighbouring countries, where the forests have already been largely destroyed. It is encouraged to conserve by restrictions placed on imports from countries within the European Union and by some other countries, which refuse wood and other forest product imports not coming from sustainable forests. In recent years, Lao laws have come into force banning the export of logs. Such laws are difficult to enforce in the remote areas where timber often grows best and where local populations are often among the poorest in the country.

Environmental Organisations

In Laos:

- Wildlife Conservation Society, PO Box 6712, Vientiane, tel: 021-215400, email: WCS-lao@wcs.org
- International Union for Conservation of Nature and Natural Resources, 15 Thanon Fa Ngum, Vientiane

Outside Laos:

- Asian Society for Environmental Protection, GDG-SEAPO, Asian Institute of Technology (AIT), Bangkok 10501, tel: 579-5266
- Traffic East Asia, 20/F Double Bldg, 22 Stanley St., Central, Hong Kong, tel: 852-2530 0864, email: tea@asiaonline.net

The reduction of poverty itself creates a situation that may harm the environment. In neighbouring Thailand the spraying of pesticides is widespread and results in low prices of Thai fruits, cereals and vegetables on Thai markets and exports. Lao farmers can often not afford the pesticides. To market produce as organic can help exports, but also means higher domestic prices.

In the end, the very factors that have restricted the development of a domestic market—the comparatively sparse population and poor communications—may prove to be the most important feature in conservation of the natural environment. But these factors will not last forever, as immigration from the East and North grow at a pace which is already in places changing the Lao nature of Laos.

PRE-HISTORY

Pre-historic times, by definition, have no recorded accounts of how people lived. To find out, we rely on paleo-anthropology and archeology. The first tells us that the area of the Vientiane plain and across the Mekong River into what is now northeastern Thailand, was inhabited at least 10,000 years ago. From remains of the early inhabitants, we know only that the people were short and probably died young. Substantive excavation of the plain areas of Xieng Khouang have yet to take place, but it is quite possible that these areas were also known to early Man.

Archeology brings us much nearer to the present day. Finds at archeological digs, principally in the northeast of Thailand in areas near or on the Mekong River, leave no doubt that people in the area had a bronze age over 3,000 BC, hundreds of years before the inhabitants of Mesopotamia and China gave up their stone implements. The early occupants of Laos lived in communities on both sides of the Mekong, forged implements from bronze, planted and reaped rice along the fertile banks of the Mother-River, and introduced pottery to the world. At a time when the forefathers of Chinese civilisation were subsisting on wild millet, the early inhabitants of Laos had rice as the base of their diet, and stored water in decorated baked-clay pots.

Present-day Laos is among the poorest countries in the world. But the reconstruction of pre-history suggests that early civilisations grouped along the Mekong River led the world in establishing permanent communities.

HISTORY

A popular Lao legend provides the link between pre-history and history. It maintains that a mythical Lao king/apical ancestor (Bulom) cut open a gourd in a place now known as Dien Bien Phu, which is within what is now northern Vietnam (by coincidence the historic site of French defeat in 1954). From that gourd, the seven sons of the apical ancestor of the Lao-Thai peoples stepped out and started to populate the world.

Whatever the symbolic truth contained in the legend, by 300-200 BC the lowland peoples of the Mekong basin were interacting with their neighbours near and far. It was during this time that Lao-Thai became Theravada Buddhists, and perhaps around this time the first adaptations of Sanskrit writing to fit the Lao language were being tried out.

In the 8th to10th centuries, a flourishing Lao-Thai state existed in southern China, in which the inhabitants spoke a form of Lao. From this state, waves of Lao-speaking migrants further populated the Mekong River areas. At that time, the nation states of China, Laos, Thailand and Vietnam did not exist, at least not in the way we think

The reason why the burial 'Jars' were constructed on the Plain of Jars remains a pre-historic mystery.

of them today. It seems likely that the use of Lao-Thai languages was widespread in the villages and city-states that sprung up across the whole region of northern Southeast Asia at that time.

What is now southern Laos followed a different early history. An essentially Mon-Khmer kingdom existed in Champassak and extended into what is now Cambodia between the first and the eighth centuries. From the 8th to the 12th centuries, Mon-Khmer kingdoms established themselves further north, at Sri Gotapura (now called Tha Khek) and at Muang Sawa (Luang Prabang), both on the Mekong.

From the earliest times, both Lao and Mon-Khmer communities formed larger centres known as muang or meuang and this is still the usual word for town in Lao (a glance at a map of the country will show that Muang are to be found throughout the land).

In the 12th-13th centuries, the small kingdoms within Laos, along with the muang in their various forms, were incorporated into the Angkor Empire. This provoked a series of Lao and northern Thai rebellions and by 1238 the famous Sukhothai kingdom was established and went on to incorporate other kingdoms and principalities in Chiang Mai, Phayao, Sawa (Luang Prabang) and Vieng Chan (Vientiane). This amalgamated kingdom was known as Lan Na (million fields). Whether it was essentially Thai or Lao is a very academic question. There was probably very little difference between Lao and Thai peoples at the time, and the language of Northern Thai (Kham muang) has perhaps more in common with Lao than with central Thai, which was probably the language of Sukhothai's capital, the prosperous town of Ayudhya.

The history of Laos then took on a very personal path, led by Chao Phi Fa, a Lao prince expelled by his father from Muang Sawa (Luang Prabang) for sleeping with one of his father's wives. Lord Phi Fa took one of his sons, who was to become the famous Chao Fa Ngum, and fled as a refugee to the Angkor Court. Chao Fa Ngum married the Angkor king's daughter and he and his father Phi Fa received Khmer support to retake Muang Sawa (Luang Prabang). With 10,000 Khmer troops, Fa Ngum seized Khorat (now in Thailand), Vieng Chan, Xieng Khouang and finally took Sawa (Luang Prabang) with the intension of putting his father (Phi Fa) on the throne. However, Phi Fa was killed as Luang Prabang was taken and Chao Fa Ngum declared himself king of Lan Sang Hom Khao (the Land of a Million Elephants and the White Parasol). Chao Fa was said to be addicted to war and ruthless in the waging of it. He exiled his own grandfather, who had been responsible for kicking out Chao Fa Ngum and his father Chao Phi Fa, and continued to expand his kingdom into Champa and parts of what is now Vietnam.

Chao Fa Ngum was a nationalist and a conqueror. He has been accorded a special place by the socialist regime as a founder of the Lao nation and a liberator. In Vientiane today, he is remembered in the name of the road that runs beside the Mekong and in a statue at the small park and road junction outside the Novotel Hotel, on the way out of town towards the airport.

But the history of Laos did not stop with the conquests of Chao Fa Ngum. He himself again suffered exile when his ministers collaborated in a coup against him in 1373 and sent him to live in Nan, now a quiet town in northern Thailand. The ministers installed Chao Fa Ngum's eldest son, Oun Heuan, on the throne. Oun Heuan took the title *Phaya Samsenthai*. This is further evidence of the compatibility or confusion between Lao and Thai identity. The name means 'Lord of 300,000 Thais', referring to the number of adult males said to be living in the kingdom in 1376. The name Samsenthai lives on in Vientiane as the name of the main shopping road, which also houses the National Cultural Hall, the National Museum and the Lao Plaza Hotel.

Samsenthai had a more peaceful outlook on life. He married two Thai princesses, in the process forming alliances with Chiang Mai and Ayudhya, which greatly enhanced Muang Sawa (Luang Prabang) as a trading centre. It was also an important centre for Buddhism, which became Lane Xang's state religion resulting in the construction of a great number of *wat* (Buddhist temples). Phaya Samsenthai reformed the structure of his state on Siamese lines, at the same time maintaining good relations with the Khmer to the South.

The Khmer, who shared the religion of Theravada Buddhism, presented Samsenthai's successor, King Visounarat, with the Pha Bang (at that time pronounced in Lao with an 'r', as Phrabang), a cast gold Buddha image. The veneration of this image in Muang Sawa eventually prompted the change of name of the town to Luang Phra Bang (Royal Buddha-image Bang) and the image became one of the sacred symbols legitimizing the kingdom and its king.

Peace and prosperity do not last, even with a sacred symbol to indicate the real king. By around 1420 Lane Xang was beset with struggles between factions, which vied for the Pha Bang and power for the next hundred years, during which time the kingship changed hands 12 times, eventually ending up in the hands of a woman, Nang Keo Phimpa, who became Lane Xang's only queen. She was on the throne just a few months before being deposed and suffered a sorry end tied to a large rock, where she was abandoned to the vultures.

In 1520, King Phothisarat, faced with the prospect of losing his kingdom to the invading Burmese, moved the capital to Vieng Chan. This astute move was followed in 1545 by the capture of the Kingdom of Lanna, which became fully Lao with the installation of Phothisarat's son, Setthathirat, on the Lanna throne. Setthathirat is remembered in his statue in front of That Luang, the national symbol, in the road bearing his name, which forms the middle of the three main parallel roads forming Vientiane, all of them named after kings. After his father was trampled to death by an elephant, Settathirat moved to Vieng Chan on becoming King of Lane Xang. He brought with him the sacred emblem associated with the Lanna kingship, the Buddha image known as Pha Keo (the Emerald Buddha). He built Wat Pha Keo in Vientiane to house that image (the current Wat Pha Keo, next to the President's Palace, which used to be the King's Palace, holds a replica of the Pha Keo). King Settathirat also constructed the largest Buddhist Stupa in the country, That Luang. That Luang remains the national symbol of Laos and the name of the area in which it stands, which also hosts the National Assembly.

Settathirat disappeared in 1571, probably ambushed by dissident hill peoples. This left Lane Xang without an agreed successor and factionalism again entered Lao politics. Warring Lao factions made the country easy prey for the Burmese, who came and went several times over the next 60 years, during which Lane Xang declined.

In 1637, King Suriya Vongsa beat off the opposition to take the throne, and ruled for 57 years (the longest reigning Lao monarch ever). These were years of comparative peace and prosperity, during which Lane Xang recovered its territories and power.

What goes up must come down, and this is certainly true of kingdoms in Southeast Asia. When Suriya Vongsa died in 1694, Lane Xang split into factions again and separate kingdoms were established in Vieng

Chan and in Champassak in the south.

During the last quarter of the 18th century, Burma annexed Luang Prabang, Vieng Chan fell increasingly under Annamese (Vietnamese-Chinese) influence, and Champassak was taken by Siam in 1778.

By the end of the 18th century, Siamese control was evident throughout much of Laos. Siam installed a Lao prince educated in Bangkok as its vassal in Vieng Chan. This vassal was Chao Anou. Like so many vassals in history, once he had a taste of power, Chao Anou did not follow the precise line intended by his masters. He restored the city as a trading and administrative centre, prompted a renaissance of Lao, rather than Siamese, arts and literature, and extended his influence to Luang Prabang. Arguments between the vassal and his masters erupted into skirmishing between armies. During one of these, Siamese troops entered Vieng Chan and stole the Pha Keo, the emblem of the Lao King's authority. This was installed in Wat Phra Keo in Bangkok, built for the occasion.

In the 1820s, the Lao vassal rebelled against his Siamese masters. This was to be something of a last hurrah for Lao kingdoms. Chao Anou invaded the northeast of Siam and briefly held a large part of Siam. For a time it looked like he might recapture the Pha Keo from Bangkok, but he was inevitably beaten back to Vieng Chan. The Lao-Siam war ended in 1828, with Siamese troops crossing the Mekong and, with the exception of Wat Si Saket, razing Vientiane by fire. All Lao living on the left bank between Vieng Chan and Champassak (i.e. most Lao in Laos) were ordered to leave the country and live under Siamese control in the Northeast of Thailand. This was a fairly normal way of waging war in Southeast Asia. People were wealth, the northeast of Siam was scarcely populated, and the involuntary migrants were subject to pay tribute to their Siamese masters. This mass movement explains partly why there are now more Lao (Isaan; Northeastern-dialect Thai) speakers living in Thailand than there are in Laos; it also assists in explaining why contemporary Laos has such a low population compared to its neighbours.

Chao Anou is regarded in contemporary Lao history as something of a hero, and he is remembered in the name of the street which crosses and joins the other main roads named after monarchs. The Anou Hotel, renovated in 2007, is also one of the oldest in Vientiane.

The nineteenth century saw an expansion of Siamese control and influence in Laos. This was not always unwelcome. Northern Lao states particularly saw Siam as a protector against invasions from warlords in what is now Vietnam and China. The Siamese interest in Laos at that time was principally as a buffer state against expanding French military presence in Vietnam, and to a lesser extent against British colonial interests in Burma.

The situation was novel and complex when Oun Kham, the King of Luang Prabang agreed in the late 19th century to become a French protectorate against Siam. The series of French military adventures and treaties in both Laos and Siam that followed led in 1896 to an agreement between Siam, China and Britain that more or less established the current borders of Laos. By 1907 Siam had pulled back to the west of the Mekong, leaving Laos as an extension of French interests in Vietnam. Thus the current borders of Laos can be traced not only to Lao history but to an understanding between the two major colonial powers in the region. Siam sided more with the British, but was happy to agree to the French presence in Laos because it retained its position as the only Asian state to escape direct colonisation by a European power.

THE STRUGGLE FOR POWER

The years of World War II saw the Japanese come and go as in other Southeast Asian nations. They left behind the seeds of independence from the returning colonial rulers. The Lao king Sisavang Vong declared independence and Prince Phetsarat formed the Lao Issara (Free Lao). This group opposed the return of the French in 1945. They were allied with Ho Chi Min's forces doing the same thing in Vietnam. The Lao Issara was badly mauled in 1946 and most fled to Thailand, where they set up a Lao government in exile. This alternative government was itself split in three directions. Prince Phetsarat refused negotiations with the French, insisting on immediate unconditional Independence, Phetsarat's half-brother, Prince Souvanna Phouma was for negotiations to achieve independence, and Souvanna Phouma's brother, Prince Souphanavong, wanted combined action with the Viet Minh under Ho Chi Minh.

The French went ahead without any consultation with any Lao Issara faction and recognised Laos as an independent state within the French Union, which allowed it to join the United Nations. Lao Issara dissolved and in October 1953, by that time fully involved in fighting in Vietnam, France granted unconditional sovereignty to Laos. Had the French acted more rapidly and perhaps more realistically, Laos might have followed a very different post World War II path—as indeed might Vietnam and the whole 'cold war' era. But the obvious mistakes of history are only evident in retrospect.

The person most generally seen as the Father of the Revolution began to make his presence known at this time. Kaysone Phomvihane was a Lao of mixed Lao-Vietnamese parentage, born in Savannakhet in 1920 of a Lao mother and a Vietnamese father. He is credited with having worked among the tribal minorities of Xiang Khouang and other eastern provinces bordering Vietnam during the post-world war period, drawing many of them, especially Hmong, into support for the Indochinese Communist Party, an umbrella Party which existed in Vietnam, Laos and Cambodia.

It was at least in part thanks to the earlier work of Kaysone that Prince Souphanouvong in 1950 established in Eastern Laos the Lao Resistance Government to fight the French. The dramatic defeat of the French in Dien Bien Phu in 1954 gave heart to a Lao resistance to the government in Vientiane and Luang Prabang. That government recognised a constitutional monarch and was led by a French-educated elite. It controlled the towns, but did not control most of the countryside, where the majority of Lao lived.

The Pathet Lao

Pathet Lao means simply 'the country of the Lao'. This remains the name most commonly used for the country in the Lao language, and has no political implications apart from those involved in any national boundary. The term was picked up by the international media in the 1960s as shorthand for the Lao People's Liberation Army (LPLA), which was supported by Vietnam in its opposition to the US-backed constitutional monarchy.

The difficult political and military situation was recognised by the Geneva Conference in 1954, which sanctioned control of the northeastern provinces of Hua Phan and Pongsali by Prince Souphanavong's alternative Government.

In 1955 in Sam Neua (Hua Phan Province), now revered as the birthplace of socialist Laos, the Lao People's Front (LPF) was formed. The LPF was a forerunner of the Party that today rules Laos.

The LPF agreed in 1957 to enter a coalition government with the Royal Lao Government (RLG) under Prince Souvanna Phouma. Thus, the two princes and brothers appeared for a time to have found a peaceful solution to differences in a Government of National Union. This, unfortunately, was not to last. In 1958, elections to the National Assembly gave a majority to the left-wing LPF of 2 to 1 seats. The US reaction to these democratic election results was to cut off all aid to Laos and encourage a right-wing backlash which arrested Prince Souphanavong, and all LPF ministers and deputies. The LPF again found itself in the countryside and the coalition collapsed.

Souvanna Phouma was shunted off to be Lao ambassador in Paris and the right-wing Phoui Sananikone was installed as prime minister. Right-wing army officers justified their actions by claiming that the LPF was using regular North Vietnamese troops in a plot to take over the country, a claim that was investigated by the UN and declared to be untrue. In 1958, Prince Souphanavong and many of the LPF escaped and led the resistance from the countryside.

In 1959 open fighting broke out between the two sides on the Plain of Jars, and both America and Vietnam

Hua Phan Province is seen as the seat of the Lao Revolution. This former residence of Kaysone Phomvihane, in Vieng Sai District, is now a place of modern pilgrimage. The New Regime sent difficult cases for re-education to this district.

became increasingly involved in the conflict. By 1960 Air America began its operations in Laos which were to fuel the 'secret war'.

In August 1960 a neutralist military faction led by Kong Le seized Vientiane in a coup d'etat that recalled Souvanna Phouma from Paris to serve as prime minister. Kong Le was ousted by a combination of actions inspired by the CIA and the Lao military right, and fled to Xieng Khouang, where he joined forces with the LPF and their Vietnamese allies. The Soviet Union stepped in to supply arms to the rebel forces and within a year they controlled much of northern Laos.

A second attempt at a Government of National Unity was made in 1962-3, with the same principal players involved. It fell apart for various reasons, one being a split between Kong Le and the LPF, which led Kong Le to align with the rightists. The LPF leadership countered by allowing seven North Vietnamese Army divisions into northeastern Laos.

The period 1964 to 1973 was marked by saturation bombing of eastern Laos by B-52s stationed in US bases in Thailand. Souvannavong and Kaysone responded by moving into the comparative safety of the caves of Sam Neua. It was at this point that the US formed its famous 'secret army', under the Hmong general Vang Pao.

This secret army was hardly secret to anybody living in Laos at the time. Based in Long Cheng in the highlands, the army was trained in mountain warfare by CIA and Thai forces and entirely US-financed. Contrary to popular myth, it was not entirely Hmong, but included individuals from many other highland areas and even some Thais. Hmong fought on both sides in the civil war, at first only with Kaysone and Souphanavong, then increasingly with the US-supported army.

Once more, in 1973, as home opposition grew to US involvement in Vietnam and Laos, ceasefires were declared and a Provisional Government of National Union was declared. At the time the forces loyal to Souphanavong and Kaysone controlled 11 of the 13 provinces then in Laos. America looked for a way out, and in June 1974 the last Air America planes flew out of Laos to Thailand.

The rapid ouster of the US forces from Saigon and Phnom Penh in 1975, together with the crushing defeat of RLG-Hmong forces at Muang Phu Khun, was the final battle of the war and one that left the road clear to control Vientiane.

The Refugee Exodus

The right-wing military fled in large numbers to the safety of Thailand, from where they were offered refuge in the US. Over the following months, an estimated 45,000 refugees, mostly members of the secret army and their families, left for Thailand and the US. The structure of the Provisional Government of National Unity was dismantled quietly and with no opposition, and on 2 December 1975, the Lao People's Revolutionary Party (LPRP) declared itself in full control of the new Lao People's Democratic Republic (LPDR). After such a long contest, the changeover was bloodless, at least in Vientiane.

Throughout highland Laos, thousands of Hmong who had been involved in the secret army were left without US support, in both the military and subsistence sense. The new government in Vientiane had its hands full and could anyway not have stepped in financially to provide subsistence to these old enemies. Some Hmong reverted to mountain village life, some surrendered, some fought on from high peaks, but many left the country as the first of the many refugees from Laos.

The first refugees were almost entirely hill tribe. But as economic conditions throughout the country worsened, individual Lao Loum who had been in positions of authority were sent off for periods of indefinite re-education. Lowland Lao began to leave in large numbers only in 1979—four years after the change of regime. Not all intended to stay away from Laos, but most found economic conditions in the large camps established with international support in Thailand to be far superior to life in Laos during the years following the 1975 change of regime. The unpopular and short-lived attempts to introduce collectivisation were compounded by fate, and Laos suffered from droughts and floods for three years after the change of regime.

The Seminar

The decade following the change was one most marked by the 'seminar'. This mild word conjures up a sleepy afternoon of academic discussion. Indeed, when seminars started in the new Laos they had something of the unreal-academic about them. Almost everybody had some experience of the seminar. Even UN agencies were required to release their staff for set periods to allow them to participate in some form of re-education. For most low- and middle-range functionaries, this meant going along to meetings instead of going to work, listening to political commentary, taking notes and making supportive statements. People were expected to support themselves at such activities, which were not voluntary, but there was no rough treatment. Things were not so easy for those who had been in a position of authority. Thirty-four people were sentenced to death, but not one death sentence was carried out; in a very Lao way, all thirty-four had left the country before sentence was passed.

Perhaps one of the worst things about re-education was its indeterminate nature. Many Lao happily went deep into the northern mountains expecting to learn a new political line and to return to their families in weeks or months. Very few did; most spent five years or more away, with almost no communications apart from occasional letters carried by those released. Conditions in the re-education camps varied. Some people were incarcerated in prison-like conditions for years. Others spent the first six months physically behind wire, attending political education and learning to work on the land. After this time people who demonstrated a correct attitude were usually released from camp but had to remain with a peasant family with whom they were billeted and were expected to work as part of that family in agriculture. The work and conditions were perhaps no harder than for the average farmer in the mountains, but to French-educated members of an elite, the climate, diet, work and lack of medical care definitely constituted hardship.

Most of those sent for re-education returned within five years. Some were kept longer. Some stayed on in their new homes with new wives and families. Few are known to have escaped. Some were allowed leave to visit their families and later in the experiment wives were allowed to join their husbands at their places of re-education, although most had children to look after and could not make the difficult journey.

Re-education returnees were generally offered their old jobs back in their old ministries or offices, but at one rank below that at which they had left for re-education. Some took those jobs and stayed, many others took time to say goodbye to old friends in Vientiane and left with their families for the camps in Thailand and eventual resettlement in a third country.

Some one-tenth of the population (as estimated in 1975, the population was three million) left Laos and was resettled overseas. Somewhat paradoxically, remissions of money sent back by those émigrés to family relatives in Laos have helped support the population and its government during the lean years which followed the 1975 victory.

Laos and Thailand at War

It surprises many people to know that the last war fought by Laos was with Thailand. It occurred in 1987, the very year that Laos declared its new economic policies and opened up to the world and Thai investment. The conflict was localised to three villages in Saynabouly Province and lasted three months, claiming over 3,000 lives before Laos was declared the winner and disputed territory was returned to Laos. Not one villager in the small piece of Laos claimed by Thailand took advantage of the situation to become Thai. During the entire three-month period, the flow of electricity exported by Laos to Thailand was not interrupted for a single hour.

Repatriation

One aspect of the refugee exodus that has received comparatively little attention is the repatriation to Laos of people who had often been in camps for over a decade. Following UN agreements, dribbles of returnees came back from the early eighties. The majority of repatriates, however, were those who did not want resettlement in a third country, and the majority of these, somewhat surprisingly, were Hmong. With the new economic policies of 1987 and the opening up of Laos to the outside world that followed, and with the compassion-fatigue that had taken hold among resettlement countries and in Thailand, a number of refugees returned, through the UN or spontaneously, before the camps were finally closed in the mid-1990s. Since then, many Lao, armed with US or Australian or French passports have returned to visit the new Laos. Many of these visitors are Hmong, with fathers who fought against the current regime. All have relatives who remained in Laos and just about all are pleasantly surprised to see that life in Laos today has no resemblance to the way things once were or to stories and fears they might have heard overseas. In a way, things are coming full circle and the differences and animosities of the past have no place in the forward-looking Laos of today. The Lao PDR, so long in the making, has found its place in the region and in the world.

Kaysone Phomvihane

Kaysone spent his life serving the Revolution. Instrumental in organising the Lao Issara in the 1940s, a leading figure in the long civil war, A man fluent in Lao, Vietnamese, Thai, Shan, French and English, he was the first prime minister of the new Laos and remained in power until his death in November 1992. He is remembered in framed portraits in some government offices and in the large statue outside the Museum carrying his name at kilometer six.

The Bombs

Laos has the unenviable distinction of being the most heavily bombed country ever, anywhere. B-52 pilots on bombing runs within Laos or Vietnam were ordered to release any remaining bombs in Laos. In Vietnam pilots were under orders to avoid bombing within the vicinity of a temple; no such orders were issued regarding bombing in Laos. Unexploded ordnance continues to litter parts of the country and, in spite of the admirable and dangerous efforts of international disposal teams, continues, over three decades later and unintentionally, to kill and maim. In addition to explosive bombs, many hundreds of thousands of gallons of defoliants were dropped on potentially hostile areas.

Conversations with the Lao

The visitor is free to talk to any Lao on just about any subject. Such conversation is limited by language barriers rather than political restriction. It will also be limited by the comparatively narrow world view of the average Lao. Graduates of secondary school may have difficulty identifying a picture of the Eiffel Tower or their own prime minister, and graduates of the one university in Laos may have trouble locating Singapore on a world map. They might have learnt the name Karl Marx at school or during their training as monks, but don't expect anybody to have heard of Trotsky or to know the difference between a Bolshevik and a Menshevik. The average Lao is quietly proud of his or her country and will not be critical of anything to do with religion or politics. At the same time, ask leading questions and you might get the answer 'yes', which is often less of an agreement than a convention of polite conversation.

The Forgotten

More than three decades after the 'change of regimes', to use the most frequently heard reference term for the 1975 transition, history has not so much been rewritten (the written word in the Lao language remains an infrequent medium of communication) as re-remembered.

Significant personalities of the civil war years who have practically disappeared from public memory include, rather surprisingly, the 'red prince' Souphanavong, and Faydang Lobliayao, the ethnic Hmong leader who worked alongside Kaysone before and following the 1975 regime change. Until the mid-1980s (and still in a few cobwebbed Nai Baan's offices) the row of portraits of the Great Men included Marx, Kaysone, Souphanavong and Faydang. Today even Marx has gone. Only Kaysone remains... and not everywhere.

In modern Laos, the only noted monument to any revolutionary leader is the single statue of Kaysone Phomvihane in front of the museum that bears his name, inaugurated in 2001, six kilometres outside of downtown Vientiane. More evident today are the statues of two Lao kings, one at each end of the main road leading into, across and out of Vientiane.

RELIGION
Buddhism

Laos shares Theravada Buddhism with its neighbour Thailand and many exchanges of monks and ideas take place. A monk from Thailand in Laos is recognised in every way as equal in status and respect to a Lao monk, and vice versa. The same cannot be said for a monk from Vietnam or China, who comes from a quite different tradition.

During the years after the change of regime in 1975 there were many priorities for the state apparatus and promotion of Buddhism was not one of them. It is important to realise that while the practice of Buddhism is important, particularly for the lowland majority, Buddhism is the religion of only some 60 per cent of the Lao population. This contrasts with the 94.6 per cent of Thailand's population which considers itself Buddhist. Of the remaining population in Laos, Christians make up 1.5 per cent, perhaps more, and Muslims count for less than one per cent of the population. Over 37 per cent of people say they have no religion. This is not so much a reflection of Marxist ideology, as it is a recognition that many minorities do not belong to any major religion, but practice animism or participate to some degree in bits of several religions without feeling themselves in essence to belong to any of them. This being so, Buddhism remains by far the most important of the world's religions in the Laos of today.

A Buddhist *Khu-bha* (Lao for monk) should be beyond considerations of politics. However, in the many years leading up to the change of regimes in 1975, it was very difficult to maintain true neutrality and the reality was that many monks offered moral support to the Lao People's Revolutionary Party and its humanistic and socialist rhetoric. This undoubtedly influenced many Buddhist farmers to support the revolution, as is shown as early as the elections of 1958.

During the year following 1975, the authorities took a different view of Buddhism. Attempting, through the seminar system, to reach all Lao and teach the basics of Marxism, the political authorities came into conflict with some Lao Buddhist practices: particularly the vows forbidding monks from turning the soil and thereby growing their own food (and unintentionally killing worms and insects) and the long tradition of *tak bat*, where lay people place food into bowls held by monks during their early morning alms round or into rows of bowls set out at *boun* organised by families.

The new order urged monks to grow their own food in the same way as all citizens. Civil servants and teachers were expected to spend the first few hours of each day growing food. Many of Vientiane's roads were in such bad repair that cereals and vegetables could be seen growing on roads that carried little more than ox-carts; it was not considered a good example for monks to be exempt from the common activity, and it was certainly true that following the success of the People's Revolutionary Party, every scrap of food was valuable. Rather than forcing the city population into the countryside, as in Phnom Penh, Laos turned almost every unneeded corner of Vientiane into an area serving social and economic needs. Thus the bars and brothels that had typified Vientiane before 1975 were given up to homeless families, and the gardens of rich villas, schools and even ministries were all made available for the growing of food. Initially, the revolutionary faithful tried to persuade the people to use time spent feeding monks to grow food needed for themselves, and hoped the monks would lead by example. This never happened. Fewer young men entered the monkhood but those who did found bowls of food left in their wat by ordinary people who felt themselves in greater rather than lesser spiritual need of the merit gained by supporting monks following the rigours of war.

The authorities quickly realised their mistake and completely reversed policies. By the end of 1976, the Government provided a daily ration of rice to the Buddhist Sangha of monks. The education of monks in Marxist philosophy continued, much as it did for the general population. As time went by, political figures could be increasingly seen taking part in Buddhist activities, even the casting of new Buddha images. Many Lao, even some of those high up on the political hierarchy, stated privately that they saw Buddhism as a religion that maintained Lao identity in the face of daily Soviet and Vietnamese secularism. Today, restrictions on Buddhist activity have been lifted and Lao monks are free to study at Buddhist universities in Thailand. Thai monks also come to Laos and visit the more elementary Buddhist University in Vientiane. Non-Lao visitors will find Buddhist monks and novices (*nenh*) particularly receptive to practicing their English and learning about foreign lands; by all means interact as fully as you wish to do, but do remember that if political restrictions have been lifted the social restrictions that control monk-layman relations remain very much in force.

Monks

Lao monks are as far removed from arrogance as it is possible to get. They are also, in the eyes of the Buddhist population, the most superior beings on earth. Go to almost any meeting or show at the Cultural Hall, and the front row seats, or part of them, are reserved for monks. High ranking officials will sit immediately behind them, but if they come in after the monks are seated, they will inevitably raise their hands in a *nop* of respect. Lesser mortals, like foreign ambassadors, will have seats reserved just behind the monks.

Should you happen to be using the same entrance and passing in front of a line of seated robes, or even a single monk, you might wish to follow the Lao example and *nop* before passing, while at the same time bending your back a little, which shows that you are at least trying not to tower over very important people. If your first exposure to monks has been in Thailand, you might find the Lao clergy somewhat less formal and rather more rustic. However, the difference is one of nuance and degree and does not change the essential respect shown by lay inferior to a robed superior. In Thailand, if speaking

Thai, you would be expected to use a high-respect form of language when talking to or about monks and Buddha images. The same is true in Laos. For the foreigner who knows a little Thai and a little Lao, the distinction in terms may be confusing. In Thai, any monk is a *phra*, a title of excellence. In Lao, a monk is a *khu-baa* and the term *pha* (Thai: *phra*) is reserved for Buddha images. in Lao monks are usually addressed as *nya pho*. In Lao, the term *doy* or *doy kha-noy* (I, your little slave) is used for the first person when addressing monks and sometimes by servants when addressing masters. It was thought to be demeaning and was frowned upon after the change of regime, but, like the *nop* it is now back in fashion. As a foreigner, particularly if a man, *doy kha-noy* is likely to sound a bit strange coming from your lips and if it is the only Lao you are using in a conversation in English or French, it might have a tint of the sarcastic about it.

Safe is to introduce yourself by first name and simply to use your first name as first person throughout the conversation. You can do this with just about everybody without sounding childish (Robert likes Lao food, etc). Nuns exist as in Thailand and have the same second class position in the wat. Rather than simple *nang*, which is respectful enough for most women, *mae sii* (mother in white) is a more respectful term you can use for nuns.

There are several ways of seeing the privileged position of monks. If you have the view that these semi-sacred beings should really go out and get a job, better keep that view to yourself. The more general view is that monks earn the respect accorded them. They do so by learning the Buddhist scriptures and by taking 227 monastic vows. Prohibition against working and storing food makes the monk dependent on the laity for subsistence. Prohibition against sexual activity and taking alcohol or other stimulants keeps their minds on the job, and prohibition on eating after midday gets them early to bed and early to rise. Of course, you might occasionally see monks sitting in a café in the afternoon, drinking ovaltine, smoking cigarettes, and leaving payment on the table. This is Laos; too much discipline is *bo muan* (no fun). This is the only explanation necessary. Totalitarianism is not for the Lao.

Buddha Images

Images of the Buddha are most often found in the *wat* and in the home. They may occasionally be placed in other surroundings of significance, such as up high on a small knoll, inside caves (the caves at Pak Ou—where the River Ou comes into the Mekong is probably the most famous concentration of such images in Laos), and occasionally carved into rock faces. All images are the subject of veneration and among the worst things you could do in Laos, stealing an image or treating it badly must rank near the top of the list. Images are regularly 'fed' with small plates of fruits, and watered, sometimes with a Pepsi-Cola complete with straw, and provided with burning incense and flowers. These offerings are always accompanied with a polite nop and a quiet prayer. Some people treat their Buddha images on *wan pha*, when they might also feed the monks in the morning or go to the *wat* to listen to a sermon and top up their merit.

The respect accorded Buddha images is entirely because they represent the Buddha, who, on achieving enlightenment and extinction, stands as example of the perfect being. The average Buddhist in Laos has no great hopes of enlightenment in this lifetime, but he or she would like to think that this lifetime has meaning in so much as it inches the individual further towards that final goal. Death and rebirth are not something Lao look forward to, any more than most other people. The Lao associate these things with suffering, although this does not mean they are not happy when their children are born!

Wan Pha

Wan pha falls four times in a lunar month, at full moon, new moon, quarter moon and three-quarter moon. Before the western weekend took hold, a day off at *wan pha* was the best an average Lao worker could hope for. Today, if a worker turns up late or not at all and pleads *wan pha*, it is very difficult to argue.

Buddha images may be 'folk style', crafted by farmers from local wood and often painted. Some of these may look somewhat bizarre to the visitor more used to seeing bronze images in museums, especially if painted pink, but all have the individuality of their maker. These are the images more likely to be picked up, sometimes quite cheaply, by foreigners; Lao will go for more classical features and materials. Giving a Buddha image to a Lao family is very fine indeed. Large or small, it should preferably be conservative, made of bronze or another expensive material such as jade, or silver or gold-coated. Lao are likely to appreciate new images rather than those with antique value. Don't be surprised if the recipient sends the image to the *wat* for three days: this is a sure sign your gift is appreciated and will be given a properly reverential place within the family.

While monks and their robes cannot be touched by women, and while monks will revere Buddha images much as laymen revere them, women are free to touch Buddha images. However, women and men should treat such images with great respect. It is fine to have any number in your house (although you will need permits to take them out of the country), but do place them high up, away from foot level. When moving or cleaning an image, strictly speaking, the image should receive a *nop* first and receive your excuses.

Smaller images may be worn around the neck, much as a Christian wears a crucifix (don't assume that a Lao wearing a crucifix is Christian) and for much the same reasons. The Lao considers a Buddha image has powers of protection against evil spirits and can even protect in the case of vehicle accidents—the power of belief having nothing to do with empirical reality, which suggests that riding a motor bike in Laos is one of the most dangerous activities in the world today.

Animism
Almost 40 per cent of Lao will say they have no religion, or reply very vaguely that they do not really believe

in religion. This percentage was probably much the same before Lao became a People's Republic, so any assumptions linking socialist ideology and religious belief or practice should be avoided. Among that 40 per cent will be many who believe in the existence of spirits which animate the world for good or bad.

This belief continues among all Lao to some extent, and while some popular ceremonies like the ubiquitous *basi* (*baci* is a frequent transliteration), may be garnished with some Pali chanting from the master of ceremonies, no monk will officiate as such occasions, which are an integral part of specifically Lao identity but very much identified with maintaining and re-animating your life force through almost magical transmission of good luck and the binding into the body of the 32 guardian spirits or *khwan*. (If a *khwan* wonders away from the body, or is attracted away, a person may fall ill or may be unlucky in an enterprise.)

In animistic thinking, which is seen as a "religion" more by anthropologists than the people who just do it, objects can possess spirits as much as people and animals. Thus, some rocks or mountains are seen as particularly spiritual. Spirits can also inhabit house pillars and even pillars holding up temple roofs—thus, you will see people making offerings to the central pillar in Wat Si Meuang, in its original form one of the oldest temples in Vientiane, which is said to contain the guardian spirit of the city.

Minorities who do not speak Lao as their mother tongue (Hmong, Akha, Khmu, etc.), and those that speak a different form of Lao (Thai Dam, Thai Khao), will most often say they have no religion, but will have elaborate concepts of a world after death, and a complex view of the interaction of spirits in the world of the living, which includes shaman (spirit doctors to treat the sick). Their lives are every bit as full of propitiation and ensuring a good rebirth as are those of the lowland Lao.

In daily life, many Lao hedge their bets by acting within the context of several religions. Thus it is quite common for a household on an important occasion to invite monks to chant in the house and to bless new undertakings; once the monks have been fed and leave, a *su khwan* (another term for a *basi*) may be held to which people of any religion or no religion may be invited and will attend. This form of activity is known in anthropology as religious syncretism, things become mixed up, with no one religious line of thought predominating. To the average Lao mind, it makes sense to placate any spiritual force, either to neutralise possible harm or to get that force working on your side.

Perhaps one of the most prevalent activities visitors may witness is the propitiation of the *pha phum*. This is a class of spirits which resides in the land. Many Lao families will build small spirit houses for the *pha phum*, usually somewhere quiet within the compound grounds or in any available space in a townhouse. Such spirits must be consulted before any building works take place, or even before a foreign embassy moves its flagpole (although it is likely to be done before the Ambassador comes on the scene!): thus when the pile driver is in place, it will not start work until the spirits agree. Failure to treat the spirits of the land properly can lead to endless problems in the house and grounds later, it can even lead to sickness and death of animals and human occupants. Remedies are expensive, much better to keep the *pha phum* happy.

Christianity

The majority of non-Buddhist Lao are Christians of the French Catholic type, and several churches in Vientiane and throughout the country exist to serve the religious needs of this group. Missionary activity is no longer permitted from abroad, although people may change their religion if they wish to do so without any need to register with any authority. Religious freedom has fairly recently been introduced formally into the laws of the constitution: the essence of the law is that all citizens have a right to the religion of their choice and nobody has the right to interfere with that choice process. This law remains open to interpretation and there have been occasional problems, mostly affecting evangelical Christians who consider it their duty to proselytise among Buddhists and others.

Islam
Very few Lao are Muslim. The majority of these live in Vientiane, where they attend one of two mosques, one established by descendants of Arab and Indian merchants, who can trace their roots back to the 17th century, and one built by Cambodian Muslims who came to Laos as refugees from Pol Pot in the mid and late 1970s. In addition there are some rural villages of Muslim Haw Chinese, mostly in the north near the border with China.

THE ECONOMY
Overview
There is now very little to distinguish the structure of the Lao economy from that of its neighbours. The decade following the introduction of the New Regime in 1975 saw experimentation with socialist praxis. The Party tried to exercise centralised control, there were a few early attempts at collectivisation, official exchange rates were artificially set, non-Soviet visitors were limited to the few embassies and UN agencies, and private enterprise was almost suffocated. As a result of these policies, funding did not reach the provinces, farmers were discouraged from cultivating more than their immediate needs, the kip went into freefall, a black-market became rampant, hard currency fled the country, the tourist industry zeroed out, hotels and restaurants closed their doors and even rice had to be imported from Thailand. Visitors to Laos, and young Lao today, find it difficult to imagine the extent of poverty and depression of a nation in decline, where Lao grazed goats on the grass pushing through the tarmac. Fortunately, economic policies were reversed in 1987, foreign investment was welcomed, tourism gradually picked up, kip rates were realistically set, and small enterprises reopened, providing a small but urgently needed source of revenue to the government.

Then, 1997, the Thai economy sneezed and the economy of Laos caught a cold. For a time it looked as if Laos had entered the free-market at precisely the wrong time. And, while the recovery in Laos was every bit as quick as in other Asian countries, the unexpected economic collapse of the neighbouring Asian tiger sounded gongs of warning that were well heeded by the leadership of Laos.

Laos made no foolhardy rush into capitalism, there was no fall of a Berlin wall, but year by year subsistence became more assured and foreign investment cautiously entered the economy bringing with it the enormous sums required to finance the hydro-power and mining projects that are today seen as the great promises of the future.

Poverty Eradication

In recent years, Laos has set itself the goal of leaving the ranks of the Least Developed Countries (LDCs) by 2020. After consultation with the International Monetary Fund, World Bank and Asian Development Bank, this goal has been declared possible if a real growth rate of 7 per cent per year is maintained. The assumption behind plans is that leaving LDCs will mean national and individual poverty has been greatly reduced or eliminated within the Lao PDR.

Current national poverty may be represented by GDP purchasing power parity. In 2005 this measured US$ 11.92 billion, a figure around one fiftieth of the similar figure for Thailand in the same year. Per capita purchasing power parity for the same year in Laos was US$ 1,900, compared with US$ 8,300 in Thailand.

In Laos some 80 per cent of the labour force remains in agriculture, a figure that was true of Thailand in the 1970s. Today, in Thailand, less than half of the labour force is engaged in agriculture.

When GDP is analysed by sector, agriculture is seen to be five times as important in Laos as in Thailand, while the relative per cent of GDP in industry and services in Laos is around half that of Thailand.

In Thailand, less than 10 per cent of the population lives below the official poverty line; in Laos the figure could be as high as 40 per cent. (Statistics are unreliable because so many Lao work unofficially in Thailand.)

Comparing Laos with Thailand is important because Thailand is by far the largest export and import partner of Laos: around 60 per cent of imports to Laos come from or through Thailand, compared to 10 per cent from China, 7 per cent from Vietnam, and 4 per cent from Singapore.

In many ways Laos can be seen as Thailand 30 years ago. Since Thailand is no longer an LDC and stands on the threshold of NIC (Newly Industrialised Country), the Lao dream of overcoming poverty by maintaining a comparatively high growth rate is realistic. However, there are other significant factors that need to be kept in mind. Over the last 30 years the birth rate and average family size has been reduced so dramatically that the Thai population may soon begin to experience problems of support for an ageing population, while Laos at the other end of the age continuum, continues with problems of high infant mortality and achieving universal education. If, as expected, Laos will follow Thailand's lead, we should expect developments in Laos in the years and decades to follow as has happened in Thailand in the years and decades gone by.

Economic Prospects

In addition to other problems, the Lao economy suffers from the size of its domestic market. This is very small, not so much because the population is small (the Lao population is almost the same size as that of Switzerland and larger than some of the most prosperous European countries), but because the population is poor. Thus, unless Laos jumps straight from being an import economy to an export-oriented economy, the growth of domestic production of goods and services will depend on the growth of some kind of substantive domestic market. Currently, the increasing tourist industry fills some of the functions of a domestic market through purchases and consumption within Laos, but tourists who buy Lao textiles, a packet or two of Lao coffee, perhaps a six-pack of Beer Lao, and carry them out of the country will not be taking with them, or sending by freight, heavy Lao hardwood furniture. So, growth in production will move more or less in step with domestic demand, and domestic demand will grow only as poverty declines.

Within the next decade export of electricity, mostly to Thailand seem set to double in importance. This should greatly increase revenues in Laos. At the same time exporting energy fuels development of Thailand and the other border neighbours of Laos, strengthening competitors for the world markets of similar products but also strengthening regional trade passing through Laos.

WTO membership is imminent and the USA has removed most restrictions on trade with Laos, while upgrading its embassy. The economy remains import-dominated, with most prices higher than their source in Thailand. Wages remain low enough to encourage a large migration from Lao villages and towns to work semi-legally in Thailand's factories and service industries, Thailand was in the same situation a couple of decades ago, with many of its citizens going to work in the Middle East in order to send money back home. When Laos can provide reasonable wages or reduce prices, Lao labour will return.

Nothing succeeds like success, and on balance foreign investment has done increasingly well in Laos. However, speculators remember bad news to good news at a factor of 10 to 1. Failure of some medium-large and prospering foreign companies in Laos (Securicor and Gem-Mining come to mind) have tended to qualify or even neutralise the good publicity of foreign companies like Lao Westcoast Helicopters, the huge Oxiania mining and several very large hydro-electricity projects, which have all done extremely well from their ventures in Laos and will probably do even better in the future.

The current situation seems to indicate rather more confidence from foreign investors than at any point since 1975. Large sums have been put into hotel development on the assumption there will be customers for first-class hotel rooms, a couple of 'boutique' hotels have recently opened, the excellent coffee in the south has regained its international price enough to make it profitable to export, Beer Lao has achieved export of a high quality product to several European countries and even to its neighbour Thailand, which forbade sale until 2007. While many other countries have suffered from natural disasters and terrorism, Laos has become a haven for a fast-growing tourist industry. All good news.

Thriving exploitations of gold and copper in Savannakhet Province, gem mining in Bokeo that promises to rival Burma's stagnant industries, timber harvests (if the sustainable aspects of forest exploitation can be controlled), and first and foremost a prospect of very significant expansion of electricity generation and export. The future has perhaps never looked brighter for Laos. While recession rocked the world in 2009-10, Laos managed a real growth rate of 6.4%. But political problems in Thailand in 2010 emphasised the reliance of the Lao economy on its southern neighbour's welfare.

Talat sao—Vientiane's morning market. Objects of Buddhist worship and merit-making are some of the most frequently seen products in Laos.

To a traveling visitor the infrastructure might look rudimentary, but enormous advances have taken place over the last decade. Surfaced roads now join all main centres of population between Luang Prabang and Pakse, three bridges cross the Mekong, two of them international, and more are planned. Transport costs of Lao products to Thai ports remain a problem, but the alternative, if much smaller, port of Danang in Vietnam is now attainable by road (although shipment from Danang usually requires transshipment in Singapore). The road joining Thailand with China, passing through a northeastern Lao corridor is almost complete (2007) after many years delay, and Laos, as the land in between five neighbours, stands to gain from increased regional trade.

The Lao population remains small, restricting domestic demand, and very young, limiting the number of skilled professionals, but ahead lies a couple of decades in which most Lao will fall into the productive age span

A street vendor pushing his wares. Street trading and the informal economy will still remain important to Laos for some time to come.

with sufficient education to meet the many opportunities available, and hopefully with sufficient cash in their pockets to provide a domestic market. Better education is coming, very poor health services can only get better, there are some indications of quality-control awareness and a shift in development policy to favour micro-finance. Membership of ASEAN and other international bodies has raised the status of Laos in the world and there is every reason to believe that it will be able to maintain a growth rate of at least 7 per cent and leave the ranks of the world's poorest economies on schedule in 2020. All in all, prospects don't look bad.

PEOPLE

CHAPTER 3

'May rice fill your granary,
may grandchildren fill your house.'
—Blessing at a Lao marriage

IDENTITY

The people of Laos and the people of Thailand are often referred to as 'the same but different'. The same could be said of the various people within Laos grouped as Lao Loum (Lowland Lao), who speak regional dialects. And the same could be said of all peoples within the greater Lao-Thai identity. The languages spoken by Lao-Thai groups, even if they have been isolated in remote mountain valleys for centuries and greatly influenced by other languages, remain essentially Lao. If Laos is the Land in Between, the Lao language of Vientiane might be seen as the Lao 'in-between' the Lao-Thai dialects as spoken in parts of China, northern Vietnam, Isaan, Chiang Mai, Bangkok and as far south as some villages in northern Malaysia.

The difference between Thai and Lao peoples is certainly greater than an apparent preference for Coke or Pepsi (readily explained by the fact that Laos produces Pepsi, it does not produce Coke). Differences were sometimes emphasised in the years after the revolution, when exposure to Thai and Western dress and habits were restricted in Laos: during those years almost all lowland Lao women were expected to wear the national dress and to keep their hair long. The national dress for Lao women is, however, based on the long and beautiful *sin*. This is the same dress (with perhaps different patterns) that Thai think of as their national dress, and is even called by the same term.

The difference is one of degree: Lao women in the decade following the change of regimes would rarely be seen in public without their *sin*, Thai at the time would rarely be seen in their *sin*. The situation today is that many in Laos continue to wear *sin* daily, all wear *sin* to enter government offices, most wear *sin* for any activity related to Buddhism or at a *basi*, and most continue to wear their hair long (often tied up). During the period following the 1975 change, reception of Thai TV was discouraged; today, booster stations throughout Laos ensure that Lao can receive Thai TV and cable in town has brought the world to the Lao family.

Ethnicity: Man and Woman

One thing all the 94 or 132 or even 500 ethnic groups in Laos (how many depends how you count) have in common is that the various types of men wear their ethnic identity literally on the sleeves of their women. Male ethnic distinctions in dress exist, but today most men dress in western style; most women, however, continue to wear the traditional clothes of their ethnic group, at least on formal or special occasions. Thus, in the 21st century, men are identified by their women.

It is largely because of the exposure to Thai TV that almost all Lao, at least all lowland Lao, can speak and understand Central Thai. There has been no such exposure of Thais to Lao, and, with the exception of those who come from the Lao-speaking region of Thailand, Thais have difficulty understanding Lao. Even if living and working in Laos, few Thais make the change from Thai to Lao—such change is unnecessary, they will always be understood. Such linguistic dominance is perhaps indicative of the feeling between both sides, which is evident to some extent in both Lao and Thai: the Lao are the little brothers and sisters of the Thais. The obvious difference in wealth on both sides of the Mekong is one of the most powerful forces attracting Lao to Thailand. The refugee business has closed shop, but the ebb and flow of movement continues.

And Lao, as the old saying relating to temporary economic migration suggests, really do leave with one gold piece in their hand, and return with ten.

Laos-Thailand Symbiosis

On an area of land roughly twice the size, Thailand supports more than ten times the population of Laos. This does not indicate a problem for either country: rather it indicates the potential for symbiosis between neighbours. Sparsely populated Laos has plenty of rivers in terrain ideal for the construction of hydro-power installations: Thailand is power-hungry, requiring fuel to support its thriving industrial-export sectors as well as a continuing, increasingly mechanised, agricultural-export sector. Thailand is also labour-hungry and Lao fulfill that need, while remitting hard currency to help the folks back home.

Age Structure

The median age in Laos is a low 18 years, almost the same median as in Thailand 30 years ago, when Thailand was at a similar stage of development as today's Laos. The indication is that Laos has a young and strong population about to enter the work force. If well-enough schooled, fed and immunized, it could provide a large proportion of educated and skilled labour that will be around for a long time before complications of care for the aged come into play. On the negative side, the large numbers currently under 18 create significant problems in funding education and training. Thailand on the other hand has an average age of 30, which means most of the population has been through school and any military obligations and are currently active in a skilled labour force. The significant amount of intermarriage between the two nationalities almost always follows a symbiotic pattern: Thai elder man, Lao young lady.

Thailand's age structure, as much as its economic prosperity, is behind the move towards a middle-class life style in which most adults married later in life than their parents but are now married and settled, and prefer to parent a small number of children who can be well educated and cared for within available household resources. The majority of Lao, in spite of comparatively early marriage patterns, are unmarried, without the responsibilities of parentage and, while maintaining responsibilities to their parents, have often left the discipline of the family structure and the village, to live in dormitories and work in urban factories in Laos or in Thailand.

Youth

The existence in Laos of many urban teenagers semi-detached from parental discipline, while they might be on the whole better behaved than teenagers in the West, has exaggerated problems of drug and alcohol abuse, which are thought to be as common in today's Laos as they were in Thailand a couple of generations back. The young, comparatively free, urban population of Laos inspires and provides sex-service industries. Discos and beer bars, which are often thinly-disguised fronts for prostitution, have grown in number and size to meet demand. Note that this has very little to do with the increase in western visitors; if the sex-industry relied on foreigners, it would collapse overnight.

Motor cycles rather than cars are imported from China for this young population, at half the price of superficially similar machines made in Thailand. In spite of the comparatively empty roads in Laos, the combination of youth, alcohol, lack of driving tests and sometimes unsafe 'copy' machines, produces accident rates that are among the highest in the world, just one more factor contributing to the low life expectancy.

Ethnic Make-up

The ethnic make-up of Laos and Thailand is similar but with very different emphases. In both countries traders and entrepreneurs tend to have a Chinese background. In Laos this is less evident because towns are much smaller and indigenous commerce less developed; also many Chinese-Lao either left the country during the decade following the change of regimes (when relations between Laos and China were bad), or suppressed the Chinese half of their identity. Chinese New Year—in Thai towns more notable in closure of facilities—passes almost unperceived in Laos. Vietnamese, almost all from northern Vietnam, certainly make up for the comparatively invisible Chinese presence. But most Vietnamese are either in Laos temporarily as cheap labour on house and road construction, or permanently in which case they are often as much or more Lao than Vietnamese.

The hill tribes are mostly the same groups in both countries, but in Thailand integration into mainstream Thai life is currently proceeding well. Signs are that Laos will follow the same pattern and hill peoples, particularly the historically-important Hmong, are already represented at the highest levels of political authority and minority-based insurgency is in decline. In Thailand, the large Muslim population in the southern provinces has not integrated; in Laos, the tiny Muslim population lives in peace and invisibility.

The proportion of Thai and Lao who consider themselves to be animist or of syncretic (mixed) religion, is very different in the two countries. Thais identify themselves in terms of one of the big three religions, whereas many Lao do not. But most Thai and most Lao see no contradiction between following some Buddhist practices and at the same time maintaining communications with the spirit world, particularly that part of it which lives in their family house and land, or which, as departed ancestors, watch over the welfare of their descendants—if treated right.

Back to the Future

The difference between Laos and Thailand is perhaps a temporal one. Comparison between the countries 30 years ago and a projected comparison ten years ahead suggests that the people of Laos, at least in statistical terms, are following where the people of Thailand have gone before them.

Since the significant year of 1975, the population of Laos has grown by over 100 per cent. This in spite of a large outflow of refugees, and the large numbers of Lao who have settled in Thailand. Increase rate is now slowing a bit but there is concern that the fertility rate remains too high. Urbanisation and education should reduce that rate in Laos, as in other countries. It has been questioned, however, if increased urbanisation in Laos will necessarily be a good thing.

While there is certainly room for an expansion of Lao industry, there are also planned increases in agriculture and forestry sectors and, at least until mechanisation is introduced into these sectors, a significant population is needed in rural areas if national subsistence is to be maintained and nutrition improved. There are also very large hydro-power projects under way and on the drawing-board that will require a substantial amount of unskilled and skilled labour in currently remote locations; if Lao do not fill these positions, labour will come in from neighbouring countries. Roads built to these remote hydro-power locations will open up new areas to agriculture and sustained forestry. The hydro projects once completed will also have spin-offs in fisheries and tourism.

The current and projected urbanisation rates as noted officially could be misleading. This is because many of those who currently come into Vientiane to work, often in garment and furniture industries or semi-casually in restaurants and beer houses, do not register themselves as living in Vientiane. This is evident at various times. In elections to the National Assembly, where all Lao must vote by law, and vote in their place of house registration: at such times, like at Lao New Year, all who come into Vientiane go back home. They must also go home to get married, attend funerals, and so on.

In addition to those living and working in Vientiane but registered in an up-country village, there are many migrant workers who see Vientiane only in passing or not at all. Thus, there are villages in Champassak, which shares a land border with Thailand, where hardly a family does not have at least one or two members absent in Bangkok. Most often, these absentees are young unmarried females. Perhaps more go to work in Bangkok's factories than in sex-related service industries, but a very large number marry Thai men. (Far fewer marry Western men.)

The situation is one of comparatively porous borders: there is a Thai tolerance of Lao as 'not really foreigners', a need for cheap manual workers who understand Thai, links of marriage between Thai and Lao families, a sharing of dialect with Thai-Isaan, and general physical and cultural similarity between Thai and Lao that makes both sides feel comfortable. In such situations 'illegal' migration by Lao into Thailand is easy, frequent, not really regarded as serious, and very, very difficult to quantify.

Also difficult to predict is how far Laos will follow Thailand's example in promoting birth control. While anti-AIDS campaigners and health workers generally think much can be gained by following the Thai example, not all Lao think such control a good thing, and cite the comparatively small size of the lowland Lao population and the comparatively large influx of Vietnamese as cause for concern. There is certainly no Lao equivalent of Meechai, the tireless campaigner on behalf of the poor and birth control, to popularise the use of condoms in Laos. Recent studies of sex workers in urban and rural Laos suggest there is at best an equivocal attitude to use of condoms, while among young people outside of the sex industry, condoms are hardly ever used in spite of wide availability. This could all change quickly and significantly, as it did in Thailand. But when?

EDUCATION AND LITERACY

Laos has a mean literacy rate of 68.7 per cent. Among those aged 15–24, the rate is somewhat higher at 78.5 per cent. Of those literate, 77.4 per cent are male, 55.5 per cent female. School enrolment rates are 85 per cent in primary education (enrolment is compulsory). This declines to 35 per cent in secondary education. Of those who enroll in secondary education, the majority drop out before graduation.

The situation is worse for upland and highland (tribal) populations, particularly highland women, but it is also quite possible to find lowland teenagers, particularly girls, living in Vientiane with access to school guaranteed and required by law, who cannot read or write in any language (although they can probably understand and speak Thai as well as Lao).

The poor education is exemplified by the fact that Laos comes 129th in school enrolment status (all levels) in UN figures comparing 177 countries. This figure would be much worse were it not for the government's recent expansion of primary education, largely financed by overseas development agencies.

The National Library

The National Library, in a beautiful French-colonial building off Fountain Square, is open every day except the 29th of each month. It provides free access to books and has reading rooms available. Very few people use it. Almost nothing is available in the Lao language and knowledge of French or English is therefore required. Apart from a few government publications, much of that available is unwanted or old books given by expatriates leaving the country. There are links with national education and literacy programmes, but more than anything else the National Library epitomises the poverty of education in Laos and the simple fact that for those Lao who can read their national language, there is precious little available in that language for them to read.

Foreign-language Skills

Thus the foreign visitor, whether here for a short stay or working in Laos, could not only find himself faced with a language problem, but also problems related to pre-literacy and education limited in scope. Many Lao, particularly women, may have learnt to read at school, but ten years after leaving school they are again illiterate.

Even university students graduating in English and able to read English may have great difficulty in speaking the language. The reason for this is simple enough: poor teachers, poor facilities, poor system. There are of course some very notable exceptions and some Lao who have been sent overseas to study quickly become very fluent in foreign languages. This may not help the visitor since earlier students were sent to Czechoslovakia, the Soviet Union and East Germany, with minorities to Poland and other countries then in the Eastern Block. Others studied in France, but probably today more speak Vietnamese well than any other foreign language.

Class and Family

While speakers of foreign languages are not necessarily from the privileged class, the chances are that a good speaker of English or French belongs to a top family, is usually a Lao Loum, but often with a large dash of Chinese or Vietnamese. Every family in Laos has a different surname, and while some families are so big that members of the surname group do not know every other member, most are families rather than clans. As in other Asian countries, families tend to stand and fall together, and wealthy families in Laos are usually represented in the bureaucracy, often in the political structure, and in business. They are also often the larger landowners, form marital alliances with other important families, and tend to live somewhat segregated from poorer families. Well-placed parents will often establish structures of protection for their children, particularly where a daughter's virginity and reputation are concerned. The middle-class exists in socialist Laos every bit as much as any other country, maybe more than many. And they are not about to throw away their comparative privileges.

THE THREE CATEGORIES OF LAO

Laos, before the 1975 change, chose to rationalise its many ethnic groups into only three categories: Lao Loum, the people of the lowlands; Lao Theung, who live in middle altitudes of 400–900 metres (1,313–2,952 feet); and Lao Soung, who generally live above 1,000 metres (3,280 feet). These general categories are based on historical origins more than contemporary reality. Thus, a Lao citizen does not change category on changing altitude—a Hmong born and bred in Vientiane remains a Lao Soung wherever he or she lives. The terms may confuse as much as they clarify, and they are not officially sanctioned by the post-1975 regime. In fact the current regime does not like them. But nobody can think of a better way of reducing the hundreds of ethnicities and dialects to a manageable number. It is not within the objectives of this book to consider arguments for changing these categories. The foreign guest in Laos for some time will certainly hear them. They are now entrenched. This does not make them any more real, but the visitor needs to be aware of them.

Lao Loum

The Lao Loum generally live on the plains and in valley bottoms under 400 metres (1,313 feet), grow wet rice on permanent fields, practice the same Theravada Buddhism as is found in Thailand and Sri Lanka, and have more in common with other 'Thai' than with the various minorities of Laos.

The Lao Loum—lowland Lao—are the majority ethnic group of Laos forming about 60 per cent of the total population, and tend to be dominant when it comes to national language, politics and culture. They are an essentially homogeneous cultural group, with significant regional differences of dialect. People generally maintain their mother-dialect and regional identity even when living in Vientiane for many years. This is partly because 'standard' Lao has not been encouraged or enforced in the way that Thailand has adopted Central Thai from Bangkok as the National Language.

That the central authorities have not pushed the language issue is partly because regional identities and ties to villages of origin continue to be very strong in Laos, and partly because people are used to the situation: a Lao from the southernmost border area of Champassak, will speak that dialect among relatives living in Vientiane (who belong to the same dialect group), but also to a Lao from northern Hua Phan speaking his own dialect, which is significantly different to the language of Champassak. Dialect group affiliation is obvious immediately and an official noticing that somebody speaks the way he or she does might well ask which part of the dialect area an individual is from, and before many sentences have passed, the two will have villages, friends and even relatives in common; it's a great way to get served first! It is not just the foreigner who gets asked where he or she is from.

Lao-Thai fall within the Lao Loum category, or maybe just within it. These sub-groups are 'Thai' only in the greater sense of the Lao-Thai family, which tends to use the words Thai and Lao synonymously. Their language is essentially Lao, although with some additions, often Vietnamese or Viet-Chinese. These groups are found in greater numbers in northern Vietnam and some of them came to Laos to serve the French colonial masters. Just 20 years ago there were two distinct villages of Thai Dam (Black Thai) within Vientiane itself. At that time, in the village, traditional Thai Dam costumes were worn. Today, the people and their descendants continue to live in Vientiane but there is little apart from a dialect to distinguish them from other Lao Loum. Similar distinctions are evident with the Thai Khao (White Thai), and Thai Pa (Forest Thai). There is another group self-identified as Thai Neua, this is particularly confusing because the translation is 'Northern Thai', which is the way the inhabitants of Chiang Mai and Chiang Rai are called by others within Thailand. The Lao-Thai practice irrigated rice but also grow rice on burnt-off fields on hill sides. They may also be less attached to Buddhism in that some villages have no temple and are closer to animism in religious practices. In these respects their culture in some ways has elements of both lowland Lao and upland montagnards, as the Lao highland peoples are often called in the earlier French literature.

In the Lao language, Lao will often refer to other Lao as Thai-Vientiane, Thai-Savannakhet, etc. In this sense the term 'Thai' has more the meaning of 'origin': *Chao men Thai Champassak, bo*? May be translated as, 'Do you originate/come from Champassak?' Do not become over concerned with the use of the word 'Thai' in Lao. It doesn't worry the Thai or Lao, so no reason for it to concern you.

Lao Theung

The Lao Theung are most commonly to be found on the mid-level mountain slopes. The largest group is the Khmu, who are also probably second only to the Lao Loum in total numbers within Laos. Other groups are the Htin, Lamet, Loven, Katu, Alak and Khatang. These peoples are thought to be 'Austro-Asiatic' and more akin to the Mon-Khmer groups in the southern province of Attopeu (who generally live at low levels). Some have developed a servile role, working for the mountain peoples usually found higher up the slopes. Khmu and Htin might have been among the original inhabitants of Laos. The two groups speak mutually intelligible languages and are generally poorer than their highland or lowland neighbours. Estimates depend on who and how you count and who does the counting, but are in the range of 15-20 per cent.

Lao Soung

This category refers to villagers who habitually live above 1,000 metres (3,280 feet). Some came in from China through northern Vietnam and have many Chinese aspects in their features, cultures and languages.

The three most important Lao Soung groups in terms of numbers are the Hmong, the Mien (also known as Yao or Zao) and the Akha. All rely on slash and burn cultivation, although some incorporate irrigated rice fields in the form of permanent terraces. All were the principal opium growers until the recent successful five-year plan which almost eliminated opium and caused many Lao

Soung to move down to lower levels, in conformity with government policies of preserving upland watersheds and forest lands.

The Hmong and Mien are said to be related. This is certainly not obvious in terms of physical features, and languages are not mutually intelligible. Both groups are to be found equally in southern China, northern Vietnam and Thailand. The Hmong have several sub-divisions: in Laos these are principally the Hmong Njua (whose women wear *batik*, pleated skirts of a blue indigo colour—Green in Hmong ways of seeing, which accounts for the translation as Green Hmong) and the Hmong Deu (White Hmong, whose women wear blue trousers except at Hmong New Year, when they wear plain white skirts). A further group, which speaks the same dialect as the White Hmong, is the Hmong Gua N'ba, whose women wear armbands of patchwork on their jackets.

Unlike the Hmong and Mien, who have Chinese surname groups ordering their patrilineal clan structures, the Akha came in from the northwest, Burma and China.

The Hmong are by far the most evenly spread, with large majorities in Xieng Khouang, Hua Phan, Luang Prabang and Saynabouly. Many Hmong now live at low altitudes and practice permanent rice. There are large concentrations in various lowland areas, principally KM52—the 'village' is known only by this term, although it is now a permanent town and holds 8,000 plus Hmong and many Lao Loum. Within Vientiane, Hmong are to found in most areas, including government offices, and one, a woman, who initially headed the Committee for Minorities in the National Assembly, has recently taken the 11th place in the 11 person Politbureau, the leading political body in the country. Hmong are some 8 per cent of the total population of Laos, and Lao Soung together make up perhaps 15 per cent.

The reader wishing more comprehensive information on Hmong culture is directed to the further reading at the back of this book.

CULTURE

I define culture in the widest sense. It is both the norms and values of a society (what people recognise they should do and think) and what people actually do, and why, how, when and where they do it. There is of course a relation between what people should do and what people do, but the two never match up perfectly. This is why anthropologists, in studying how people behave, need to participate in a society and base analysis on what they see people do as well as what people of the society tell them they do. I am well aware that people do not always do as they should do, and that if a person really wants to do something, he or she will do it and think later, if at all, about rationalising actions in terms of what should have been done.

The word culture is used actively to include all being and doing, including thinking and not thinking, and passively to include the environment, social and material, in which being and doing take place.

There is a natural human tendency of all peoples to present a sanitised version of their culture to the outside world. Therefore it is not enough simply to ask Lao about their culture, although this is a good starting point for a visitor newly arrived in the country—as long as he or she remembers that real culture is as culture does. Culture can be envisaged as the many slats of a fan that, when waved, move together to perform the required function of a fan. But when the fan is closed, is it still a fan? When Vientiane fountain is dry, as it has been for many years, is it a fountain?

Culture can also be envisaged as the 52 cards that make up a pack. Some cards appear to have a greater value than others, but only in comparison to the others. Different games can be played, using the same cards but following different sets of rules. All cards are required or the pack is incomplete and cannot complete its function correctly. Of course, it is possible to cheat in all games, as in all societies, but to do so requires knowledge of the rules for playing each game. And of course, culture is not static like cards asleep in their box—culture is changing all the time, evolving through its own dynamics and through interaction with other cultures and a changing material environment. New games are being invented all the time, with new rules. Lao society is adapting to play those games; at the same time it seeks to maintain a certain 'Lao-ness'. So what are the essential components of 'Lao-ness'? Some of these are very familiar to the culture of the reader, others are more distinct. Let's start with a distinctly Lao one.

LAO WAYS OF THINKING

Some Lao may be able to quote Jean Jacques Rousseau and Karl Marx and Simone Signoret. The comparatively few Lao who have even heard of these names will almost certainly have learnt them overseas, probably at a French university. For the majority population, however, intellectuals are about as common as in England.

The Lao world is divided into good and bad. There may indeed 'be no good nor bad yet thinking makes it so', which the Lao might see as a good reason not to think too much. Thought itself is neutral but too much thinking is as bad as not enough; in Laos it is often very difficult to hit on the appropriate amount of thinking. As a guide, it is the minimum required in any known situation.

A Lao Joke

Keo: Who're your favourite writers?

Roger: I like the works of Marx-Lenin

Keo: I asked about writers not fruits.

(Explanation: 'Marx' is pronounced *Mak* in Lao—exactly the same word means 'fruit'. It precedes any fruit, e.g. *mak kuay* is banana, *mak nao* is lime, *mak Lenin*…)

The Lao do good in order to get good, and when they get bad presume it is because they have done bad, i.e. not enough good. Some things cannot really be bad. Relatives never do wrong. Even if banged up in a police cell, they must be fed and supported morally and physically. So, to a degree, the Lao will say *bo pen nyang* (never mind) about right or wrong, stick with your family. But the Lao will not say *bo pen nyang* if it's you the foreigner involved; no reason for a Lao to take your side. If Lao culture is a pack of playing cards, a Lao individual can be seen as a card in that pack, the Lao family is the suit of which the individual is part, the combination of suits is Lao society, and the cultural norms and values are the rules of the games the pack can play. So, where does that leave you? Think about it. Joker? But don't think about it too much. It will just give you a headache.

Muan

Whatever culture is: being, doing, thinking, drinking, dancing, singing, reading; and whatever culture is: not being, not doing, etc., in Laos it should be enjoyable. *Muan* in Lao, like *sanuk* in Thai, is often translated as fun. But fun in the usual sense of the term in English is a rather exceptional state—the English, Germans, French and so on go about their daily activities following some kind of normative straight line where fun is something special above that line. Westerners usually do not expect life to be lived at the peaks of pleasure and laughter. Neither do the Lao. Lao, on the other hand, do expect the daily life-line to be *muan*. It is the exceptions which are *bo muan*, and to be avoided.

While fun is a usual English translation for *muan*, it is not really all there is to *muan*. *Muan* encompasses such Englishness as nice, but only when referring to an activity, even if that activity is lying down in a nice place, or to a subject of entertainment, like a movie. A movie can be *muan* even if it scares the hell out of you, if you find it in any way enjoyable.

If a Lao asks Robert, "Robert *muan, bo*?" This does not mean, "Are you fun?" Such a question would be an unsympathetic statement. "Is Robert enjoying himself?", is a better translation, being a sympathetic enquiry of concern that Robert may be a bit down in the dumps. There is a world of difference between the two. Unfortunately, Lao grammar has built in ambiguities that often make the language only fully understandable and translatable in particular situations and with reference to Lao culture rather than the exact order and meaning of words.

For the visitor to Laos, the important thing to know is that when asked if something is *muan*, you always answer positively that it is, not honestly that it is boring or a waste of time, even if that is in the heart of your thoughts and on the tip of your tongue. If you progress in Lao language, there will be exceptions even here: "Was your visit to the dentist *muan*?" is play talk and provokes either an exaggerated *Muan*!! (yes!) or just a smile or a laugh. But you never ask a Lao if a funeral was *muan*, even if you personally enjoyed it immensely.

Life itself can be *muan* or it can be *bo muan*. If the former, the speaker does not have to be a playboy or a millionaire, 'enough to live, enough to eat' is not just a common Lao saying, it really is (or should be) enough to make life *muan*. So, *muan* is not a difficult state to achieve or maintain—if it had to be in any sense strived for, it would not be *muan*. Use of the word *muan* implies that life is comfortable without any great hassles, indeed without any hassles at all. If a Lao is stuck in a *bo muan* situation, he or she will try to get out of it, even if it means return to a poorer standard of living.

Muan is definitely a thought-related process, but it is not one which requires a great deal of thought, which in itself is *bo muan*. The Lao psyche avoids what is not comfortable and is difficult. As psyche's go, the Lao one is not great at coping with stress, but is pretty good at avoiding stress.

Khay Luuk

Khay luuk (baby eggs) are the eggs with the chicks formed inside them. Often sold at the roadside, they are a favourite with Lao travellers, and you might find yourself sitting on a bus next to a large lady peeling off the shell around a curled up unborn chick and sinking her teeth into the unborn flesh. *Khay luuk* are part of Lao material culture and they also typify Lao thinking.

A Lao, told that westerners don't like this sort of thing, might shrug his incomprehension. He will not verbalise it, at least not to the foreigner, but he might be thinking: these foreigners are a rum lot—they eat chickens and ducks, and they eat eggs of various birds, yet they don't eat the food that comes between the chicken and the egg. Lao do.

What came first, the chicken or the egg? Lao don't think about this question. With *khay luuk* they get chicken and egg at the same time.

Bo Pen Nyang

Bo pen nyang means never mind. Literally: 'there isn't anything'. By extension, we arrive at: there isn't anything bothering me. Perhaps 'No Problem' would be a better translation. The Thais used to have *bo pen nyang*, but they called it *may pen rai*. They lost much of it when they took on the benefits of a real education and the responsibilities of modernisation, with all its angst. The Lao still very much have it. In Laos, there are no problems that *bo pen nyang* cannot solve.

Bo pen nyang is also the answer to *khop chai deu* (thank you very much) and in this function it encapsulates the Lao view of thinking: 'think nothing of it'.

You will be getting the idea that the Lao don't think that much. This is true. Most still live a traditional life style where action has meaning but at the same time is spontaneous and repetitive. Try tying your shoelaces when really thinking about it: chances are you'll get into a mess. The Lao can get through most actions of their daily life in the same way you tie your shoelaces. Laces still get tied, and are better tied for not thinking about the process.

Thoughtfulness and Nam Jai

Monks, when they are not learning the scriptures by heart, can and do think. See the monk eating. Before doing so, he thinks his food mud. See the monk on the morning alms round. See the beautiful young girl put food in the monk's bowl. See the monk, eyes cast-down, thinking of her as piles of skin, hair and bones. Back behind the walls of the wat, the monk will certainly not be thinking as he ties his shoelaces, since he almost certainly has none to tie, but he might well be thinking of every little movement of every little muscle as he walks barefoot and mindfully across the temple grounds.

Such concentration helps him pass beyond thought to meditation. He walks very, very, very slowly. A meaningful action, so full of thought that thought becomes its meaning. This is great for the advancement towards enlightenment of monks, but, can you imagine, in a land where lay people anyway walk slowly, what would happen if everybody did everything this way? In daily life it is often better not to think too much.

On the other hand, the Lao have *nam jai*, which is thoughtfulness in the English sense of the term and comes top of the values. If you can be thoughtful enough of the old and sick to spend your time with them and help them to the toilet, this is much, much more deserving of respect than giving them US$ 10. Just think about that the next time somebody asks you for ten dollars. But don't think too hard.

Bo Pen Nyang

Roger: Tell me, does Lao life have anything like the Spanish *manyana* in it?
Keo: Well, the Lao have the *bo pen nyang* attitude to life.
Roger: How would you translate *bo pen nyang*?
Keo: Well, it's a bit like *manyana*... but without the urgency!

Nop

The *nop* has no easy translation in English. It is the same as the Thai word *wai*. The *nop* is in the realm of meaningful actions for which no thought is necessary (for the Lao, that is). *Nop* is the action of raising both hands, palms flat and joined and lowering your head. It is not just a way of saying hello without words, it is more a public literal demonstration of the 'height rule': in any social encounter between two or more people, the social inferior takes on a physically inferior position and the social superior assumes a posture of physical superiority.

If talk of such social distinction in a socialist society worries you, you will be glad to know that it worried the leadership of Laos for some years after the 1975 change in regime. At the time, use of the *nop* seemed to run counter to the ideas of equality that the new leadership wished to introduce. For a few years, the *nop* was frowned upon and it almost disappeared. During this period people still needed a way of greeting each other, and, strangely perhaps, the handshake of the French colonial masters was used, even between men and women, and thought to be more egalitarian. Gradually, the *nop* returned and the handshake retreated. The handshake never disappeared completely, and comparatively high up men and women might still prefer to use it, particularly with foreigners, so don't rush into a *nop* unless it seems to come naturally, which it might well not do for a foreigner.

The *nop* itself has not regained all its ground and compared to the Thai *wai*, which in extreme cases involves the flattening of the whole body on the ground, eyes turned to the ground and joined hands held up above head level, the Lao *nop* has clearly lost its most powerful demonstrations of inequality.

In the Laos of today, the *nop* is in daily use but the visitor may not see much of it. Girls who take your few kip for a coffee are most unlikely to throw in a *nop* of appreciation, as they might do in a similar situation in Thailand, not even if you step outside of Lao custom and leave a large tip.

Since spontaneous use of the *nop* is only between lowland Lao, that means about 60 per cent or so of the population, the visitor might decide to stick to a verbal *sabai dii* as greeting enough. On the other hand if somebody throws you a *nop*, you might be tempted to reply in a similar manner.

This reply is not really necessary, as the social rule is that the inferior always initiates a *nop*. If the *nop* comes from a servant or another obvious social inferior it is better not to reply, or to reply with a smile of acknowledgement. This is because the *nop* in Laos, like the *wai* in Thailand, is a symbol of respect between unequals.

It doesn't matter what the person behind the *nop* is really thinking, he or she is just conforming to current social convention. Convention is much stronger in Laos than in a European country, but even so some simple parallels can be made. In the West, the man cutting your hair or assisting you at the supermarket may call you sir or madam; you don't think much about it, but you almost certainly don't reply to the barber with sir. Same with the *nop* in Laos. If the social distance between two people is very great, the *nop* is not returned.

The *nop* is a respect continuum. The lower the head comes down to meet the thumbs of both hands, the more respect is demonstrated. In daily practice, without thinking about it, this respect continuum has three main positions and many in-betweens:

1. Hands held together close to the chest, fingertips reaching to around neck level but not above the chin, head only slightly inclined. This position is used between equals. It is also used by strangers dressed in a fashion to suggest equality who are unknown to each other and unaware of social differences. In Laos this *nop* is seen far less frequently than in Thailand, unless people are coming together in a formal occasion such as a wedding feast. Many people prefer to smile their greeting, a few will shake hands, some will say or do nothing at all—which should not be read as a slight.

2. Head lowered so that the fingertips reach above the tip of the nose. Used by an inferior initiating social interaction with a superior. It may also be used by a beggar asking for money as an alternative to the outstretched palm.

3. Forehead lowered to the base of the thumbs held in the *nop*. Accompanied by a bending forward of the body, Japanese-style, from the waist.

The simple rule is: if you receive a *nop* of high respect, reply with something a little lower. If greeting a monk, use your most respectful *nop* and expect none in reply.

The *nop* is more in daily evidence in an urban than a rural environment. Indeed, in an agricultural village, where everybody knows everybody, language and social actions are equal and the only place you might regularly see any indication of formal respect is in the *wat* or between schoolchildren and teacher. When introductions are taking place, either a *nop* or a handshake is appropriate. There is no need for both, although some Lao faced with a foreigner are as unsure as you are as to how to interact and might throw in both, in which case the *nop* comes first.

When entering the house of a Lao, at least for the first time, *nop* the owners. If they are standing in a group, one *nop* is enough, you can swing it to take in everybody.

It is a sign of the times, particularly the English-language *Vientiane Times* which is one of the least controversial papers in the world, that the newspaper has run over the past year several articles on local culture and encouraged parents to teach their children to *nop* their elders and betters. This represents a complete turnaround on the position of authorities in the years following the change of regime in 1975, when the *nop* tended to be seen as reactionary and outdated.

When somebody is tying thread (*mat khen*) on your wrist in a *basi* ceremony, hold your free arm in a half-*nop*. You may also *nop* your thanks with both hands as the knot-tying completes. (This is Laos: none of this is obligatory.)

Whoops

There is no established Lao term for this most Lao of actions or noises. Once more, it is an action that appears totally spontaneous and belies thinking. I call it a *whoop* but it could as easily be called a *whee*. It is a sound made by a group of Lao gathered together in a non-formal social situation, usually eating together, or just drinking or chatting. At some point, one person will say something that strikes a note with the group, something funny or a play on words, and at precisely the same moment everybody present, and that means everybody except you, will let out a *whoop*. There is no parallel in western cultures.

Applause might come close, but applause has indicators for the participants to follow: the show has ended, or perhaps an ice-skater has performed a particularly difficult triple leap with amazing beauty and skill—but even then one person usually leads the applause and others follow. And with spontaneous applause it can go either way, the leader might not be followed, or the following might be strangled rather than enthusiastic, and the clapping can either change the whole experience or tail off embarrassingly. Not so with the Lao *whoop*, which issues mystically with no perceived signal from every single Lao in the group. Never does one Lao *whoop* alone; you can't make *whoopee* all by your self. Spontaneity rules. To be Lao is to *whoop*—not because everybody else is *whooping*, but because it just happens without thinking. The *whoop* over, the group resumes its shared activity, its cohesion and homogeneity confirmed.

Your first encounter in a group of *whoopers* might leave you sitting on the sidelines. Never mind. You are witnessing the essence of being Lao: togetherness. At the same time, you are probably experiencing a most un-Lao sensation: being left out of the group: being alone. Perhaps an hour will go by before the next *whoop*, perhaps a dozen will follow rapidly one upon the other. Group spontaneity won't be tied down to a schedule.

Togetherness

The *whoop* is the archetypical sound of spontaneous social interaction among the Lao. It is the sound of togetherness. And togetherness is vital to the Lao psyche. In Lao society, one person does not stand alone, as long as there is any alternative. Many Lao have never been alone in the sense the western reader will have experienced and perhaps even enjoyed. The idea of spending a night alone in a hotel room is, for most Lao inside Laos, perhaps unfortunately necessary, but it is certainly not something to be enjoyed. Lao who have never slept alone in a room will sometimes rationalise their fear in terms of unknown spirits, even if the room is in the only house they have ever lived in. Most Lao will go to great trouble to avoid being alone: if the husband has to go away, the wife will invite a relative to stay with her and sleep in the same room. If her husband is a western foreigner, she might marvel at his courage, but if he says openly that he enjoys occasionally being alone, she might suspect he has something wrong with him (or suspect perhaps another motive).

If your maid leaves her comparatively easy and highly paid job with you, and leaves the nice, cool room you gave her, to return to sleeping on the floor above the furniture factory with the other girls, the deciding factor will undoubtedly be that working and living alone is *bo muan*. Of course if you have two maids and they share the same small room, you may not encounter this problem. A Lao alone can survive, but cannot thrive.

The very gregarious nature of Lao: the almost-fear of being alone, provides a natural check on anti-social behaviour. The slightest whiff of the anti-social and a Lao loses face among those he or she cares about: family, friendship group, village, neighbourhood. Lao keep themselves in line just by being together in reasonably large numbers, at least numbers larger than one.

Wow-lin

Wow-lin (play talk) is often but not always associated with alcohol. A friendship group might get together regularly for drinking sessions, but might include some non-drinkers. Drinking rarely reaches large proportions and aims at mellowness rather than outright drunkenness. Often, in the countryside, a single glass is used and one person pours a drink for another, whether it is home-brew or beer. The pace of drinking limits drunkenness and encourages chit-chat. Such get-togethers perhaps have more to do with social control than with social license. As in other societies, the passing of alcohol allows a certain leeway in acceptable behaviour and talk on these occasions might get quite risqué. Some speakers are cleverer than others, and the cleverest can almost criticise husband, wife or neighbour

---

Wow-lin in Social Context

An outspoken women who may want to tease the young man sitting opposite with his new bride, may just ask him: "*Mak mia laay, bo*?" ("Do you like your wife a lot?") Pause. "*Leu mak mia noy*?" ("Or do you like your wife a little?")

The first sentence, given the ambiguities of Lao grammar, can also mean, "Do you like a lot of wives?" And the second can also mean, "Or do you like your minor wife?"

The young man is faced with an impossible choice: does he like a lot of wives or does he like his mistress? He can only laugh. Not to do so would mean that he, and not the outspoken woman, would lose face. In fact talk of losing face in such situations suggests there might be some tension in the air. There usually is not, and the laughter will be genuine, perhaps terminating in the spontaneous Lao group *whoop*, which may be seen as another release of tension.

while making them laugh. This is done through the telling of stories slightly exaggerated, often as if they were quite true. A verbal parry-riposte might develop with some razor-sharp quick-fire repartee. The aim is to make people laugh—itself a release of any tension for the 'performer' and the audience. Laughter is a well-known healer.

When people are engaged in such tall story-telling, or just throwing in an outrageous line or openly telling untruths, they are said to be engaged in *wow-lin*. This is a favourite Lao activity, whether in a group, where it will be readily appreciated, or just between two people, where one may 'send up' another. If one of the people is you, and even if your Lao passes muster, you might not recognise that you are having your leg pulled until your Lao partner says, "*Wow-lin*" ("Just joking").

Wow-lin is joking, but goes beyond telling jokes, often using word play in a social context that might be described as making jokes.

A Wow-lin Joke

At the market, a woman complains to the vendor of *sai gop*, sausages.

"When I bought sausages from you yesterday, you told me they were a mixture of buffalo meat and pork. When I ate them, they were full of bits of metal!"

"But, *nang*," the vendor replied. "Have you not heard that the *khwai lek** is everywhere replacing the *khwai*?"

* *khwai lek* (iron buffaloes) is a term for the motorised ploughs that run on two wheels instead of four legs.

People who develop a reputation for skill at *wow-lin* are admired. They animate the social group and thereby perform a service to all its members. *Wow-lin* is essentially interaction between friends. It can also enter the spontaneous repertoire of the *mor lum*, a professional singer hired for an evening's entertainment at an event or at a private home that might go on all night. The *mor lum* may be a woman—indeed some are very attractive young women. They are the nearest thing Laos has to a stand-up comic, although they usually sit down. They quickly perceive the little quirks of the unknown audience and can get away with comments that would be quite outside the pale of a normal conversation. The Lao are not alone in the world in allowing things to be sung which would be risky to put into the spoken word. Eskimos have a similar institution and the Hmong of Laos allow a women to sing of her woes in a way that would not be acceptable were she to say it as it is. The difference with the *mor lum* is that her calypso-like spontaneity must be *muan*. As long as it is fun, even some political commentary may be included. Thus, *wow-lin* serves more important functions than just raising a laugh—although it does that too.

Gin Khao

At some point early on in your stay, you will hear the ubiquitous call, '*gin khao*' (often transliterated *kin khaw*), it simply means 'eat' or more literally 'eat rice'. If people say it to you, it is an invitation to eat. They may or may not mean it, and may or may not particularly want you to accept, but so engrained is the idea of eating together that people automatically invite you to eat with them, if, that is, they are sitting down eating at the time you turn up. Don't worry, a refusal will not offend. In fact it is polite to refuse with the simple formula '*gin layo*' (eaten already). If, on the other hand, you have just walked in on them in a restaurant, that excuse sounds a bit odd, so you pick another one like, 'just waiting for my friends to turn up'. Of course, if they are your friends or you want to join them, go ahead.

Any social event that you are invited to (except for official openings or large government affairs such as the national day parade), will always be accompanied by eating. To invite somebody to your house, either by invitation card or simple verbal mention, will always involve some communal eating. Normally, you do not leave before eating.

It follows from this that eating alone is a rather sad state of affairs and many a Lao would rather not eat in public if alone. Togetherness sometimes seems to the foreign visitor like a fear of being alone. A Lao might feel sorry for you if they see you eating alone, but if you say you prefer to eat alone, the Lao will be left thinking that you are a bit weird (although a little eccentricity is accepted within the framework of Lao tolerance.)

TO SIN OR NOT TO SIN?

Traditions are anything that has existed over time, and for a long time. They have existed in the past and continue through the present. Logically, they should be set in stone. However, in reality, Lao traditions are much like Lao history. They are what people remember, and to an extent what people want them to be, either to fit in with the political requirements of the present or the current fashion. Thus, one example: traditionally Lao women wear the long, close-fitting *sin*. This is often described as a 'wrap-around skirt'. It is not really wrap-around but tubular like a Malay *sarong*, one climbs in, and folds the slack around the waist; the gold or silver belt often worn is largely decorative, the *sin* being held up by a simple hook and eye.

After the change in regime of 1975, every woman seen in public was wearing a *sin*, as this was part of a dress-code favoured by the new socialist government. In some ways, therefore, the new progressive socialist regime gave new life to an old conservative tradition. Wearing the *sin* reinforced identity as Lao, and in a way reinforced traditional social values that conformed to what was wanted of the new Lao: a return to honesty, hard work, unselfishness, community and an end to the decadence of prostitution and deviance that had become so prevalent in Laos during the long years of civil war.

Today, the wearing of *sin* in public is certainly okay, but more young woman do not wear the *sin* as normal daily dress. The majority of young people wear jeans or other items of universal culture. Young women, like their mothers, will don a *sin* to enter government offices, and most will wear a *sin* if required to do so because they work in any office—even one selling airline tickets. All, or almost all (and there is a great difference indicated by 'almost') will wear *sin* if making merit through *takbat* (giving food to monks in the street) or attending a wat for any reason. Today, the non-Buddhist *basi* (thread tying ritual) remains central to any important social occasion and is a specifically Lao tradition (albeit that variants are found in Thailand's northeast and north), but young women attending a *basi* might today not bother to put on their *sin*, or may change from *sin* to jeans for the party that follows.

There is more to Lao tradition than women wearing *sin*, but this is emphasised because of the durability, and even resurgence, of wearing *sin* as a symbol of Lao identity. This dress-code was sanctioned by the same authorities who tried unsuccessfully to adapt other traditions, such as the feeding of monks, in the period following the great change of December 1975. The dress-code was accepted because Lao women love their traditional dress, changes in religious practice was rejected because people loved the traditions of their religion.

Thus, in Laos, we cannot draw up two cultural columns labelled 'tradition' and 'change' and throw everything before a certain time onto one side and after a certain time into the other. Reality is a bit more complex than that. To put this another way, in the salty words of one foreign old-hand: 'Laos is still the land of whores and virgins, but today the two qualities may sometimes be found in the same person.'

There is hardly a Lao woman who does not possess at least one *sin*. These can be as cheap and everyday as a pair of jeans or very carefully crafted and expensive. They typify Lao tradition rather than change. The golden road to prosperity now directs Lao out of traditional life, so the time of the *sin* is perhaps as numbered as the remaining days of the buffalo.

TRADITIONAL BUDDHIST VALUES

This is not the place to go into the hundreds of sutras that make up the equivalent of a Buddhist bible, or even to summarise the principles, practices and traditional values of Buddhism. The interested reader is directed to Gerald Roscoe's excellent little trilogy for this information. However, since every Lao schoolchild will know them, or should know

"The children are at school, the young girls in Bangkok, who will look after the buffalo and wear the *sin*?"
—Lines sung by a traditional *mor lum*.

them, it is appropriate to jot down the five great 'Do Not' commandments of Buddhism. These are things that all Lao Buddhists should obey. They are not the same as the Noble Eightfold Path that is advisory rather than required.

> **The Five Basic Precepts**
> 1. Do not take life
> 2. Do not steal
> 3. Do not commit adultery
> 4. Do not tell untruths
> 5. Do not take intoxicants

Most Lao recognise these five requirements much of the time. For the occasional failing, *ka'ma* can hopefully be re-balanced by a spot of merit-making.

Taking Life

This means killing anything, both the higher forms of life, which include elephants and people, and the lower forms, which include cockroaches and mosquitoes. Vegetarianism is rare in Laos, particularly among the monks, who must calmly eat anything placed in the bowl by design or by accident. Luckily, the art of rationalisation provides the way out. Fish and meat purchased in the market would not have been killed if nobody bought it; but the customer is not usually involved in the killing, so that's all right. And when, as does often happen in both rural and urban scenes, frogs need to be tapped on the head before being skinned and grilled, and chickens need to have the throat cut before being plucked, well, they are completing their destiny, and there is always the balancing act of merit, where the best bits will be given to the monks before the rest is cooked and eaten by people who like to eat a lot of leaves and vegetables, but usually to the accompaniment of some animal protein—indeed, it would be quite insulting to invite somebody to eat and not have at least one animal protein dish. As for spraying the air against flying and crawling bugs—the bugs can, in theory, always get away or, at least, always live somewhere else.

Theft

Very few Lao steal. Which leads to the question of why many Lao go to lengths to secure their doors and other entrances with roll-down metal shutters, bars on windows, and padlocks on gates. Perhaps they are simply helping others to avoid temptation.

Adultery

Adultery by a man's wife with another man, whether or not the other man is Buddhist, is clearly very bad. On the other hand, a man's visit to a guest house (not the one next door) where he has a few beers and a roll with a young girl is usually not considered as adultery. Not unless the girl happens to be married, and married to the man's friend or relative. So, in spite of the comparatively high place accorded Lao women in maintaining home, religion and economy, double standards are alive and well in Laos. That being said, the incidence of sexual gratification outside the marital bed may be smaller in Laos than in some other Southeast Asian countries. Maybe this has something to do with the Lao woman's control of the purse strings!

Telling the Truth

Truth and untruth are debatable concepts. Not that a Lao is ever likely to be caught debating them. Like most people, most Lao like to be flattered and apparent self-deprecation is often an appeal for flattery. When Lao say they are too dark, you say, "Oh no, you are just perfect, indeed any whiter and I really would be dazzled by your beauty." It is really not good to say, 'But I like a bit of dark meat', even if you do.

Occasionally, the Lao can appear very frank and sometimes, quite acceptable Lao speech habits sound odd in translation. Lao lies may appear gratuitous, maybe even rude or mean, to the foreigner. If somebody calls to ask if you know where your *fan* (boy or girl friend) is, then tells you the love of your life has just got into a Thai-registered taxi with a hulking foreigner, your '*bo pen nyang*' may not come easy. Things are not made any easier when you phone your *fan*'s number and her mother tells you she has just popped out to the market.

You may call an hour later and father says she has just popped out to the market. Eventually, you will realise that when the whereabouts of a person is unknown, they have always just popped out to the market. This may seem a frivolous point but it is significant. Like everybody, a Lao has a secret life not worn on the sleeve. This is considered further below.

Life-saving Operations

Many foreigners get rankled when it seems like everybody and their mother needs a life-saving operation and will die unless the foreigner pays for it. The correct reply is to ask how long they have got before they die, and when told two weeks at most, say 'call me in three'. They will.

Intoxicants

Many people think *Beer Lao* the best domestic product in Laos, and the most successful industry. They might well be right. Advertised everywhere, on sale everywhere. Should a Buddhist society be so keen on promoting intoxicants? You do not ask such questions, of course.

Many Lao, particularly women, simply cannot drink a small glass of beer without going first red then silly, then passing out or vomiting. It doesn't stop them from repeating the experience. To believe Lao women, all virginities are lost following drinking sessions. Getting happy should be *muan*, and it should not give guilt feelings. Lao say they don't think of beer as really alcohol, but they would never offer it to the monks along with the Pepsi-Cola.

Other intoxicants include opium, heroin, marijuana and amphetamines. All of these have been produced in Laos. Marijuana was, until recent years, a part of the flavouring of *pho*, a noodle soup of Vietnamese origin that became the Lao national dish, and almost the only available restaurant fare for some years after the change of regime. At the time when there were crackdowns on many things, an armful of dried marijuana, wrapped in a foreign newspaper, could be had for one dollar at any stall in the tobacco section of the Morning Market, where opium would be placed in the trader's drawer, not so much for fear of the police as to protect a valuable commodity. All that has changed now. The marijuana is kept in a sack well at the back.

Opium

It was only into the third millennium that Laos launched a five-year plan to eradicate opium cultivation. Foreign donors were skeptical of the plan—after all it had taken 20 years to reduce opium crops in Thailand, and Thailand grew less than Laos. After initial successes greatly reducing cultivation, the 2010 harvest was back to the high levels at the beginning of the century. Modern designer drugs have taken over among the young disco-going crowd in Vientiane. Pill-poppers are a lot more difficult to identify than chaps who lie around for hours drawing on pipes of opium. The pipes themselves, or reproductions, are on open sale on Sam Sen Thai Road in Vientiane. Opium is more than just nostalgia for the bad old days.

So, how do the Lao score in maintaining the Five Basic Precepts of Buddhist life? Maybe none too well. The Precepts seem to belong more in the realm of the ideal than in the reality. This, however, does not make them one jot less important to a Lao.

THE SECRET LIFE OF THE LAO

The world around a Lao can be a dangerous place. If the spirits don't get you, gossip might. For this reason, a Lao needs the possibility of retreat to a familiar place where he or she is safe, where the drawbridge can be pulled up, all 32 pieces of the *khwan* can be serviced, repaired and retied into the body. This place is the familiar world of the family. Some timid creatures, male or female or in-between, feel so threatened by the world outside that they rarely leave this familiar world. Others can physically step out into the greater social environment but feel the need for a mental recharge through periodic trips home.

Remember when you were young? The big world beckoned and you went. Remember when, for the first time, you left your familiar bed, home-cooking, mum and dad, the family dog, and the stairs that creaked comfortably not threateningly? I bet you were homesick. Maybe that's all it is with the Lao. A sort of homesickness. A deep-felt need to belong. If you could turn back the clock and satisfy that need, wouldn't you do it? Well, the Lao can, and do. The Lao can home better than any pigeon.

A Lao can *kit hot*, miss something or somebody, when a familiar person is barely out of sight—sometimes when they are right there but asleep or writing at a desk, in a different spiritual world. A Lao can also forget, or pretend to forget, an unwanted experience or person that threatens the link with the spiritual homeland of family, as soon as the familiar home is regained. Most Lao has the uncanny ability to turn off his or her thought process and withdraw from whatever is threatening. A Lao is the superficial emblem on your computer desktop beneath which a whole book can be invisibly saved.

The connection between the superficial emblem and the hard-disk essence is an important and personal one, and it is a connection for which a Lao is unlikely to give you the password.

Does the Lao now fit more the stereotypical western image of the inscrutable oriental? He or she should. There is a lot more to a Lao than a smile, a *sin*, a *nop*, merit-making, even more than a strong preference for the *muan*. You should realise this. But you are not required to delve into this secret essence, this *khwan*. In fact you are required not to delve in, at least not too far.

How does this image of the Lao fit with the myriad of questions that are asked on first acquaintance? Where do you come from? What do you do? How much do you earn? What food do you like? How old are you? And how does it fit with life in the goldfish bowl, where it seems impossible to be alone and more than slightly deviant to want to be?

How does this image fit with the apparent self-disclosure of personal problems to a monk or to the boss, when such self-disclosure may cover the most intimate problems of social or even physical relationships with a spouse or loved one?

Well, there is a fit. And quite a tight fit at that. And what may appear as contradiction become complement when the nature of the fit is understood.

The secret life of the Lao is very much to do with the *khwan*. It has nothing much to do with *khwam lap*, 'a secret'. The Lao are not very good at keeping secrets. On the other hand, they are very good at keeping the soul. *Khwan* itself implies *khwan lap* (a secret inner presence). The secret nature is vital. The Lao soul is not laid bare.

There is nothing sinister in this. The secret life of a Lao is not the same as the secret life of an English person. The English say that everybody has a skeleton in the cupboard. The English extend this to include almost everything.

It is considered somewhat un-English and impolite to enquire about the kind of things a Lao wants to know about, particularly how much one has in the wallet at the end of the month. Americans from both sides of the Panama Canal, like Latins in Europe, tend towards the other extreme and disclose and request personal

Each Lao has a secret life below the surface and most are reluctant to reveal more than glimpses of this life. Predictable and known on the surface, unknown and unpredictable below the surface. Which is the real Lao? The superficial one or the deeper, unknown one? The answer is that both are equally real: the known and passive surface protects what is underneath—an incredibly fragile soul.

information more readily, seeing openness as a virtue where the English tend to see reserve between strangers as appropriate to norms of social life. The Lao fit into both moulds: they will disclose the comparatively superficial aspects of their existence in a very open and transparent way, but clam up or go berserk when something or somebody touches their souls. This has nothing to do with dark secrets of a past life and is the same for whores and accountants; good or bad, people do not like to have their souls touched.

The *khwan* originates in and in a way remains with the family. *Khwan* interlinked by family bonds tend very much to behave in the same way. Another way of saying that is: like begets like.

This does not mean that a Lao is happy to bare the soul in a family environment. A girl, or a boy, goes home to Mum but doesn't necessarily cry on Mum's shoulder. Periodic refuge in the family is the best way to repair a soul that might be getting a bit worn around the edges. This is because each person's *khwan* comes from the womb of the family and, like Superman returning to Kripton, needs to check-in for a recharge occasionally.

So, what do you do when you need to know more about a Lao than what you see and hear on the surface—and you do so need if you plan to marry them or take them into business partnership—after all you can't really trust someone if you don't really know the person, can you? Well, the last thing you want to do is disturb somebody's *khwan*, so there is not much point in asking the person in question. In any case, would you trust the answer? Ask a businessman if he intends to keep the promises in the contract he is about to sign and you might not get a truthful answer. Much better to employ detective-like anthropological methods and observe what a person does than trust they speak true when they say they do. Anthropological method does not exclude asking others about the subject of your enquiry—just make sure those you ask are not direct relatives. In the eyes of a relative, no Lao ever does wrong.

A Lao knows that the *khwan* is an essential part of his or her Lao being—and is that individual being. They also know that the world is full of naughty spirits that will attach themselves to a weak or lost *khwan* and drag it down. Parallel with the naughty spirits is the world of human gossip. To placate or control human gossip is sometimes more difficult than keeping the capricious spirit world happy. While a family member can almost never do wrong ('almost' is important—a family member who commits incest or hurts another family member always does wrong), non-family are fair game. A man or a woman can be dragged down by gossip every bit as much as by spirit-attack. In fact the two act together, whenever the *khwan* is weak. And when the *khwan* is in danger, it needs support and repair. A *sukhwan* or a *basi* is in order. And, prevention being better than cure, regular doses of *mat khen* at a *basi* will strengthen the individual soul to withstand any attempts at attack by spirits or gossip.

And with prevention being better than cure, there is no need to cultivate 'self-disclosure' as a virtue when clamming up is safer. So, if you really want to know a person, give them time and don't delve too far or too obviously beneath significant surfaces. These have little to do with the superficial and material questions of Lao speech habits, but much to do with questions that can offend by disturbing the *khwan*. If you do seriously disturb somebody's *khwan*, even if you have no intension of doing so, you will be met with a withdrawal—perhaps the person will physically disappear from your world or perhaps they will just avoid you until the *khwan* gets back on form. In extreme situations, where the *khwan* feels itself under real attack, it will lose its tenuous hold on reason and enter the spirit-like world of capricious violence, lashing out without thought of the consequences. By then, it will be a good moment for you to practice your fleeing-the-scene technique.

MERIT-MAKING (*HET BOUN*)

Merit-making in daily life means little more than giving money or food and other things bought with money, to a wat and its monks. It functions to hide or correct a multitude of sins and can be seen as the balancing mechanism between the ideal of what people should do and the reality of what they really do. To use Marxist terminology heard more in a French university than in Laos, it resolves a contradiction without antagonism. For it to behave in this way, the Lao have to believe in the effect of their merit-making actions in changing their world in this life or the next. Never question this belief.

There is a status factor in merit-making, which is done in public, so that everybody can see what is being given. And if the monk-recipient may think the food mud before it is eaten and think of the woman giving the food as a pile of skin and bones, lay people around certainly do not think in these terms and the merit items are likely to be the best they can afford and each person will have gone to some trouble to make themselves very presentable. Thus, especially at the mass alms-givings which accompany significant events such as the beginning and end of Buddhist Lent, long queues form inside the most important temples to place items of food and subsistence in the many monks bowls set out on tables. The lay public carry their merit-making items in pretty *khan*, sometimes made of valuably-worked antique silver and kept in the family for generation, and all friends and neighbours can see precisely what and how much each person gives. Most people in the queues will be women—those same women who cannot become monks are the most prolific in meeting the daily needs of the monks—and they will be dressed in their finest *sin* for the occasion, have their hair done and carry just a touch of facial make-up.

How far do you get looking at all this from the perspective of western logic? Logic: Those people who give the best and most on these occasions, have the greatest need to redress the balance between their actions in the real world and karmic determination of their future existence. This is certainly not how the Lao think. While some Lao say the amount of money spent on temporary pleasure should be balanced by that given to the permanent

A Lao woman holding her khan at a merit-making ceremony in a temple.

treasure of religion, merit-making is not redressing the balance through confessional-type actions of prayer or flagellation. Individuals do not punish themselves to redress the balance, instead they do good: *Do good, get good. Do bad, get bad.*

Like everything else in Lao society, making merit is done in the company of others, but the significance of the act is individual in the extreme. Merit can and is transferred to others, particularly the dead or sick or old, certainly a lot ends up with mother and grandmother, but this merit-transfer is a very private aspect of merit-making. It takes place in the temple grounds, usually at the base of the large and sacred *boh* tree which stands in every temple as a reminder of the tree under which the Buddha achieved enlightenment, and where part of the ashes of Lao are scattered after cremation.

Merit transference is usually accomplished while pouring water over the fingers or joined hands while saying in the mind a Buddhist scan and perhaps thinking where the merit should go. Since nobody goes alone on such occasions, there is always a friend or relative to take turns slowly pouring the water. The individual gets merit for transferring the merit. If you are that friend, you can pour the water, it's a good act; but don't even think of asking where the merit went—wherever it went is part of the secret life of the Lao. And if this is getting conceptually difficult to grasp or calculate, don't think about it.

The Three Fundamentals of Het Boun

Merit-making (*Het Boun*) in Lao, brings together three fundamentals of Lao life:

- Individual *karma* which eventually determines an individual's rebirth.
- The community of the living of which the individual is part, and
- The community of dead family members.

As such it is an action that reinforces religious belief at all levels of the Lao identity.

THE LAO FAMILY

An individual Lao, whether in Washington, Jacksonville, Brisbane or Bangkok, will feel himself mentally and morally bound to his family of birth. Migrants, temporary or more permanent, will tend to go to or regroup in localities within Laos or overseas where they have family. Even the most distant migrants will expect to return not only to Laos but to the home household. When such possibilities of periodic return are denied, a Lao will wither—whatever the benefits and advantages of the new location.

Upon marriage, a Lao woman traditionally stays physically with her home family. When this is not possible, she remains with that family in every sense of the term except residency, and returns to it as often as feasible to recharge her social identity and, in a sense, "reinvigorate her soul". A Lao man, upon marriage, enters the household of his wife.

Psychologically, his *khwan* (soul) remains attached to his family of birth and, whenever he feels a bit down, it is to his family of origin that his mind will turn for succor, particularly to his own mother and grandmother.

Upon death, the *khwan* returns to the community of dead family ancestors while awaiting rebirth. A man returns to his mother, a woman to her mother. Rebirth is determined by *karma*, which can be influenced by the actions of contemporary and future family members.

Urbanisation and expatriation (even if only to neighbouring Thailand) has exacerbated the problems of social identity, with a wife intent on return to her family home, with or without her husband but with any children, at Lao New Year, and the husband forced to choose between families on such occasions—and usually going to that of the wife, since this is expected. If both families are in the same rural village or neighbouring locations—which used to be more frequently the case not so long ago, problems may be minimised, but when a Lao Loum man from Phongsali in the north marries a Lao Loum woman from Champassak in the south, psychological problems associated with *khwan* identification and travel time (home identities are separated by three days of bus travel) may lead to real marital problems. Unofficial estimates are that some 50 per cent or more of marriages in Laos end in separation or divorce, a figure almost identical to that in the industrialised west but comparatively high for a nation where 80 per cent of the population lives and works on the land. This estimate is way above the official one, which only counts registered marriages and divorces (on paper, Laos has a low divorce rate).

Marriage across ethnic boundaries can involve interaction between almost opposing social systems. Lao Loum matrilocality and matrifocality and Lao Soung or Chinese patrilocality and patriliny. Such unions can create identity problems for the children if the parents divorce but somewhat paradoxically sometimes entail less problems of *khwan* identity than where both partners to a marriage are Lao Loum.

Such mixed marriages often involve two distinct cultures, very different languages and large distances between home locations. All these factors suggest strain on relationships. However, significant events in the ethnic social calendars, particularly Lao Soung and Lao Loum New Years, do not coincide or conflict; both partners may therefore maintain pre-marital identities along with a joint marital identity which is neither and both.

Marrying a Lao Family

The many activities, interviews and copious documentations that precede a Lao-foreigner marriage are considered under the chapter 'Fitting In'. At this point, it is enough to note that such marriages follow infinitely more complex procedures than marriage between Lao, although most of the traditional procedures, as described here, are incorporated.

Some, probably most, Lao go through a traditional wedding in the home of the bride and never get round to the legal documentation. The bride's family is happy—as long as the full bride price has been paid. Should the marriage founder before it is legally recognised and certified, the bride and her mother are left standing, but standing in the family home and with a comparatively large amount of money as compensation.

> Given such close *khwan* ties, if you are not Lao Loum, nor a Hmong or even a Chinese, how do you, the guest from abroad, fit into a Lao Loum family structure on anything more than a strictly temporary visit?

The nuptials can be as complicated and protracted as the families involved care to make them—or they can be almost non-existent. Much depends on the status and wealth of the two families being linked through the marriage. If both Lao Loum, families are often of similar social standing. Where there is an obvious difference in status and wealth, the marriage is most often between an older man, possibly one already married, and a young and attractive girl. Marriage with foreigners, including Thais, often fit this pattern.

While the families are vital considerations in any marriage, Lao brides and grooms are not obliged to marry against their will. Wealthy parents of high standing may however use strong persuasion on a son or daughter who wants to marry a partner of whom they disapprove. To employ a rationale used by many Lao: good families and bad families do not mix.

Weddings can involve invitation cards and expensive restaurant-based feasts accompanied by fine whisky to mark the engagement and the marriage, or a simple once-off operation focused around a conventionally routine *basi* and a 'wedding breakfast' accompanied by home-brewed *lao-lao* in the home of the bride, to which relatives and neighbours may be verbally invited at short notice or just turn up.

Bride Price

However extravagant or modest the nuptials, the bride's mother is not likely to forego the bride price. This is non-returnable. Unlike those of some Lao minorities, Lao-Loum brides come with no guarantee.

Traditionally, the amount of bride price is settled before the *mun*, often translated as 'engagement', which can in itself be as grand as any wedding or which can be little more than a meeting of the two families or their kin-representatives. The mun can also be dispensed with altogether—any negotiations being settled between the groom and the bride's parents. The amount of the bride price depends on several factors—a high bride price means a high status for the groom, but an even higher status for the bride and her mother. (It is not completely unknown for the bride's mother privately to give a poor Lao groom some extra money so he can give it back publicly.) Traditionally the groom will move into the house of the bride, or build his own house in her compound if there is room. Land and house and rice fields traditionally pass from mother to the daughter(s)—a fact that surprises many foreigners with a preconception that Lao society is male dominated.

How much is a reasonable bride price? Between Lao of average status, around US$ 1,000, plus at least two *baht* (weight) of gold in the form of necklace and/or bracelet, worth some US$ 500 more. A 'wedding ring' can also be part of the gold package, but the foreign visitor should be aware that this is not really a symbol of marriage, a ten-year-old child might have one and a married mother of three might not. An uneducated girl of poor family and unattractive is not likely to hold out for the US$ 1,000. A Lao man who cannot pay, even after borrowing from his family of origin, can defer in the hope of paying later. Until he pays his debt, he will work a lot of the time without pay and without much of a share in produce on his wife's mother's land. The bride's parents host the wedding at their house and should host (and pay for) an evening reception either at the house or in a restaurant.

Traditional practices associated with marriage and inheritance continued unchanged during the long and periodic civil war, which may have reinforced the practice of holding land in female hands, allowing a man to leave for war and providing a security for the widow if he did not come back. Peace and increased aspirations have led to a situation where many rural households are seen as a base from which the younger members leave to work in the factories of Vientiane, as yet comparatively few, or, as is more likely, in various activities in Thai towns. This often results in a Lao groom not taking up his right of residence in the bride's compound; instead he and his bride leave to an urban environment, where they may both work. The bride's parents are equivocal about such a move: they would prefer the couple to stay near at hand, but appreciate the regular sums of money that come in to them.

A western man marrying a Lao is most unlikely to want to live in his wife's mother's house and gets no obvious benefits from his new support group. Economic rationality says he should pay less, social realities require him to pay more, usually twice as much. The Lao logic is that he will take the girl away, not only from her parents but also from the country. Unspoken is a distrust:

Even if it is pretend, it is normal for the groom to give, publicly, somewhat more than the amount agreed with the bride's parents, indicating that his donation is completely voluntary and should in no way be seen as buying a wife.

the girl might be stranded overseas and the extra money needed to bring her back. This fear is the reverse of almost all realities—the formally married Lao overseas-wife can always get money from her husband, even well after a formal divorce, and even when she is entirely responsible for the divorce. But this kind of argument when negotiating bride price would certainly not be appreciated.

Some rich Lao will pay a high price partly for status and partly because they expect to get a beautiful young girl who is still living with her parents or a close relative and has little, if any, sexual experience. Bride price negotiations are real enough, but money is not the only consideration. A man should show the kind of patience and respect for his prospective in-laws that will be required when he marries-in. Negotiations may be extended in time if necessary but they should never become unpleasant. In the end, most Lao tend to get what they pay for, and to agree to US$ 5,000 for a virgin, who has been to university and comes from a good family would be a good settlement. Of course, if the wealthy man marrying a poor but beautiful girl wants a reception to fit his status, he will need to meet all or most of the reception costs, which should traditionally fall to the bride's parents.

Payments made at the wedding are only the beginning. And here a man, Lao or foreigner, may console himself with the thought that never will anybody be able to say that he married for money. The bride might help her husband in his work or business, or she might be a perpetual drain on his resources. She might, as is traditional, handle all household expenses frugally, or she might greatly inflate them, insisting on two maids and a gardener-driver, daily trips to the beauty parlour, quantities of shoes and clothing that remain unworn until given to the constantly-visiting siblings.

Having a beautiful, young wife will only add to a rich man's status if she is faithful. Having an educated wife will only really add to his status if she comes from an important family—in which case that family will be looking for a useful marriage alliance and the bride price payment might be secondary, although high because of the need to maintain status.

Love and Marriage

With all the talk of bride price and status, where does love fit in? You might well ask. At the reception, guests put the envelope containing their money gift, clearly marked with their names, in a heart-shaped box: that's probably as near as the public world comes to symbols of love. But Lao nuptials are not without consideration of love. Even if it sometimes seems that the prime consideration is love of a bride for her mother.

Kinship Terms

Within the family, when talking to or about a direct relative, personal pronouns are usually replaced with kinship terms.

The distinctions inherent in kinship terms are indicative of superiority and status. The elder are always superior to the younger—a younger brother or sister will fetch for an elder; an elder bother or sister will help out or treat a younger. While actual feelings can differ in degree depending on the individuals involved and the age gaps, all younger family members feel some level of *kengjai* towards elder family members. *Kengjai* is often translated as 'consideration'. It is the duty of the young to be considerate to their elders and betters. Thus, a wife, presuming she is younger than her husband, and in spite of her control over household finances, feels *kengjai* towards her husband: that's why she may clip his toe nails, pluck his nose hairs, squeeze his spots and massage his aches and pains.

Kinship Terms

(These can be extended to include non-kin:)

Mae = mother

Phor = father

Phor thaw = father of mother

Pu = father of father

Mae thaw = mother of mother

Nya = mother of father

Kinship Terms

Lung = elder brother of father or mother

Na bow = younger brother of mother

Aw = younger brother of father

Pa = elder sister of mother or father

Aa = younger sister of father

Na = younger sister of mother

Ai = elder brother

Euay = elder sister

Nong = younger brother or sister, further distinguished:

Nong say = younger brother

Nong sao = younger sister

Lan = cousin, further distinguished:

Lan sao = niece, also granddaughter

Lan say = nephew, also grandson

Extension of Kinship Terms

Real feelings of kinship remain between direct blood relatives, of whom a current fertility rate of 4.77 children born to each female ensures there are a great number. Kinship terms are extended to non-relatives. Such extension has less to do with friendly feelings of being in the same family than with conventions of showing respect to elders. When a kinship prefix is attached to the first name of a non-member of the speaker's family, it is something like saying Mister or Mrs before a family name in English. With non-family, the term indicates age relative to the speaker and given a choice, the more honorific term is used: thus, if meeting an old man and wanting to call his attention, no matter if he is a car park attendant or gatekeeper and you are driving a Mercedes Coupé, call him *Lung* (elder brother of father), not *Aw* (younger brother of father). You can also call a man *Phor*, if he is old enough to be your father, or *Ai* if he is older than you.

When addressing a monk you can either use these kinship terms preceded by the honorific *Luang* (*Luang*

Phor) or more simply use *Khu Ba* (monk) as a pronoun. When talking to an older woman you might use *Mae* and should use it when talking to a nun (*Mae Si*—"mother in white"). There is also *Mae Khua/Mae Bahn* (Mother of the kitchen/house) used for a female cook or servant who is not a young girl. A male cook can be *Pho Khua*. Use *Nong* for any young household or restaurant staff (boy or girl). A Lao can use *Ai* and *Euay* for elder equivalents of the same, but you might be better regarded if you stick to *Nang* for any adult female staff, even if they are younger than you (but not too young).

Note: Thais will tell you *Nang* is used only for married women, and so it is in Thailand; in Laos it is used for all adult women, married or not—above 18-years-old. *Nang* is also a fairly common name, so if attaching the respect prefix to somebody called *Nang*, you get *Nang Nang*, which might sound a bit odd to your ears but not to the ears of a Lao. To distinguish between a married and an unmarried *Nang*, use *Nang-Sao* for Miss. Be aware that *Nang* (mid-tone and short vowel) means 'sit down' and *Nang* (high tone and long vowel) means Miss/Mrs—so try not to tell the lady to 'sit down' (unless of course you want her to do so).

To relate Lao speech habits to European, think of the extension of 'Uncle' and 'Aunty' to non-kin as a form of respect. In Europe this is used mostly by children and is limited in extent—although everybody can call a priest 'father' and the somewhat old-fashioned 'mum' is a contraction of 'marme' which in itself comes from 'madam'. So Lao use is not unknown to you, it is just a bit more complex and extensive.

While use of terms is based on the age-respect rules involved in social interaction, people regularly using such terms, particularly *ai-nong*, with non-kin may be very close friends and more or less equal. Terms are used as spontaneous speech habits and too much should not be read into their use or non-use. Feelings of *kengjai* may be indicated by use of such terms, but not necessarily. Thus two girls, or two boys, may be almost inseparable friends, and may feel no *kengjai*. A husband and wife, on the other hand may use the term *thi-hak* (darling) when addressing each other, but the wife may well feel *kengjai* towards her husband—and a good wife should do so!

The extension of Lao kinship terms into the English language is frequent by Lao. This is because English contains so few terms of respect based on age and status, respect being shown in more subtle uses of the English language which are not taught in language schools or at Dong Dok University. The visitor must be aware that a person introduced as an 'aunt' or an 'elder sister' may be precisely that, may be a friend so close that a bond equivalent to kinship exists, or may be somebody who is barely known. It is not taboo in such circumstances to ask if the sister is a 'true sister', and by all means ask if it is important for you to know, but don't overdo it.

Bloody Classy Relatives

A German recently married to a Lao was at a loss to know who his wife's real relatives were. So he lectured her on the difference between blood-relations and classificatory relations. The next day his wife, in English, introduced yet another two relatives with the words, "This is my bloody elder brother and his classy wife."

Social Security

The socialist state has far less in terms of social security for its citizens than its neighbours to the south. There is no state pension scheme, medical care provided free in hospitals and clinics is minimal, any scholarships are provided by outside assistance, and state orphanages have been called early recruitment centres for a poorly-paid police force. In this situation, the extended family continues its traditional role of security against sickness and old age.

As a unit of social and economic security, the family does not come free. All members contribute. Traditionally, all will help in the labour-intensive periods of agriculture, such as the harvesting of rice and cash crops such as coffee. Today, members may take leave from their work or studies to return to the family and help with such harvests, but this is sometimes hard to do because of long travelling times and a lack of paid holidays. For those working away from home, it usually makes economic sense to send money to hire labour in their place. This is not always possible, as labour-intensive activities often mean all families in an area are stretched at the same time, and labour for hire may be unavailable or expensive. It is also less than satisfactory because it introduces non-kin into family activities.

Vientiane, and to a lesser extent the other urban centres of Laos, contains some families for whom agricultural activities are a comparatively minor consideration or no consideration at all. Some families have 'always' lived in Vientiane. Such families may be comparatively wealthy or much poorer than the average smallholding family that typifies the rural urban Lao. There are indications that wealth and even class differences are increasing rather than decreasing as socialist Laos follows a path to prosperity that is almost identical to that followed by its richer non-communist partners in ASEAN. Whether an urban family is rich or poor, all members will be expected to make some contribution.

Children of better-off families will complete their education and get a comparatively well-paid job in a foreign company or development agency, or they will go overseas, most often to the USA, and work for a while and send money home. Some of these 'second-generation' economic migrants marry overseas and adopt foreign nationalities; almost all will maintain connections with the home family, urban or rural, sending remittances and revisiting whenever possible. Such overseas Lao will probably never call on the home family in times of need, but they continue to contribute. Within Vientiane it is possible to find complete family units where not one member seems to be paid a wage. Few of these rank among the poorest of the poor; a close look will inevitably show that relatives overseas are sending back significant sums of money. Given the low wages paid in Laos for unskilled work, such non-working families may be better off than working families with no overseas relative; they may squat in a shack and live on the edge of legality, but all will have a TV set, and many find no problem in getting to the disco at night. The one or two attractive females in such families rarely work in the normal sense, and while such groups will welcome foreigners and are always available for a *thio* (trip out), and therefore can be good fun, they are also among those families thought of by Lao as *bo dii*. Getting too deep into such a family, where usual family solidarity applies but few other values and rules are followed, can cause problems for visitors, particularly financial problems.

Children

With the median age of the Lao population currently at eighteen and 41.6 per cent under the age of 15, Laos is not a good place to be if you hate children. For the Lao, many children in the family is a continuing value and a Lao woman married in 2010 can expect to give birth to 4 or 5 children. The fertility rate is currently 4.77, a reduction from the 6.2 of 1975, but still around the fertility rate of Thailand in 1975. The infant mortality rate, while still among the highest in the world at 91 per 1,000 live births is half what it was in 1975, meaning more children survive the dangerous years of infancy.

Children born out of wedlock in Laos are rarely supported by the father, if indeed the father is identified. They may be raised by a 'single mother' within the family unit, but more usual is for the care of such children to pass from the genitor mother to the grandmother, or another relative who may be better off. Some such babies are sold at birth and looked after by their adoptive parents. Few Lao bother with cumbersome adoption procedures and some obtain birth certificates which are considered fully legal showing adoptive parents as the genitors.

Just about all Lao love children and love to play with children. However, when the child grows past the cuddly stage, often before the onset of puberty, which at age 13 plus is comparatively late, it may find itself attracting the interests of child traffickers, usually women. I am not talking about street children here, who are very few in Laos, but normal children with parents and a family. Traffickers purchase the children for a certain time and may take them out of the country to Bangkok or Pattaya in Thailand, where they work long hours in locked-door factories or in locked hotel rooms. Even the comparatively respectable among the mothers within 'bad families', who may balk at sending their daughters to a life of sin in Pattaya, will often cooperate in selling the virginity of the daughter, giving the rationale: 'If it is not sold for good money, it will only be given away in exchange for an ice-cream.' Indeed, even where mothers are not involved in the sale, plenty of young girls do sell their only asset, or give it away to a nice man who buys them cakes.

Such trafficking of children by mothers, or by the children themselves, is unfortunately not an extremely rare occurrence. A good Lao will not get involved if they know such things are happening. Involvement by the police is likely to be limited to taking a cut. And while the Ministry of Social Welfare hosts an anti-trafficking unit, there is no known case of such abuse of children resulting in a single prosecution of mother or trafficker. Perhaps the most surprising thing is that the strong bond between mother and daughter, which is the fundamental relationship of Lao society, survives such mistreatment. Any daughter will tell you: her mother can do no wrong.

KHATOEYS AND TOMS

Most countries make do with two genders; heterosexuals team up with the opposite gender and homosexuals stick to their own gender. In those countries, gender-benders may or may not be frowned upon but are unlikely to be very evident in public. Laos, on its official forms, is no different; just a choice of two. However, a visitor is not likely to be long in Laos before he or she realises that four genders exist.

Laos is a particularly tolerant country when it comes to men wanting to be women, and dressing and behaving according to the beauty-parlour imperative of the Lao woman, and women who want to be men and slouch around in outsize jackets, a fag hanging from unpainted lips, in exaggerated imitation of Humphrey Bogart.

The Lao Khatoey

How to recognise a *khatoey*? Chances are that if the lady has the following characteristics, she is no lady at all, but a 'lady-boy' as *khatoeys* are often called by Lao who think they are speaking English:

- Extreme mini-skirt
- Large feet in gold shoes
- Matching gold handbag
- Blouse buttoned at upholstered cleavage
- Exposed midriff
- Visible plastic bra
- Hair long and detachable
- Overdose of fake Channel No. 5
- Blood-red high-gloss lipstick
- An exaggeration of rouge and powder on the cheekbones

Note: It is politically-correct and gentlemanly to refer to *khatoeys* as 'she' in English (Lao language does not use gender distinctions) and to allow them into the Ladies Powder Room.

Not all *khatoey* work in the sex industry. Some are trusted servants in the homes of normal heterosexual Lao—usually the poorer ones, since few servants come cheaper than the *khatoey*. Many others work in the kitchens of restaurants as cooks or in beauty parlours as hair-dressers. These 'working *khatoey*' can be as honest and reliable as anybody else, and usually work harder for less money—which is why they are employed. They are skilled at washing clothes (but check that your wife's underwear is returned).

On the other hand, the non-working *khatoey*, or those who sell their services in the sex industry, often from the curb-side, have a reputation for dishonesty. This is perhaps no more deserved than real girls who work the beer-shops and street corners of Vientiane, Savannakhet and many other places in and outside of urban areas. The *khatoey* is also known to be a useful gossip, sometimes providing information on a business rival or an unfaithful paramour—but check out such information before acting upon it, and think at least twice before entrusting a *khatoey* with a secret (unless it is something you would like discreetly broadcast), as the *khatoey* is not known to be the soul of discretion.

Khatoeys can be amazingly outrageous and get away with it because of Lao tolerance, which tends to recognise outrageousness as the gender-bender *khatoey's* right to be.

Lao know what some foreigners and *khatoeys* get up to. At several places and times *khatoeys* have been banned from bars and places of entertainment frequented by Europeans. Many foreigners have heard before coming to Laos that sexual relations with Lao are forbidden and that contravention of the law can lead to a hefty fine and even deportation; the law covers same sex liaisons as well as heterosexual ones. So do not think that a tryst with a *khatoey* is in any way getting around the law.

Toms are a very different kettle of fish. The name comes from the English 'tomboy', but whereas a European tomboy is likely to be a bit rough and tumble but essentially feminine, the *tom* has decided that she would much rather be a man. Whereas a *khatoey* (a man who wants to be a woman) keeps the company of women and may even innocently share a bed with a Lao woman with few hairs being turned, and inevitably dreams of settling down with the perfect man, who will understand her and treat her like a woman, a *tom* behaves like a man but rarely establishes a sexual relationship with a woman, unless it's another *tom*. They rarely do well in the sex trade, since customers are inevitably men looking for women or women substitutes or other men, but *tom* can excel in the snooker hall. *Toms* have a reputation for dishonesty.

Are there more people of transient sex in Laos than elsewhere? Maybe, maybe not. The apparently large number in Laos may simply be a manifestation of the tolerance of the Lao and the intolerance of many other nationalities. On the other hand, some anthropologists have suggested that the strong role of the mother, the coddling of young boys and the generally close relationship between a man and his mother (she needs him to become a monk in her place, he looks to his mother for succor of his *khwan*), leads to a male personality that is both spoilt and far from macho. This personality is perhaps further confused by the legal role conferred on the man in all documentation as head of the family—in spite of the clearly matrifocal nature of Lao society, family names are taken from the father, not the mother. Many foreign ladies (and homosexual men) have been taken by the gentle charms of the Lao man; few marry them, sometimes feeling that they could never compete with the man's mother and sisters for his affections and sometimes feeling they could not cope in a cultural system which places the man as family head on paper but expects the wife and mother to hold the purse strings and socialise the children.

NAMES
Family Names
In spite of the comparative equality of the Lao language compared to Thai and a comparative homogeneity of culture between the rich and poor, Lao are status conscious. Perhaps the most important indicator of status is the family name. Each family name is different to any other Lao family. A few of the top names belong to families that have so grown in size that members no longer know everybody in their 'family', which becomes more like a clan. But if people share a family name, it is likely they are in some way related.

Although land and house traditionally pass from mother to daughter, family names pass through the male line (making Lao society, in anthropological terms, 'bilineal' rather than matri- or patri-lineal). This situation means that women should change their names upon marriage to the family name of their husband. Many do, but many do not, retaining instead the family name they were born with. This name would also be taken from a man, but the father rather than the husband. Whether a woman changes her name on marriage or not is not going to create any ripples of disapproval among Lao. It could however be a possible source of confusion or ambiguity, particularly if no wedding ring or children provide visible evidence of marriage and particularly if no official certification has been obtained.

Status Indicators

A Lao will establish your country, age, occupation and perhaps wage on first acquaintance, probably by asking you directly. If you don't want to disclose these superficial aspects you can lie—a 60-year-old with no beard but with some hair on his head can say he is 50 and, in a land where male life expectancy is 53, probably be believed (and if you are not believed, it doesn't matter). Some Lao think Europeans consider it impolite to ask age, so you can hide behind that explanation without fear of challenge. If you don't want to say how much you earn, you can smile and say *bo bohk* (I'm not telling). As a rough guide to status, be aware that a Lao is likely to assess other Lao on the following criteria:

- Superficial Appearance
- Family name
- Means of transportation
- Status of the person you are with
- Age
- Occupation
- Wage/organisation
- Who you know
- Education

Lao meeting each other do not automatically check out family names. If introduced by a third party, the family name may or may not be given. Family names are almost always on name cards and invitations and any documentation. Asking a Lao for his or her family name is okay, but is not a usual Lao speech habit. Family names are by no means secret, but they are not automatically disclosed. No assumptions should be made about "self-disclosure" as this is a habit in many Southeast Asian societies where one name, or even a nickname, is used.

People sharing a family name are likely in some way to be related and therefore should not have sexual relations or marry. In reality, the diaspora of Lao to many countries and the possibility of keeping the original family name calls the extended incest taboo into question.

Family name and wealth are correlated. The correlation is nothing like that in a caste society, but most members of the top families figure in the top 10 per cent of Lao society, owning 30.6 per cent of total wealth, while very few, if any, members of such families are to be found in the poorest 10 per cent of households, who own just 3.2 per cent of the total wealth and all live below the poverty line. (Figures are from a *Focus Asia* analysis of the 2005 GDP and per capita purchasing power.)

Given Names

Family names are an important indication of a Lao's wealth and education. Given names on the other hand indicate nothing at all. Lao given names are essentially the same as Thai given names, with differences of pronunciation, and the very important difference that Lao names are not indicators of gender. Most Thai names are male or female specific, like most English names; all Lao names may refer to either a male or female. This is not likely to be a source of confusion for most foreigners, but is a constant source of misunderstanding between Thais and Lao. Thais and Lao do not consider themselves 'foreigners' in the same way as both consider nationals of other countries, but culture shock related to language use differences is more evident between Lao and Thai than between Lao and any other people. This precisely because both peoples and both languages are at once very similar and yet very different.

Given names are the names that should be used by foreigners when talking to or about a Lao. There are prefixes to indicate Mr and Mrs, but these are very readily dropped in Lao (to Thai ears this makes Lao sound very upcountry, familiar and even rude). When talking to a stranger, use may be made of the prefixes *Than* for a man and *Nang* for a woman, married or unmarried. These prefixes are not usually used to mean "you", instead the term *Chao*, sometimes transcribed *Jau* or *Jao*, is used for both male or female. Chao originally meant 'Lord', but has completely lost that meaning in modern Lao—except when referring to lords of the past (Chao Anou, etc) and in some modern religious contexts.

Nicknames (Seu Lin)

Nicknames are given during the first days or weeks of life, but can change. Almost all Lao have nicknames, although some may prefer the formality of using their given name at work. Nicknames are not used on official documentation. Some Lao have multiple nicknames, one given by the parents and used in the home environment, one self-selected and used with friends and workmates, and possibly one which is easy to say for a foreigner and used essentially with foreigners. This can confuse the foreigner looking for Top, if Top is known as Nga at work and Thui at home. Lao of Vietnamese or Chinese descent may also use one name with other Lao and a different name when speaking their mother tongue.

Apart from nicknames used with foreigners, which are often one syllable taken from the multi-syllabic given name, nicknames usually do not, as in the west, represent a contraction of the given name. Thus, you can work out that Bill's real given name is William, but no way can you guess that Phet's real name is Bounteua or Tippaphone or anything at all. And it doesn't matter—you can go on using the nickname and never know the 'real' name, as most Lao do.

Nicknames are easier for the foreigner to grasp than given or family names. For a start they are always one syllable only. They are the same for male or female (as with Lao given names), they usually have an easy translation which can expand your Lao vocabulary, and are fewer in number than given names. It might also help that half the population seems to be called Noy (small)—although it can also be a problem when talking about a particular Noy. Tonal differences, consonant aspirations and vowel lengths can also mean that a single transliteration in English perhaps refers to several different names (if read in Lao)—this problem is reduced in multi-syllabic given names.

Nicknames take the place of given names and people are often introduced by the nickname only. Like given names, respect prefixes, including kinship terms, may be used on nicknames, although friends don't usually use them. Nicknames can also be used for 'you' as an alternative to *chao*.

By all means learn the literal meaning of nicknames, but don't be put off or led on by the fact that they may mean anything from fertiliser to diamond.

Titles

Modern Lao is now comparatively free of the status-filled titles that exist in Thai. These are still sometimes heard in Lao, but foreigners can happily ignore them.

Academic qualifications, while conferring status, are not usually used as attachments to names, at least not outside of the tiny academic circle. They may be written on your name card to impress, but don't expect a Lao to understand what a doctor of letters is. For certain respected professions, the professional appellation can be used as a pronoun. In English this is limited—you can say 'Hello Doctor' but not 'Hello Massager'.

This Lao speech habit may confuse the foreigner: for example, a medical doctor is *mor* and you may refer to him as *than mor* or just *mor*; but a masseur or masseuse is also *mor*—or *mor nuat* to be precise, and a type of traditional singer is *mor lum*. And so it goes on, with a *mor phi* (spirit doctor), who will attempt a cure through contact with the spirits aggravating your *khwan*, *mor berng nyang* who will tell your fortune and a *mor phon*, who will officiate at the traditional *basi* that characterises all important occasions in Laos.

The morning markets of Laos offer a variety of goods, ranging from fresh produce to handicrafts and silver jewellery. Goods may be priced in Lao Kip, Thai Baht or US Dollars.

Built in 1818, Wat Si Saket is the oldest intact surviving temple in Vientiane. Its cloister walls feature many thousands of bronze, wood and fired-clay images of Buddha.

The Royal Palace was built in 1904 during the French colonial era for King Sisavang and his family. It has now been converted into the Luang Prabang National Museum.

Operations to clear unexploded ordnance (UXO) continue in the eastern provinces of Laos. Up to 200 people are killed or maimed by active UXO each year. Current victims are cared for at the Rehabilitation Centre on Khou Vieng Road, Vientiane, which is open to visitors.

The entrance to the modern Lao PDR parliament, constructed in close proximity to the ancient That Luang national symbol. All but two members of the popularly-elected National Assembly belong to the ruling Lao People's Revolutionary Party.

Lighten Up!

A Lao patient went to a very renowned medical doctor and admitted that before coming to a modern doctor, she had consulted a *mor phi*, a *mor berng nyang* and a *mor phon*. The doctor looked at her in disapproval, "And what sort of useless advice did all those charlatans give you?" he asked.

"They told me to come to you!" said the patient.

STATUS AND FLATTERY

The status game is not played the same in Laos as in the west, although the final objective may be as near as makes no difference. Lao may in fact show as much reluctance to blow their own trumpets as the traditional Englishman—although nobody objects if somebody else blows your trumpet for you. Humility is in itself a mark of good breeding. Not crawling on the ground humility as in some Asian countries, but simply not rushing to disclose that your family is top drawer, that you have an advanced degree in rocket science and that your uncle is a high number in the Central Committee.

It follows that when the person who cuts your hair, or the girl who cleans your room or the boy who carries your golf clubs, asks you apparently personnel questions, they are not so much establishing your status in relation to their status. That is already obvious. What they are doing is flattering you by giving you the chance to say nice things about yourself in answer to their questions, such things as you might be reluctant to disclose because of the modesty of your fine breeding. You can wallow in the status, why not? When being pampered in the beauty parlour, it doesn't hurt to have your ego massaged along with the other bits. You might also treat the whole repetitive performance as a series of language lessons. After a few weeks or months in Laos, if you can say nothing else, you will be able to give your name, age, marital status, occupation, wage, reason for coming to Laos and the price of your conveyance, all in reasonably understandable Lao. And if you find it a bit boring, look at it as work. You are building friendly relations. Many of them you will not need. But you are learning all the time to establish acceptable relations with Lao. And that could be the key to a harmonious and productive relationship. Keeping things on a friendly level is safest for everybody.

COOL HEARTS

There is something more to the avoidance of anger and violence than simply staying out of conflict situation. Anger not only disrupts the peace and unity of a person's *khwan* and the *khwan* of the adversary, it disrupts to some extent the community of which the conflicting individuals are part. In an agricultural community, where people cooperate on such labour-intensive activities as rice harvests, uncontrolled anger can threaten the welfare of two or more families, and if sides are taken, the welfare of the entire village community. The Lao have had enough tragic examples of what happens when large segments of the population take sides in a conflict. War is one outcome. Malevolent spirits wait for just such opportunities to meddle in the affairs of Man, and when they do, and Man is caught off guard, traditional thinking has it that droughts, floods, famines and epidemics can follow. A people facing such social disruption is then easy prey for more organised violence, and a whole nation can fall to its enemies because internal disputes affect its inability to defend itself. *'For the want of a nail a kingdom was lost'*. Tiny beginnings can have tragic consequences.

DISASTERS

Modern explanations for natural disasters, together with programmes to irrigate drought-prone land and protect against floods, and health-extension services, have perhaps to some extent undermined belief in the power of the spirit world to affect individual, economic and social development. But Vientiane and all other urban centres in Laos are really no more than a collection of villages, with communities focused around traditional markets.

Belief in spirit propitiation and the need to maintain a unified *khwan* remain strong. Even the university student studying for final exams will enlist the help of the spirits to pass, and will almost certainly make some vows to be performed if and when successful. Even the leaders of the secular government will participate in the casting of Buddha images and renovation of temples, making merit on a national scale. When bird-flu struck dead Lao citizens in March 2007, the Lao of Vientiane complied with orders to kill their chickens and to sell no chickens or eggs, at the same time many people conducted propitiation rituals for the spirits behind the epidemic. As the prohibition on sale of eggs continued, individuals went across the river to buy their eggs in Nongkhai, Thailand, which appeared untroubled by the epidemic—a different place and different spirits... and everybody knows that most spirits have difficulty crossing water.

Whatever the cause of bird flu attacking Vientiane but not (it seemed) nearby Nongkhai, the consequences of uncontrolled spirits on the loose can not easily be foreseen. Logic doesn't really enter in. More important is for each individual to be in control of himself. In practical terms that means avoiding anger, and keeping cool (*jai yen*) if faced with violence. This is often hard to do, but the person who achieves a reputation as *jai yen* (cool heart) earns respect of the community. So, if you want to help yourself and help the community around you, know that you will not do that by becoming angry, no matter how far a particular situation deteriorates. Of course, easier said than done. But a Lao manages it... most of the time. They believe that hot hearts lead to disaster; cool hearts keep best and stay fresh longest. Thus, when you feel anger surging, just put your heart in the fridge for a while.

SPIRITS

Just like the people they help and plague, spirits fit neatly into the good and the bad. The good are the *phii heuan*, spirits of the house or ancestral spirits, remembered at certain times of the year and appealed to in times of crisis. Western logic finds family spirits a little difficult to work out. Theoretically, ancestral spirits are treated well at their death and soon thereafter. Lots of merit is sent to them by the survivors in the family, who send merit even to those ancestral spirits so distant they live on in no family member's memory. With all this good merit, it may confuse the western mind seeking to come to terms with Buddhism, spiritualism and reincarnation that these good spirits are still living in the house up on a high shelf on which they are fed daily and not enjoying a jolly time in their reborn identities.

The explanation has everything to do with time, which enters different dimensions after death. Unlike Tibetan Tantric Buddhism, reincarnation isn't immediate upon death, no matter how good somebody has been and no matter how much merit they have built up during a lifetime. Lao cannot possibly know when, if at all, they will be reborn, and they certainly cannot assume that all their ancestors, names long forgotten, have been reborn. There must be somebody left on the shelf—look how the offering of Pepsi Cola goes down. This is a very Lao explanation, and for once we cannot use anthropological method to observe the process of rebirth—there might just be other reasons for the decline in Pepsi level, but we can't observe any. Anyway, all that matters is that Lao believe this is the way things are. Reincarnation is not a precise science. Neither is anthropology.

As long as you treat them right and keep them fed, the *phii heuan* will cause you no trouble; indeed their job is to look after all the family and ensure its good fortune. Of course a quarrelling pair of newlyweds could disturb the *phii heuan*—although if these *phii* are doing their job right, there should be no quarrelling in the first place.

Also within the good category are the *pha phum* (spirits of the land). These spirits live in the nice spirit house built specially for them in a quiet corner of the compound and enjoy servants and horses and dancing girls and maybe a little Mercedes. If you look inside their door you will see the *pha phum*, or at least their effigies, sitting quietly and harmoniously at the back of their house, looking out at their land which they must protect. You can cut the grass on that land and pick the mangoes (don't forget to give one or two to the *pha phum*), but don't go putting in posts or building fences without consulting them. Keep on good terms and they will look after your compound for you.

Spirits keep closely to their job descriptions. There are spirits for everything. For example, the rice spirit can ensure a good harvest, but cannot protect your house against fire.

Unfortunately not all spirits are predictable and benevolent and just about all of the malevolent ones are unhappy and if given the chance, will offload their unhappiness on the Lao. These spirits are ghosts of dead people who, partly because of the manner of their deaths and partly because of the manner of their past lives are stuck between death and rebirth. They are vastly different to, perhaps the opposite of, the Buddha, who overcame suffering, reached perfect peace, and therefore overcame the need for rebirth. These spirits are prevented from rebirth because they are stuck in a state of torment, having died suddenly and violently. They are certainly not prime candidates for reincarnation. They float around in nasty places waiting for a murder or a nasty accident to happen, indeed doing their best to encourage such malevolent occurrences, as it is their best chance of jumping into an unprepared and dislocated *khwan* and cheating their way into rebirth, leaving another to take their sad and unhappy place.

These spirits are certainly nasty pieces of work. They of course have their parallels in the human world— they are very susceptible to bribery and corruption and for a consideration, half now and half when the job is done, they will make an enemy sick, and maybe make him or her die, which also gives that spirit a possible way out of purgatory.

Should you think you may be under attack by one of these

Like a British solicitor, the *mor phii* cannot act for both sides and may refuse to take on a case if he has a moral problem with it. Like the medical doctor, he will enquire after your problems in order to discover which part of your *khwan* is under attack. Unlike the solicitor, the shamanic healer is unlikely to demand payment unless you feel better after his treatment.

spirits, go straight to a *mor phii*, who will pop into a trance or use other divination methods for discovering precisely what sort of *phii* has it in for you. He should also be able to contact the antidote, another *phii* who can be bribed to attack your attackers, both the spirit and the human behind the spirit's actions, and get them both off your back. The *mor phii* will charge a fee for his work, which is not without danger, and he might also require you to provide some chickens and eggs to sacrifice.

Shamanism

Shamanic treatment of the sick is remarkably similar among the various ethnic groups in Laos. It always requires diagnosis, contact with the spirit world and rapid improvement in the patient's condition. Different groups will have somewhat different concepts of the *khwan*, but it usually involves the equivalent of a *khwan nyay*, which is the major or controlling part of the *khwan*, sometimes seen among Lao as the combination of the 32 parts of each *khwan*, and sometimes translated in terms which come close to the Christian idea of a single soul. The entire spiritual universe within which various categories of spirits live is also very similar between groups.

There are differences in the forms of practice between shamans of Lao Loum origin and animistic minorities, but a similarity of principle which permits patients from one ethnic group to consult shamans from a different ethnic group. Whatever his ethnicity, a shaman is seen as a bridge between worlds of man and spirits. Treatment requires divination, which may be achieved by various means, communication with the spirits, which is not necessarily in the language of the patient, and usually involves the shaman entering some sort of trance to journey to the spirit world temporarily (don't try this at home), striking some sort of bargain and returning to treat the patient through the means required by those spirits causing the problem or by other helper-spirits working for the welfare of the patient. In all cases, success is judged by an improvement in a patient's condition.

Charms

Shamanism, as described above, involves a cure for when one or more parts of the *khwan* have strayed or been enticed away from their home. But Lao recognise that prevention is always better than cure. For this reason they regularly attend *sukwan* or *basi* sessions in order to bind the 32 parts of the *khwan* firmly into the body through the process of *mat khen* (tying the wrists). The visitor may already have attended a *basi* without understanding its significance. On a very superficial level, the *basi* serves to get people together and, when tying on threads, to wish each other well. If nothing more, this produces a collective energy which grows as it circulates around the group, where each person is linked either by thread or by physical touch. *Basi* may take place at any time, but particularly when there is any spiritual danger in the air—births, marriages, and so on.

In addition to the *basi*, the Lao will often go in for charms, most often worn around the neck. These may be provided by a shaman, a trance medium, or a monk, or obtained from a dealer in such things, often at high prices. In addition to images of the Buddha and of famous monks, such charms may be problem-specific, involving rolled up pieces of thin metal with a written formula inside (often written in a language other than Lao), pieces of tusk or horn and even phalluses. A good charm is valuable and individuals may go to some lengths and expense to obtain one. While a skeptical westerner might admit that such charms could have psychological value, overcome fear and provide confidence, the Lao wearing them really believes in their therapeutic value. The reverse side of this is that the loss of such a charm can send an individual into depression or illness.

Avoiding Danger

Spirits love trouble. The best way of avoiding their unwanted attentions is to stay away from trouble. This is precisely the best way of dealing with any disturbance in the human world, which is intrinsically linked with that of the spirit world. Avoid people who make life difficult or who seem to revel in dangerous situations. When confronted by a difficult person or spirit, promise or say anything to get out of the situation, and having got out, avoid placing yourself again in an ambiguous situation.

The foreigner staying some time in one place in Laos will before too long, become aware that some people are just a bit weird. They pose you no physical threat and are unlikely to communicate with you, or for that matter with anybody. They might walk up and down the same street every day, heads down and muttering to themselves. They might make regular rounds dressed in gaudy colours and bright make up. They might even go down to the river for a bath, same place, same time every evening and take off all their clothes. Strange individuals, colourful in a way, well tolerated but not helped. They pose no obvious danger, but are best avoided. Why? Better safe than sorry.

THE LAO AND YOU

'One intelligent man is not necessarily right.
A host of fools not necessarily wrong.'
—Lao proverb

WHATEVER YOUR REASON FOR COMING TO LAOS, and however independent or anti-social you may proudly consider yourself to be, you will, from your first moments in the country, be interacting with the Lao. How far you interact is up to you—and of course up to the Lao. This chapter will continue to address Lao ways of behaviour and thought, but will specifically address how you fit in, if at all. From now on, the spotlight is on you.

Chances are you have not read much about the people and country of Laos before or since arrival. There just is not that much written on Laos. And another thing, I bet you don't speak Lao. A few diplomats and academics apart, almost no foreigners have learnt any Lao language before arrival. A lot of expats posted to Laos will have already cut their teeth in Thailand, and picked up a bit of Thai, or maybe a lot of Thai. Those sent to Laos are usually sent because they did well in Thailand, or because they did so badly they had to be shuttled off somewhere.

If that is your case, and through your Thailand experience you have learnt that talking pointedly is pointless, you may, with a little more coaching and patience, fit in quite nicely to Laos. If on the other hand you have developed the attitude that Laos is but an undeclared province of Thailand, and a *baan nok* one at that, then it's back to the culture shock drawing board for you. We know, don't we, that most Asians, the Lao included, have a strong tendency to agree with you, at least to your face. And we know that they have this tendency because they dare not risk any hint of criticism.

Well, yes, the book you read on 'How to Manage the Asians' has a bit of truth in there somewhere. So, how about this for another explanation, or two explanations, of why nobody in Laos is ever going to tell you that you are doing things wrong: 1) the Lao are not fanatical about their own cultural habits, and 2) they can't be bothered.

Lao know that hands should be washed before eating. That's why sometimes there's a bowl of cloudy water standing outside a better Lao restaurant, next to the utterly filthy cloth on a nail to dry your hands having washed them. And they know that only the right hand should be used when digging fingers into a basket of sticky rice, taking out a lump and plopping it onto another person's plate (if there is a plate to plop onto). But—and I am not making this up—you will not be too long in the country before you notice an unwashed hand and an unwashed left hand at that, doing just this. The Lao have not read *Culture Shock!*

Well, what are you going to do about it? Questioning such observed actions is likely to get you nowhere, and might suggest that you are trying to criticise rather than trying to understand. Maybe the water's off. Maybe the guy is left-handed. Maybe he does this all the time. Maybe this is a deviant sub-culture. Or maybe, he just can't be bothered.

Well, you will be mightily relieved to know that those anthropologists who actually really did live in the societies they studied have long noted this problem. Indeed some of the earlier anthropological texts, those carved into stone with a hammer and sickle, those same texts which made their writer's reputations and served as the very basis of anthropology, are now regarded as fanciful fiction.

Sure, the anthropologist learnt the language, talked to people, and faithfully noted down what people said they do, rather than what they really do. Why did those faithful natives lie through their teeth to the poor anthropologist? Well, maybe they wanted to please him or her.

You are probably not an anthropologist, but you still have the anthropologist's problem. A Lao, when questioned, even in the nicest and most sympathetic way, about behaviour, is most likely to tell you what should be done rather than what is done.

So, you might not be writing a thesis on the Lao, but if you really want to understand the Lao, observe what they do among themselves, as well as ask them what they do. The truth, a changing and capricious concept in itself, lies somewhere between the two—in fact it probably bounces between polar opposites.

Now, some people may say, "How do we observe the sex-life of the Lao?" It is difficult. And if you observed through participating, you would not be observing the sex life of the Lao, but the sex life of the Lao with a foreigner. I think we might be getting there. You can't really observe everything, and you certainly can't believe everything you hear (or read), because what you are observing includes you, and what you are hearing also includes you.

And…finally…this is the whole point. Don't bother with things that don't include you. Direct your attention to the Lao and you. Don't bother with things that don't concern you.

But don't shut this book and flee the scene just yet. It really doesn't matter all that much if you are interacting with Lao on a personal basis—after all, many of them eat half a baguette and drink strong coffee in the morning, so what is Lao is not set in stone. What matters is that you want to appear well-mannered rather than ill-mannered and want people to like you rather than hate you. I suppose this is why you are reading this book. So, forget about really integrating. Try to be Lao and you will probably end up pushing the Lao away. Like Nirvana, you can't get there by grasping. The more you try the harder you make it. So, do things the easy way. Take yourself as a virgin block of stone. Chip away all that looks horribly un-Lao. What remains is not a Lao, but it is also not a complete foreigner. Leave the rest to the Lao.

BODY IMAGE

Before you get a chance to say a word in any language, and even before you can knock them dead with your radiant charm, a Lao will see you coming.

Laos has been on the hippy-trail for a few generations now and Lao know that not all foreigners are rich, although most of them wonder why some come if they can't afford to enjoy their time here. If you look like the beggar in the street outside, you will still get served. Wearing a hare-Krishna haircut will certainly not help your integration, even if you could explain your particular version of the Hindu faith, Lao will think you a bit odd. Never mind, they will still give you breakfast, since that's what they do if you can pay for it.

> If you want your first impressions with the Lao to be good, you don't have to go to elaborate lengths to do so. Just take a bath and change your clothes from time to time. Pretty easy.

Body image can be positive or negative. Nobody expects you to put on a suit and tie, although if you did the Lao would not hesitate to say you looked smart, even beautiful. It's all superficial, but so what? Blue jeans, even clean shorts and tee-shirt are fine, if you feel comfortable in them, and if you are going to the noodle shop, not the Ministry. No particular need to wear socks, few Lao do; but if you feel comfortable in them and they have been washed within memory, no particular reason not to wear socks.

Most Lao are not fanatical followers of fashion. But most will attempt to wear clean clothes, even if they can afford only the cheapest, and—it has to be said—most Lao will look rather cleaner and rather better dressed than most foreigners coming to Laos.

TOUCHING HELLOS

On entering a shop, or a market stall, and finding the young lady-in-charge asleep (it does happen), do not touch her on the shoulder, or anywhere else, to get her attention (even if you are female). If you do, nothing might happen, or the girl might scream, or go and complain to the manager, asleep in the back, and he might do nothing, or he might look unkindly on you until you leave and never come back. Laos is not a touchy-feely society, although you might not believe that if you spend five minutes at the Suradit Discothèque.

So, what would Miss Manners advise in the getting somebody's attention department? Yes, of course, keep a reasonable distance and just keep saying 'Hello', as loudly as necessary. Touching somebody is bad manners, especially across the sex line—unless you have paid for precisely that. Touching or shaking sleeping people could wake them up. And it could wake them up with a start, and if Lao have to be awakened, a polite 'Hello' is okay, a hand on the shoulder is not, particularly if startled eyes are met by round ones set in the face of a stubbly foreigner. Lao are very fussy about how their soul should be treated. And being awakened with a start by a foreigner could just leave one or two of the 32 bits of their soul still scrambling to the surface.

This being said, the Lao are far less fussy about touching across the sex line when it comes to a handshake. After all, Laos was a French colony. But don't try kissing on the cheek! Don't even try kissing on the hand.

So how do we say 'hello'? Of course, there is the *nop*, but you're a foreigner, and even if you were Lao, you probably wouldn't use it. As you will know if you have really read this book this far, it is mostly used on formal occasions like weddings and funerals, and even then a handshake is a substitute that will create no bad feelings. For almost a decade after the change of regimes in 1975, the *nop* was frowned upon as an indicator of class status (which it is). It has now been rehabilitated, but the *nop* is still on parole and not everybody rushes into it. Let's say it is in restricted use, mostly as an expression of thanks on receiving a present. It may be used more by the up and coming middle-class, but it can also be used by a beggar. Since you probably get no presents, and are probably not a beggar, the Lao will be happy enough if you stick to the handshake. Indeed, when faced with a foreigner, more Lao will initiate a handshake than a *nop*. But don't overdo the handshake. In France you risk appearing rude if you do not shake hands with everybody in your immediate environment; not in Laos.

Jup Hom

The French habit of cheek 'brush-kissing' has something of a parallel among Lao in the *jup hom* (the nice-smell kiss or to translate more graphically, the 'sniff-kiss'), the Lao version is used only between intimates, and not in public, and certainly not as a form of saying hello. So, while the French cheek-kiss has spread to such staid societies as the cold-lipped British, and is now almost required in the USA, if you take a Lao lady's hand then kiss her on the cheeks—unless she has spent half her life in France or is under the age of one—she will certainly avoid you next time you come within range.

Nops Away

For those of you intent on getting kicked out of the country, throw a *nop* to a senior civil servant or a member of the Politbureau (sometimes the same thing), some of whom can remember trying to get rid of it. Since it is also not initiated or returned with those of lower status, and has little meaning between equals that is not better expressed by a handshake, you could go a long time between seeing examples of it. Then again, go to a society wedding and the *nops* will be flashing all around the entrance as people arrive. At such times one *nop* is worth a thousand handshakes, which saves a lot of time and keeps hands clean.

One place the *nop* is in order is in the wat. You *nop* a monk, he doesn't return it. (Although, in Laos, you can never be quite sure, and it has happened to me.) Even monks are likely to extend their hands to be lightly squeezed rather than vigorously shaken—but only to men, never to women. Women, of course, not only never touch a monk but never hand anything directly to a monk, which is seen as an extension of touching—and while we are on the subject, extension goes as far as touching a monks robes (when the monk is inside them), so be very careful, ladies, when climbing into a *touk-touk* if there are monks onboard. And if they climb in after you, squeeze yourself back as far as you can go and when it's time to get off, squeeze your way out past the driver. And if you can't do that, make to stand up, bent double and *nop* the monk(s), and wait until they make some sign of moving their legs to one side to allow you by, and if by that time the *touk-touk* has charged off, stay on and go around again, or bang on the back of the driver or the side of the vehicle—in the situation this is considered good manners.

If you are a Buddhist, or even if you are not but think maybe you would like to be, you will save your most respectful *nop* for the Buddha image within the *sim*, the central 'chapel' of the temple. Touching a Buddha image is a bit ambiguous, but it is certainly okay, even if you are female, if you do so in order to press on a thin gold leaf, but you should *nop* first to request permission of the image. Don't expect an answer, after all he is infinitely superior to you.

So, to summarise this little section. Lao are a bit touchy about being touched, particularly across the razor wire, and particularly by foreigners. Hellos are much the same as in England, said once when meeting, but maybe not even then—just like in England. You can even use the English word 'Hello', which is always used by Lao on the phone (with a pronounced H, not the French 'ello), although it doesn't take a great effort to learn *sabaay-dii* (literally, 'good health'), which can at a pinch double for 'good-bye'. The handshake, although introduced by the French, conforms more to English use: fine on introductions, even between genders, and maybe on departure, but don't go overboard. If you pass on the street a Lao you see every day, a mild smile is enough.

SMILING

The Lao Loum, when awake, are prone to smile. The same is not necessarily the case with the ethnic minorities. When in the town centres of Vientiane or Luang Prabang it is easy to forget that around 40 per cent of Lao do not have Lao as their mother tongue, do not structure their societies and cultures in the same way as the Lao Loum, and do not behave in the same way. In some parts of Laos, one minority or another might be in a clear majority, and their norms may predominate. Where this is the case, school curriculums should be taught in the national language, but Lao Loum living in the area usually learn the dominant 'minority' dialect, which is most likely to be the lingua-franca in the market place.

Friendly, smiling children are a common sight in Laos.

If trekking in the mountains, you are likely to be walking on paths just one person wide. You will undoubtedly meet a mountain person going in the opposite direction. Rather than *nop* or smile, that person, man or woman, would normally say to another member of her group, in her own language, some sort of greeting, which usually translates exactly as Lao translates in such circumstances: "Where are you going?" or "Where have you been?" Saying nothing in such circumstances can make everybody feel a bit awkward—on a lonely mountain path it is reassuring to hear a human voice, particularly if the strange body in front of you is unfamiliar; it is evidence of sorts that you are human and not an evil spirit. Smiling might be okay if passing a Lao Loum, but if passing a Hmong or Akha woman, a silent, toothy smile could send her rushing back where she came from. The safest thing is to forget real convention—you can't learn "where are you going" in every language and dialect—and just say the Lao *sa-bai-dii*. So, smiling is not always the easiest and most appropriate way of saying hello. Like everything else, it depends on the context.

Feel free to smile. Don't force it or you are likely to produce a grimace. Smiles are as varied as the people behind them. They have to be spontaneous to serve their function. And no matter that you have a mouthful of cracked and yellow teeth, smiling portrays a welcome and a warm beauty like nothing else can.

Most of the time, you will be interacting with Lao Loum, or Chinese shopkeepers or guest house owners who are fully Lao Loum when not being fully Chinese. Most of the time, therefore, your smile is appropriate, even if you do speak Lao. Smiling is contagious and one smile certainly makes two.

Don't go out of your way to exaggerate your smile, and if a friend tells you your smile is too lascivious, it probably is. But give a smile and a Lao is psychologically obliged to smile back—not that they think about it. And should you get a smile first, you certainly should return it, maybe adding a little interest, if that is your inclination. Cross-gender smiles are fine. And most relationships start out from a smile. But do not presume that a lady's smile means she fancies you, and do not presume that the smile of her husband sitting just behind her means he doesn't care, or that he too fancies you. A smile alone does not necessarily mean anything apart from 'Hello, I can see you'.

LAUGHTER

A Lao can smile, even laugh, when they find something funny. With a life expectancy of 53–54, a comparatively huge malaria and tuberculosis rate, and around 40 per cent under the poverty line, you might rightly ask what the Lao have to laugh about. But maybe that's the answer right there. Faced with the statistics—what can be done but laugh? And, as far as it is possible to do so, a Lao likes to enjoy life—that's the whole thing about *muan*—life is just too short to be miserable. They might enjoy somewhat different things than you, and smile and laugh at what you don't find particularly funny. But there are plenty of areas of overlap. Sit with Lao and watch Charlie Chaplin's *Modern Times*. No language problems and smiles all round. If, on the other hand, you open a bottle of Pepsi and it sprays all over the nice clean shirt you just put on, well, the Lao will smile, laugh and even guffaw. This is more than just breaking the tension: they really find it funny (although maybe you don't).

EXCUSE ME

When you climb into the back of a *touk-touk* full of little people, forcing your way through a collection of knees as you make your way through the narrow passage between them, swiping a few in the face with your backpack, hands clinging to the overhead rail and moving ape-like over your curled over body, leaving your armpits exposed to the rows of flat but sensitive nostrils and finally fitting yourself into a space big enough for at least two Lao, you are only doing what the Lao do, even if less gracefully. It's not your fault. It's not that you are too big, it's the *touk-touk*, jumbo or even the Lao bus (there are public buses in Vientiane town but this is one of the country's best kept secrets—even *Lonely Planet* doesn't know). They are all too small, or too crowded. You certainly owe no apologies for the state of the public transport system. But you might get the feeling that some sort of acknowledgement of the inconvenience you are causing is appropriate. Verbal apologies are not necessary, particularly as you are under pressure, the engine is revving loudly, and you don't have a chance in a million of getting the tones and vowels right on both syllables of *khor* (rising) *thort* (falling), which means 'excuse me'. Apart from the fact that you are much more likely to say 'please fart', 'excuse me' is not really the thing to say. A Lao in a similar situation will just throw out *khor thang day* ('make way, please') and go straight through.

Now, I am aware that you are likely to want to use some transport before becoming fluent in Lao, and also that having got past the knees and to a place on the bench, sometime you are going to need to get out the way you came in. Since you will arrive in Laos with the linguistic abilities of a six-month old, a smile is all that is needed. No need to gurgle. A nice smile as you come and go. And the Lao might just say, 'What a nice man/woman/boy/girl'. They will of course say it in Lao, but the good vibes will radiate and before you know it you'll be climbing into and out of *touk-touk* because you're hooked on radiation. Compare this with the situation back on the 73B double-decker, where you run the gauntlet of tuts and 'They're my feet, you great oaf.' And the most *bo muan* expression of all time: "What you smiling at, mate?"

Maybe, one day, a Lao will say 'excuse me' to you, either in English or Lao or in French (*pardon*). Maybe they won't. After all if something can be done with a smile, why waste words? There is also the fact that 'excuse me' sounds a bit apologetic, and Lao don't like to apologise. However, they don't mind saying *khop chai* (thank you), even if a smile would suffice. The answer to both, in English, would be, 'Don't mention it'. Similarly, one answer suffices in Lao, '*Bo pen nyang*'. But if all that seems too much trouble, just smile. A smile might not be enough if you back your Land Cruiser over somebody's parked motor-bike, but for most other occasions, it's all you really need.

BODY LANGUAGE
Head and Toe

You know by now that one Lao is divisible into 32 parts corresponding to the 32 parts of the *khwan*. None of these should be disturbed, as the Lao needs all the bits, and all in place and working, if he or she is to function at all. The chief part of the *khwan*, which controls all the rest and decides what to do if one bit goes missing, is located in the top of the head, under the hair. The taboo books on Asian manners will tell you under no circumstances to ruffle hair or touch heads. Of course this is not something regularly done between strangers. It may come as a surprise therefore to read here that there is really no need to get paranoid about the possibility of touching sacred heads in Laos. You can behave pretty much as you would in the West, norms of polite behaviour are pretty much the same on this subject. And it will not be long before you see a mixed group of young people laughing and playing, and, heavens forbid, ruffling hair. I'm not talking about very young children here—anybody, even you, can ruffle the hair of a five-year old without fear of being struck down by a cultural thunderbolt or dragged off as a pedophile. Certainly think twice before joining the teenagers in a good-old hair-ruffling session, but if somebody ruffles your hair in a friendly way—which is not likely to happen unless you are pretty good friends, same as back home—feel free to ruffle back. It is not unknown for a Lao to touch a white foreigner's brown or fair hair, such is their fascination with it, and you could certainly stroke back, as long as you say while doing so that the person has the most beautiful hair. Flattery will get you everywhere, even past the portals of so-called taboos.

As for those feet and long toes of yours. That's another matter. While it is within the realms of possibility that you will, in time, get to run your fingers through some beautiful, long, Lao hair, just don't try it with your toes.

There are correct ways of sitting when in the *wat* or at a *basi*. This is the sideways sit, where you jut out ungainly and uncomfortably, like the leaning tower of Pisa, until you slowly topple over. Even Lao find such sitting uncomfortable for long periods, and it is permitted, when hands are not in use for *mat khen* (knot tying of threads on wrists), to prop yourself up on one arm. Seeing you uncomfortable, some men at a *basi* might even tell you to sit cross-legged, which is not done in front of a monk (or shouldn't be done)—although there is usually no monk at a *basi*, so no need to worry. Of course, sitting cross-legged might also be uncomfortable for you, in which case, at the risk of making it all too obvious you are not Lao, you can ask for a chair. If you do have a problem with a bad leg or something that stops you sitting at all on the floor-mats, you can always let somebody know in advance or on arrival. Lao culture is not handicapped-friendly, but finding some seating is a perfectly reasonable request, so if you want it, ask for it. If, on the other hand, your main problem is getting up rather than getting down, rest assured that many hands will help you upright. The *basi* doesn't last that long, especially if its very hot, but count on up to 20 minutes, and if you can get an outside position, perhaps propping your back against a wall, that's fine. But don't stretch out those long legs and awful feet. Sitting on a chair is okay, but pointing your feet at other people is not.

All this being said, don't be surprised to see a young man sitting by the river, playing with the toes and feet of his girlfriend, while she lies down with her hands beneath her hair-do and her feet in the boy friend's lap. Don't be surprised even in a *wat* to see an old lady stretch out her aching legs—but away from any Buddha image. Everything depends on the situation and the people involved. Playing with your girlfriend's toes is okay in the right place, even in a public place, but putting your tongue down her throat is not okay. Laos has no equivalent of Hyde Park.

Signalling to Waitresses

Fingers should not be wriggled palm up to call a waiter or maid, or anybody. Such an action indicates that you want just one thing. On the other hand, or rather on the same hand, fingers, all of them, wriggled or waved palm downwards cause no offence at all. Of course, your polite gestures may not be seen, especially if the waitress has her eyes on the TV. In this case, you either wait for the commercials, which won't be long in coming, or resort to attention-calling noises.

In Spain you may clap, in Portugal you may hiss, in France you might get away with calling out '*Garcon*' or '*Mademoiselle*', in England you would cough politely and wait for ever. In Laos you do none of the above and do not call out 'Boy', which used to be okay, even to call girls, and is still occasionally heard in Bangkok. In Laos, you can say 'waiter', if in a western restaurant with an English, French or Italian menu, but far better to catch attention with *Nong* (little sister/brother) for a waitress or young waiter. You will occasionally hear *nong sao*, which is fine and simply makes it clear that a little sister is being addressed, not a little brother. Sometimes you might hear *nong sao ngam,* beautiful little sister, which will certainly get the girl's attention but is not considered any more rude than saying 'dear' or even 'darling' to a girl serving tea in England. The Bangkok-Thai *Nu* (literally mouse, often used in Thailand when talking to children) is not used in Laos. Real Lao would be *sao* or *sao sao*, meaning 'girl'; this is now considered a bit upcountry and the use of *nong* has come in from Thailand and is considered more polite; *sao* sounds a bit brusque coming from a foreigner, and you could get the tone wrong and end up talking to the house pillar.

You will have noted the concern with young girls in this section, this is because most people serving on tables in most restaurants are young girls. In the really cheap places, or down by the river in Vientiane, where tables are set up and packed away each day, these young girls and young boys probably get no pay, or just a little pocket money. They often come in from outside Vientiane, perhaps sent by parents who have no work for them. Many are under the legal age of employment (15 years) and work in exchange for food and a place to sleep. Lao rarely leave tips in such a place, so they really do scrape by. Some are picked up and end in some form of prostitution, others move on to work in a textile factory and live in the associated dormitory, still others get married to a customer. I know of one who is happily married to an Australian, but she is perhaps the exception. Many restaurants employ *khatoeys* (men who want to be women and usually wear women's clothing) in the kitchen, since they are reputed to be good cooks and work harder than real women; sometimes these double serving tables. It is polite to address a *khatoey* as female.

If a waitress is middle-aged or obviously older than you or (and this is an important or) if you know her to be the restaurant owner rather than a waitress, call her *Nang* (think of this as Madam or Mademoiselle rather than Mrs). You can also waggle your fingers (downwards) if you want somebody to come over, or just call out *check-bin* if you want to pay (the words come from cheque and bill, but usually involve neither). *Check-bin* sounds a bit over the top if you have just had a coffee, when the alternative *thao-daiy* (how much) is more appropriate. In the early stages of your integration, or when the music is too damned loud to make yourself heard, a downwards circular movement of the forefinger will have the same effect.

Fingers cannot really be used for pointing out people. It is seen as rude to do so. So, if you want to draw a Lao's attention to somebody, you really have to use language, unless that person is alone, when a slight upward movement of the chin will suffice. It is quite okay to say 'that fat ugly girl with the jumble of teeth' (if you can say it and be understood), but it is not okay to point at the girl. This can be inconvenient. But then so can most culture at times. And it all has to do with avoiding any possibility of causing offence or ruffling sensitivities. But if you happen to be a sergeant in the Lao army or a schoolteacher with a class of 50, you are granted exemption from this social rule. Not, however, if you are the big boss of a big company and need to get some discipline in there—wagging a finger in front of somebody's face will not help him or her focus on what you are saying.

A Lao does not go to lengths to stand out from the masses. Praise from other people is fine, boasting is not fine, and being sectioned out from the group with a finger is definitely not fine at all. Get those fingers tuned into Lao social protocol: They can squeeze pussy spots, pluck out nose hairs and count money sideways, but they cannot point at somebody.

Eyes

Eyes are the window to the heart. This expression is exactly the same in Lao and in English. And in both cultures children are told, 'don't stare, it's not nice'. It certainly is not advisable to stare. In a London pub it could be physically dangerous, in Laos it could send shivers down the spine and disturb somebody's *khwan*. So, in everybody's interests, by all means look, smile and look again, but don't stare or you might scare away what you want to attract. A few Lao ladies will avert their gaze when you look into their eyes. It doesn't mean they don't like your eyes;

Also try not to point at sacred objects, like Buddha images, although pointing out a semi-sacred object, like a Mercedes-Benz, is quite okay.

in fact most Lao are fascinated by green or blue eyes, and eyes are an important part of definition as beautiful. The girl or lady averting her eyes has been brought up to believe she should do so as a sign of propriety and modesty. She is undoubtedly within the category of 'good girl'. That does not mean that the great majority of girls who do not avert eyes are bad girls. Eye contact now goes along with smile and crosses the gender line easily; on the other hand if you too obviously scrutinise a member of the opposite sex—or the same sex for that matter—you will not be told "in your dreams, bud!", but you risk making another person feel uncomfortable, and that is a social crime. No punishment, but the object of your fascination might take to disappearing every time you turn up.

While Lao know they should not stare, they are distance-lookers. If something fascinates a group of young people, they will spontaneously train their eyes on what has commanded their attention. It may be an eminently beautiful foreigner, it may be a black person, it may be Lao behaving out of social context, it may be a particularly scruffy and dirty white foreigner, it may be a *khatoey* who has gone beyond the limits. The Lao watchers will not interfere, at least as long as they do not feel in any way threatened. They are engaged in entertainment more than anything more, so if they laugh, they find what they are looking at funny. If they exchange opinions on beauty, these opinions will inevitably be precisely the same. Lao are like that.

Whether Lao eyes hold more promise than the eyes of other nationalities, who knows? But a look in the eyes and a smile do colour first impressions. How often have beautiful eyes distracted you from fat thighs or worse? In Laos, the foreigner doesn't need rose-coloured spectacles, but can you fully trust the evidence of your own eyes?

SLOWNESS

It is now a bit of a tired joke to say that Lao PDR stands for 'Lao Please Don't Rush', but many an honest word is spoken in jest, and many clichés, having born the test of time, are worth listening to. Lao seem to move, drive, talk and even drink, slower than most Asians. For many foreigners, this is a large part of the charm of the people. For some other foreigners, particularly those assigned to do a certain work in a certain time, Lao docility can be frustrating.

The Sound of Rice
Long before the Lao PDR came into being, the French colons regarded Laos as a place in which to relax after the hectic rush of Vietnam. A semi-racist joke of the colonial period was that the Vietnamese plant the rice, the Cambodians watch the rice grow and the Lao listen to the rice growing.

LAO ENGLISH

Long before you can fit into Laos in Lao—and it can be done, however impossible it might seem at the stage when the Lao for 'near' and 'far' sounds to you like exactly the same word—you will be trying to fit into Laos in English.

As stated already, the general level of English is not high. This is certainly not for want of trying. Many Lao spend hours on extra tuition, over and above what they get at secondary school. Such tuition in English is either by a Lao who has been through the rote-learning system, which makes it cheaper, or it is by an unqualified European-looking foreigner, which makes it more expensive. Both foreigner and Lao may have purchased their ELT certificates for 1,000 Baht in Khao San Road, Bangkok.

Thus, you must come to terms with some special English. You will soon get used to people from down Pakse way saying, 'I lu dike you duvedy luk' (I do like your lovely dog). Such regional variations are the least of your problems. More difficult is the Lao capacity or incapacity to pronounce two consonants without putting a vowel in between, for example, green = ga-leen, and sometimes any vowel will do, block = bollock or bullock, unless the two consonants are at the end of the word, in which case the last gets lost. Who needs two consonants together anyway? Doesn't "I can go" mean the same as "I can't go"? L becomes N—'File it under L', 'You mean fine it under en?' R becomes L, except when it becomes H, and final consonants get transformed into the nearest of the few finals that exist in Lao—'Ask Bill and Liz for drinks. Yes, that's right, 'Ahk Bin an Lit foh drin'. And a final 's' doesn't exist, making singulars and plurals the same.

No matter how long you persist, at times you will just have to guess whether the price is 'seventy' or 'twenty', not quite the same thing in English. But pretty much the same in Lao-English. One time you can use your fingers without causing offence.

And can you believe that Lao pronounce 'ice-cream' as 'galem'? Many a foreigner has discovered that the greatest incentive to learn Lao is Lao-English.

English by Elder Sister

Phet had graduated from Dong Dok University in English and had the photographs and certificate to prove it. Her younger sister Pui wanted to follow in her footsteps but doubted she could pass the basic English exam required to enter the four-year course. So, Phet, being a good elder sister and using English everyday in her new job as secretary at a UN agency in Vientiane, went along to the examination centre in place of Pui. She put Pui's ID card on her desk and filled in Pui's details on the paper. She got straight down to work, which was an entirely written exam. When she had finished, she looked up and into the eyes of the teacher who had been her tutor in English for four years. "Aha," said the teacher, who was also invigilating the entrance exam. "Miss Phet! Did you enjoy my course so much that you want to do it again?" "Yes," said Phet, with a well-you-got-me smile. Sensing the game was up but counting on her old tutor not giving her away, Phet stood up, leaving the exam paper behind, and left the hall. A week later results came out and Pui was admitted into the English degree course.

TELEPHONES

Lao telephones have come a long way in a short time. Just six years ago the waiting time for a house phone was about three years, now it's a few days, with Internet connection added at a price. In the meantime, the mobile phone revolution has taken over. Funny how, when you don't need a house-phone any more, the telephone company falls over itself, well almost, to fit one before you change your mind. The democratic nature of the mobile phone has certainly taken any cachet out of telephone ownership.

Mind you, house phones can be useful—if you have one, you get a telephone book, which advertises many of the things and places you need in English (which does not mean that somebody will answer the phone in English). If you have never used a Lao telephone before, be prepared for some idiosyncrasies. For one thing, Lao cultural norms of polite face to face encounters are reversed on the telephone.

'Hello', you say. Practice this. Pronounce the 'h', even if you are French. Start in mid-range, dip just a fraction, then swing up into a full rising tone, making sure your 'o' is a long, round-lipped one. This is the only answer allowed when picking up the phone in Laos. Don't, whatever you do, complicate matters by giving your name and number. The caller will repeat your 'Hello', perhaps adding a *sa-baay-dii,* but never telling you who he is. If your initial hello is less than perfect, the caller recognises a foreign accent, and presuming he is not calling a foreigner, all you will hear further is the clunk or buzz as the phone is hung up or clicked off with no need for an excuse me. The same number will call again one minute later. Make sure you are speaking above a motor-cycle engine if your hello is still not perfect. The caller will recognise that you are not Noy, and will ask to speak to Noy. Should you be one of those foreigners married to a Noy, you will hand the phone across to your spouse, who will then talk for ten minutes on the phone, until you ask who your Noy is talking to, to which your Noy replies that she doesn't know. If, on the other hand you are sure your spouse does not go by the name Noy, and I mean really sure, that's to say you have checked carefully all the names by which your Lao partner—and the maid and any other person living in the house—is known in other circles and nowhere does Noy figure, you may simply say *thoh phit* (wrong call) and hang up. Do be aware though that the majority of houses with telephones do have a Noy somewhere, and the Lao know this.

Hanging up doesn't improve your Lao conversation skills very much. So, if you wish, you can practice saying,

"Who do you want?" If the answer comes that the caller wants the noodle shop, you can, if you don't want to hang up immediately, explain that this is the private residence of Lord Home-Pronounced-Hume. Almost certainly the caller will not have listened to a word you said, so much for language practice, and will ask, "Can I speak to Noy, then?" There are a million possible answers to this, but since the caller is not a listener, you might as well practice, "Wrong call", and hang up.

Speakers on the telephone abhor a vacuum, so if there is a millisecond's silence, one person says "Hello" and if there is no immediate Hello in return, proceeds to "Hello, hello, hello". Also if your partner to the call has been talking some time without getting any periodic confirmation you are still there (you should grunt 'erh' every two seconds), they will suspect you have placed the phone in the fridge and therefore go into the "Hello, hello" routine. Believe it or not, but in one out of ten telephone conversations in Laos, the only word spoken is 'Hello'. To be fair, this probably has less to do with Lao manners than with Lao telephones, particularly the mobile variety. This might be because mobiles in Laos seem to fall into water and drop from motorcycles more frequently than in other countries, but might also be because they are programmed to go beep-beep-beep and self-terminate on every tenth call.

Telephone manners are not so much deliberately rude as much truncated. The supreme example of this is the call of the 'one-ringer' (see next page). Other, more normal calls, where you are answering the phone rather than calling can also be very short in duration, with the caller any time deciding he or she has got all they are going to get out of the cost of their call, saying *thao ni* ('that's all'). Down goes the telephone or the button, sometimes leaving you in mid-sentence.

A few last words on use of the ubiquitous *meu teu*, the mobile telephone. This has the advantage of showing the caller's name in the window if you have keyed it in, so you have a good idea as to whom you are speaking. If there is no name and you don't recognise the number or the voice—and all Lao sound the same—be careful about saying, 'Who are you?' Even in tele-talk this sounds a bit brusque, and therefore should be preceded by a short statement asking if the caller is speaking from the back of a motor-cycle or in a Chinese noodle shop or taking a shower; if that's straining your Lao, a simple *bo dayyin* (can't hear you) will suffice. Before you get the name you will receive declarations of disbelief that you cannot remember somebody who served you noodle soup six months ago in Bokeo Province. Then, of course, when you get the name, it will be Noy, which reduces possibilities to 50 per cent of the population.

Some wrong numbers love to talk to a foreigner, either to practice their English or to listen to your cute Lao, and will go on for hours—this is perhaps okay if you are talking Lao and need the language practice, although such people tend to call you back at 2:00 am in the morning with no idea that you aren't too keen on answering the phone when asleep. Other right numbers are not enthusiastic about talk if they have to pay for it. These belong to a typology of two. The first calls you and says immediately, 'Call back, no money in phone' (don't). The second are the 'one-ringers', who hang up before you can possibly answer. They hope you will call them back. If you do, the chances are they will ask you to transfer money from your phone to their phone, so they can call you at awkward times, or they might simply cut to the chase and ask you for the money for the immediate surgery they need if they are not to die in two weeks (to which the only answer is, 'Call me back in two weeks time'). All in all, it is best not to give your number to one-ringers or suspected one-ringers. This does not stop them getting your number from their friend, or even your secretary—few Lao would hesitate to give your private number to any caller; indeed, telephone numbers do not fall into the Lao concept of 'private'.

SPEECH HABITS
Before going into Lao speech habits, try to be conscious of the habits of your home language and people. Walking

along the park pathway by Lake Geneva, Swiss of any language will say *Bonjour* to any passer-by. The same Swiss, going down into Geneva train station will say nothing to a passer-by unless acquainted with that person. That's how finicky speech habits are. A French joke asks how two Englishmen greet each other when meeting in the middle of an empty desert, both dying of thirst. The answer is, of course, that they do not, because they have not been introduced.

And talking of introductions: in English when introducing a young person to an elder, more important, person, who do you address first? It doesn't matter? It does according to Miss Manners, who says that the important person must be addressed first. Thus, 'Mum, this is my new friend, John'. This is just a habit of speech. But in Laos, you would turn to your new friend first, 'Tui, I want you to meet my mother'. It doesn't matter much because nobody really cares who gets spoken to first, not in Europe, not in Laos.

The Englishman who won't speak unless he has been introduced, is likely in London to thank the bus conductor for giving him a ticket in exchange for money. Of course, there is likely to be no ticket in Laos, and maybe also no bus. But go round greeting everybody, thanking everybody, and excusing yourself when you haven't done anything wrong, and your speech habits will make you seem a bit odd to the Lao. Just a bit odd. You're not yet flying over the cuckoo's nest.

Once again, it is not so much what people say that is important, it is what they think and what they do.

Flattery

The Lao love to be flattered and to flatter. This is sometimes seen by foreigners as superficial and insincere, and of course it is. If you look like you have just crawled out of the gutter, Lao practice their avoidance techniques; in all other situations they call up their seemingly endless capacities for praise and flattery. Your height, hair, eyes, nose, skin colour and clothing are all acceptable subjects for flattery. You have to conform to these social habits. If you are one of those who like to talk turkey, better button your lip. Tell somebody they have a King Kong nose—and quite a few Lao have just that—and they won't like you. There is always something to flatter. And you don't have to worry about repetition making you sound insincere. Indeed, repetition, as has already been stated, and stated again, is a way of emphasising the important.

Strangely enough, it doesn't matter how many times a Lao hears that she is beautiful, they don't become immune to flattery. Indeed the Lao world is full of people who have been taken advantage of after a good soporific dose of flattery.

> When the Lao do not conform to your particular speech habits in any particular situation, don't presume they are being unfriendly, or even rude. Or, on the other hand, when they ask where you are going, or invite you to sit down and eat with them, recognise that these are just speech habits, nobody is making advances, nobody is being super friendly, and nobody really cares where on earth you are going and they would probably be surprised if you did sit down and eat with them.

You can more or less say what you like, even across the sex-line, although if going overboard in praise of a man's wife, be aware that it is probably okay if you tell him that he has a beautiful wife, after all you are flattering him, but it will not be okay if you ignore the man and flatter the wife.

You can flatter your girlfriend's girl friend, but not as far as you flatter your girlfriend (read boyfriend as appropriate). When in the company of a paramour, do not flatter unknown girls or boys who drive past smiling in your direction. If you notice them at all, you must immediately come out with an unflattering comment like 'God! if I had thighs that fat, you wouldn't see me dead in a mini-skirt that short'.

Meaningful Conversation

According to some foreigners, it is impossible to have a serious conversation with a Lao. This is quite untrue. You can have a serious conversation about the relative qualities of Korean and Chinese motor-cycles, the best *sindad* in town, and the inadvisability of getting a reverse boob job. If talking to a Lao with an advanced degree in hydraulic engineering from Grenoble, 30 years experience working in the UN, and fluent in six foreign languages, you need not hesitate before plunging into the Freudian fear of big breasts. Too glib? Too generalised? Too patronising? Yes.

Criticism

The Lao society that attracted your favourable first impressions is one that is easy-going, look the other way, never mind, and tolerant of differences. Think about that. Any society can only be all those things if there is no disturbance within it. Indeed, the perfectly tolerant society must be made up of individuals who can do no wrong. This would indeed be paradise.

But paradise does not exist. All attempts to create paradise on earth have failed, some to the point of creating hell on earth. A few societies come closer than others to the ideal community. Some of these are extremely peaceful and have turned their backs on violence and change. The Amish and Mennonites in parts of America come to mind, communities where children are brought up to behave in one way only, the same way their parents behaved and their children will behave. The norms and values of such communities are not discussed by their members, they are learnt. The Lao can be seen as far from such a model; they have participated in wars and revolutions, and they welcome prosperity and modernisation. At the same time, they do not discuss Lao norms and values, they learn them by heart. They learn non-interference in the lives of others. They learn to value respect for others. They agree that each is responsible for his or her own destiny.

The more meaningful your talk with a Lao, as with anybody, the more likely you are to arrive at points of disagreement. Perhaps this is why even old-hands find they rarely have meaningful in-depth conversations with Lao. In Laos, friends and relatives do not disagree with each other and do not criticise each other. Even strangers do not criticise each other to their faces: what is said behind backs to a third party does not count. This will not stop a parent punishing a child if it does what the parent considers wrong, like refusing to do what the parent says is right—but this is part of learning norms and values.

Many Europeans think of the Lao as children, and talk to them accordingly. As long as the imagined child is good, the paternalistic attitude of the foreigner causes no offence, it might even approach the way a Lao boss might talk to his or her underlings, and be met with demonstrated respect rather than disobedience. "A boss must love his workers, a grandfather his grandchildren", one Lao saying that sums up this point of view. If you have somebody's respect, they will be more inclined to do what you tell them to do. The reverse side is that they will not point out where you are completely wrong and where your suggested actions might have dire consequences, but you can't have it both ways. Or can you? Let's consider this aspect more under the section on business. For the moment, we are still dealing with the fundamentals of Lao culture and how you can some way integrate into it—which does not mean that you get assimilated by it, you do not have to become Lao. But if you want Lao to tolerate and accept you, there has to be a social contract of sorts; you have to agree to a quid pro quo.

Do not expect a Lao to tolerate intolerance. And if you are critical of a Lao or of Lao ways of doing things, you are being intolerant. Does this mean you have to accept whatever a Lao does, even if you disagree completely with it? Yes, if your disagreement would be criticism or even imply criticism. You can always practice avoidance.

DEVELOPMENT

Can development projects aimed at helping a people so sensitive ever succeed? An important question, considering the billions of dollars spent in Laos over decades and the very slow rate of development. So many projects have failed miserably—a pity, and a waste of money. There are only 6 million Lao, and at the cessation of hostilities in the 1970s the number was nearer 3 million. Okay, we know the Lao have had more tons of bombs rained on them than any other nationality, but they have also perhaps had more dollars per head spent in their name than most other least developed countries.

Telling, or showing, a Lao how something is done (if he wants to know) is not criticising, it is some form of training. Telling a Lao they are doing something wrong or poorly is criticising. The Lao, compared to most Europeans, have a zero-tolerance attitude to personal criticism. Such zero-tolerance can sometimes lead to missed opportunities. It can result in Lao failing to jump when bargains or good advice are to be had. But it can also prevent differences from entering the family, the community, the society and even the nation.

Zero-tolerance towards anything does not sound very nice. But, like it or not, if you want to accomplish your mission in Laos, or just have a good time, you have to live and work within it. That means sometimes putting things on a back-boiler if you notice the Lao not jumping at an idea. Many more times, it means observing and maybe participating to an extent in the life of the people a project is to serve. It means communicating in the way Lao communicate, which is not likely to be with one man invited to sit at a table for dinner. And if you do not speak Lao, it requires a good interpreter (one who is patient and does not try to use his reflected status for personal gain). It will certainly require time. Not just time for ideas to sink in, but time for ideas to be repeated outside of your immediate circle. And it will certainly require repetition of the important points.

If a project fits in with local plans, it may be accepted. But you need more than simple acceptance, and so should the donors who put up the money in the form of aid or loans. You need community enthusiasm: this is the best encouragement to work, and such enthusiasm isn't always spontaneous among Lao. The Lao who stand to benefit from the project must be directly involved—call them the principal

The Ugly American

'You've got a good machine there. But don't think that just because it's good the Lao are going to start using it. You have to let them use the machine themselves and in their own way. If you try to jam it down their throats, they'll never use it.'

— Lederere and Burdick, *The Ugly American*, 1958 (and still as relevant as ever).

stake-holders, primary beneficiaries or whatever—they must be prepared to own the project by contributing their time at the planning stage, their labour, their funding or partial-funding (even if it means giving them a micro-loan to do so). If they show enthusiasm only for the benefits of the project but are not prepared to contribute, they are most likely being polite and logical but have no real confidence that the project will succeed—and given the number of projects that fall by the wayside, do you blame them?

TIME

Foreigners in from Thailand will be glad to hear that the special way Thais have of dividing up the day and the night into various segments and noises is not practiced at all in Laos. The Lao use the straight-forward European-American way of telling time, dividing up the 24-hour cycle into two lots of 12 hours and referring to them precisely as a European would. Bus schedules and evening events are usually referred to by use of the 24-hour clock in writing, but the 12-hour clock in spoken Lao. So the kind of misunderstandings that plague foreigners in Thailand should not happen to you here.

While at it, there are some other differences with the Thai timing system of which foreigners should be aware, since many people will presume events match up as in Thailand. The year in Laos is the familiar Gregorian year, beginning 1 January and ending 31 December. Lao generally use this Western year in conversation rather than the Buddhist Era (B.E.) year, which is frequently used in Thailand. Wow, even better news, never could work out those thousands of Thai years!

In the rare event of a year being given in Laos only in B.E., a simple formula to convert to Gregorian is to take off 543 from the Buddhist year. That will bring you close enough. Also, Laos is generally one day behind Thailand in the important festivals. Thus, Thai New Year falls on 13, 14 and 15 April; Lao New Year on 14, 15 and 16 April. The three month Buddhist Lent (moveable, July–October) is also usually declared to start (*khao phansa*) one day later in Laos than in Thailand, and subsequently to end (*ock phansa*) one day later.

One source of confusion remains for the foreigner. Months in Lao are easier and more difficult than in Thai. Easier because Lao language makes do with numbers except on the most official of communications. Thus in spoken Lao the year is divided into Month 1, Month 2, etc. Only one problem: Month 1 begins in December, so month 2 is January, and so on. This would not cause great headaches, if it were not for the fact that some educated Lao, when speaking to a foreigner in either Lao or English, will say Month 1 for January, and so on. Rural villages and most Lao in town will stick to the agricultural calendar, where Month 1 coincides with the first month after the rice harvest. A slight further complication is that so beautifully simple is the month-numbering system, that many Lao do not know the real names of the months in Lao or in English, and sometimes get them wrong. Without learning the proper names of the Lao months (which a Lao might not recognise), a foreigner can obtain precision by asking 'month 1 Lao or month 1 *falang*'. Although the meaning of *falang* (French) coincides ambiguously with the Thai *farang* (white foreigner), it doesn't matter as far as months go, since French are *farang* in both senses of the term.

Another, more important, difference with Thailand is that while Buddhist years are the same, they are also different. This is because Thai Buddhist years change on 1 January, whereas Lao Buddhist years change on 15 April. So, for the first 3.5 months of the Gregorian year, Laos is one year behind Thailand on the Buddhist calendar. Since the Lao use the Western calendar-year all the time, this will cause you no confusion at all (unless you are a monk).

Time-keeping

Perhaps a greater problem than telling the time is the interpretation of time and time-keeping. In some circumstances, Lao can be very precise. In garment factories, workers are subject to time-clocks and penalised if late. It is a bit of a surprise to see the same clocks in restaurants employing perhaps five or six staff. However, the use of such a clock, which might now be seen in some European quarters as 'dehumanising', removes the need for human criticism. Nobody argues with a clock, which has a clear objectivity, and if workers pay is docked according to the actual time they are at work, there is no explanation necessary and no criticism implied.

Time-keeping differs between Lao and circumstances. If you invite a Lao to a restaurant, he or she will presume the invitation is extended to a group of people and further presume you will not be sitting alone if he or she turns up late or not at all. People vary of course but those who retain a rural mind-set, even if living in town, are likely to be far less precise in time keeping; if somebody is very late you have no obligation to wait—if the person is important to you, these days you can always call. Written invitations, mostly to engagements or marriages, involve more precise time-keeping. If the invitation says 7.00 pm, you don't have to rush to be the first one there, as you are likely to be if you arrive right on time, but the leeway accorded an invitation in Nepal (where you should arrive a couple of hours after the stated time so as not to appear greedy) is not evident in Laos and a perfectly acceptable arrival time would be 20 or 30 minutes after the time stated. Sometimes an invitation will give the time of a *basi* (for example, those associated with babies). If you want to go to the *basi* that's fine, if not, you can happily turn up an hour 'late' and still be in time for the food. Nobody minds—unless the *basi* is for you.

AGE

Most Lao know if they were born on a Monday, Tuesday, etc. and a surprising number have a good idea of the time, because their mothers might note this for the fortune teller. Less precise is the year of birth, which would be the most important thing in the west, and many Lao cannot state a year of birth.

As in other countries, the law takes account of age. A Lao cannot have legal sexual intercourse until age 15, the same age as being able to work legally. A Lao is considered an adult at 18 and can vote at that age, obtain a passport, and can even marry a foreigner at that age. If a Lao wants to do any of these things before the legal age, it is not too hard to obtain an identity card with a different age to the real one. Some 'bad' girls may have so many identity cards and passports that they lose any track they had of their real age. Documentation in Laos cannot always be taken at face value.

Official or informal meetings with members of the government or civil service (it is often academic to distinguish the two), usually take place on time. Certainly the social inferior, if there is one, should arrive ahead of time, and this is a reasonable precaution even if you are by no means inferior but have requested the meeting and stand to gain by it. If one of the parties arrives late, it will be the important person.

A further minor cause for confusion is that Lao sometimes give their age the way a European would give it, age last birthday, and sometimes give their age next birthday, even if one has just gone by.

VISITING A LAO

When Lao invite to their homes it usually means an occasion. The occasion may not be evident, but you can ask. If invitation is by card, it almost certainly means lots of people and states time, the person inviting and the occasion. It usually also means money is involved somewhere. If you receive a printed invitation with your name clearly on the unsealed envelope, you are expected to put some money inside and return the same envelope, sealed, upon arrival. The envelope may be given to the hosts or, if a marriage feast is involved, placed in the slot on the heart-shaped box. It is important to reuse the same envelope as it has your name on it and your hosts, later on, will see how much or how little you gave. If you can't go, you send back the envelope, sealed, with money inside.

How much you give depends partly on you and partly on the status of your hosts. As a foreigner, your status is not set by that of your family or place in the community. If you want to stay around in one place for a time, Lao will talk about you, of that you can be sure. If your behaviour is considered good and you are reasonably generous, you will get a good reputation and your status will be fairly high. If, on the other hand, you are seen as mean, your reputation goes down, and with it your status. If you are attending the function of a high-status family, it is obvious they do not need your money, but remember this is all about status rather than assistance, so give more rather than less than you would give to a modest family. It is also not simply a question of more money, more status. If you deliberately give a large amount, you certainly draw attention to yourself, and your hosts might ask why. Is it because you want to cement relations with the family of a business partner? Is it because you have romantic interests in somebody in the family?

As a very rough guide, put into the envelope an amount that will easily cover the cost of consummation of food and alcohol. In the case of a very modest family, doing the cooking themselves and with the help of neighbours, and serving only cheap rice wine, this is not likely to be more than US$ 2–3 per head. However, very modest, or very rural, families do not usually invite by card, but by personal spoken invitation, often at the last moment, and for really rural families, perhaps not even that—it is assumed that anybody within range is invited and they might turn up. In such cases, friends and neighbours often help out with the food and cooking but give nothing in terms of cash. You cannot do that. If there is a card in an envelope or if there is neither, US$ 2–3 is too little for you. Think in terms of what you would pay for a reasonable meal in a foreign restaurant, which would be at least US$ 10 dollars per person. Since Thai Baht is often used on such occasions, a 500 baht note should be fine. If a really important occasion for a really important person, 1,000 baht would make your contribution stand out while not being so generous as to embarrass.

The *basi* that usually precedes such feasts will give an extra opportunity to contribute. This is done not on arrival, but at the tying of strings onto wrists (*mat khen*) that terminates the *basi*. If the *basi* is for a baby, tie your banknote (rolled lengthwise is easiest—and more obvious) onto the baby's wrist while wishing it all the best (in any language). If the *basi* is the traditional wedding, tie your bank note onto the bride (you can also tie the groom but in addition). If the *basi* is for a person leaving the area for a long time, perhaps to go abroad, tie onto that person. When no written invitation has been received, contributions are usually made at the *basi*, but if you miss it, you can always tie on later; don't forget to add the appropriate wish as you do so. You will notice many notes already tied on, perhaps notes of just a few thousand kip. Do not be influenced by these to downscale your contribution, your US$ 10 bill will stand out all the more.

Do remember that if the invitation card bears only your name but is to a large event (not a sit-down dinner), you can bring a friend. It is also polite, but not required, to call and inform you are doing so.

You do not have to wait for an invitation before visiting Lao at home. An occasion such as a birth in the family means you can go at any reasonable time and be received. The family will not invite formally until the baby is at least 30 days old. It is usual on such visits to provide a small gift of money to the mother, and if you wish to provide baby articles, this is the time. A pack of disposable nappies is always welcome. These are comparatively expensive if bought in Laos rather than Thailand, but a surprising number of Lao use them and you need not worry that your gift is inappropriate.

You may visit without waiting for an occasion. It is more usual for the inferior to visit the superior, but Lao are flexible here. If visiting an important person, you may not get past the gateman or servant unless you provide a name card for them to take inside, while you wait. If they return to say the person you wish to visit is not in, that could mean anything. If they take you in it is likely to be to a veranda area outside the house or to the 'reception room'. It is quite usual to complete your visit without moving out of that area, unless you are invited in to eat. Even some quite formal occasions, with invitation cards, take place in the garden, where tables and chairs are set up, usually under a removable awning if there is any chance of rain or sun making guests uncomfortable. One such occasion might be a variant of funeral practices: while poor people will often take the body the day before to the *wat* where cremation is to take place, the middle-class can decide to move the body out of the house on the morning of the funeral. In that case, get to the house early and eat the simple breakfast provided before the body starts it journey to the crematorium. Take all the photographs you like.

What to wear on such occasions varies. Weddings and engagements usually require a suit or respectable female equivalent, although jackets can be removed as the evening progresses. In a remote rural environment, normal daily dress is usually acceptable, a clean shirt preferably with long sleeves is formality enough. To all other occasions, including the party held by every village headman at a time near the New Year festival, smart casual is quite enough.

Visits to homes require removal of footwear at the entrance. Shoes are normally left outside the door, but you may with no offence ask if the dog has a penchant for shoes and leave them just inside. If told to keep them on, the choice is yours. When visiting the toilet it is normal to ask permission on the first occasion (unless it is a hut at the back of the garden). It is not polite to explore somebody's home or garden unless invited and accompanied. When leaving, even if there is a very large group of people, take leave of your hosts and thank them.

PAYING

If you are eating out with a group of foreigners, by all means divide up the bill any way you like. If eating with Lao, follow Lao norms. These generally involve the host paying for everybody. If there are more than one foreigner eating with Lao, by all means divide the bill, but straight down the middle unless one of you wants to pick up the whole thing.

Certainly, you will find some young Lao out for a good time on the night of the monthly pay day putting together an amount of money and eating and drinking their way through it. Sometimes this is done at the place of work, but usually in a restaurant. Sometimes they each give so much of their salary to a different member of the group each month, and this person, temporarily a much bigger person, treats them

When it is your turn to invite the Lao to your house, do make sure you have adequate food supplies available. Beer is not a problem as there seems to be nowhere in Laos that is not within walking distance of a shop selling beer by the crate.

all with their own money. And sometimes you will see Lao dividing up the bill. This is perhaps because on such occasions they spend much more than they usually would and are in a large group. But if the bill is thus divided, which is already an exception to the way things should be done (but *sin deuan*, month's end, is a rather exceptional time), no individual is going to work out what he ate or drank and pay for that alone, the total is simply split by the number of people—and this is agreed beforehand, or is an established procedure for a regular event involving more or less the same people each time.

Those foreigners who make a point of insisting a Lao pay his or her share—yes, plenty of foreign men seem to think female liberation has stretched to Lao girls paying their way, nothing is further from reality—find they are changing their Lao companions rather too frequently. It's the quickest way to develop the kind of reputation you do not want.

The bottom line is: If you invite somebody to eat, pick up the bill, unless that person pays 'behind your back'. In situations where the inviter is uncertain, the person of higher status pays—probably you. Men pay for women, unless a business woman is on official expenses and does the inviting.

SEX AND MARRIAGE

The laws of the Lao PDR allow sex between Lao above the age of consent, usually taken to be the same as Thailand, 15 years. For foreigners, sex with a Lao (male or female) under age 18 is forbidden. And it remains forbidden unless you are married. A foreigner may marry a Lao aged 18 or above, with permission obtained from the Prefecture.

The period between requesting permission and obtaining the marriage certificate involves at least three months, longer if a 'fixer' is not employed or if one partner is officially resident in a distant province or if one partner is not resident in Laos. Any cohabitation during that time is punishable by a large fine and possible deportation. At several interviews during the period leading up to marriage, the couple will be asked independently if they have had sex. You know the answer, but make sure your Lao partner does!

The law is now rarely applied, and Thais seem to be immune. But some corrupt policemen work together with some girls. The girls pick up a foreigner, go with him to their regular guest house, or even to his house, and in come the police. The chances of getting taken to court and fined—and the fine runs into thousands of dollars—is small and such problems are usually sorted out on the spot, with no trip to the police station and no being held in custody, but the unofficial 'fine' could empty the pockets of many visiting foreigners. Many do not realise that the girl is part of the trap.

Other foreign men live with their girlfriends. Such excuses as "she's my maid" do not wash if there is co-habitation. Their girlfriends visit the local village police at regular intervals and pay a few dollars each month. If, however, the couple decides to get married, they can expect to be visited by regular and village police and immigration control at the addresses they give on their application for permission to marry—which cannot be the same address.

Once married, official hassle stops. But couples can still expect visits to check their legal status. The only exceptions are people with diplomatic status.

Courtship

Compared to the rest of Asia, courtship norms are very free and easy in Laos. They are, however, likely to be rather more structured than modern Europeans may be used to. This might not be obvious since a range of models exist, with plenty of variation. As in just about all countries, the concern is with the female partner to the relationship.

It will perhaps surprise a European that traditional norms of courtship are strongest among the middle-class and those with middle-class aspirations, among the very people who by dint of education and comparative wealth come a lot closer to the European than those who have grown up in a traditional agricultural environment.

You might meet a university student or even a graduate working in a shop or restaurant or hotel. Although she might through the requirements of her work, interact with many foreigners each day, it does not necessarily mean she will be free to date a foreigner. A typical first date in Laos (of a 'good girl') involves an invitation to a restaurant.

You can invite a girl directly without the need to talk to her parents or kinship guardians first and if she wants to go, they are most unlikely to attempt to dissuade her, and if they do it will almost certainly not be because you are a foreigner or have a different religion and culture. It would be normal for a Lao to go to the girl's house and fetch her. This may pose you great difficulties, especially if you have no car (and don't go on a motor-bike because everybody would not fit onto it). It may therefore be agreed that you meet at a restaurant or at a point you know. She is likely to turn up with at least one friend, a girl friend, or perhaps a relative, even possibly the mother. For girls of middle-class families, there is likely to be a curfew, initially a quite early one. You will spend the first date, and possibly the first few dates, talking at least as much to the friend(s) or relatives accompanying. Do not be surprised if the girl arrives in a car, and if the evening is reasonably successful, do not be surprised to be invited back to meet mother or another family figure, usually female. The assumption will then be made that you know the house and your excuse for not picking her up at the home dissipates.

Some girls, even in their mid-twenties and with responsible jobs—even jobs that require travelling away from home—may continue in this way for some time. It is partly distrust of the male, partly to provide time for you to get to know the family and the family to get to know you a little. There will inevitably be times when you are left to speak to mother while she is getting ready. Quite possibly father will bring out a beer to share with you, although men often keep out of the way in such matters. These talks may take place on a superficial level, but somewhere in there you will be asked relevant questions about your work and other things that indicate status.

On the other hand, a working class girl, perhaps working in a factory or a shop, might be free to meet you alone. Do not assume from this that she is a whore, although she is unlikely to be a virgin. She is simply from a different background and her family and friends, while interested to meet you, will not feel any compelling need to rush the meeting, which might only take place after the girl is fairly sure of her affections.

Going Out with Mother

Roger courted Oy for three months. On each date he picked her up at her home and they were accompanied by Oy's mother. Roger didn't mind because he enjoyed talking to the mother while looking at Oy. Then one day Mother said Roger and Oy were free to go out unaccompanied. Roger knew this was a great step forward. But suddenly Roger and Oy had nothing to say to each other. Roger married Oy's mother.

Why this middle-class hang-up with tradition, which amounts to chaperoning? It has everything to do with status and wealth. Middle-class parents want their daughter to marry a middle-class man. That man will spend more time with the girl's family than the girl spends with the family of her husband. This traditional matrilocality is impossible in its fullest sense in an urban environment, where in-coming husbands cannot build their house in the bride's mother's compound, but the bride's former home is most often the focal point of the marriage (this is what anthropologists mean by matrifocality).

A good marriage means an alliance between families. This is unlikely with a foreigner, who might expect to take the girl away from her home and country. It is a truism to say that in marrying a Lao girl, you marry her whole family. The middle-class family is interested in what you can bring to the family. The lack of a good marital alliance is not reason to prevent the marriage, but you might be expected to provide in other ways that strengthen the family's social and economic position.

The Bride Price

Roger: I can't really believe this. Laos is full of girls who pick you up in a bar or disco and sell their bodies in guest houses or hotels or come to your home. Surely decent foreigners willing to go through correct marriage procedures, including paying a high bride price, can't be deported. Where would that leave the girl?

Answer: Sad. Possibly in trouble with the police. But counting the bride price.

TAKING PHOTOS

Most travel guides tell you to take photographs only after asking first and receiving permission, they also tell you to send back copies of pictures to the people in them. That all sounds very ethical. But follow the advice and you will have endless sets of rigid people standing to attention, and even if you note the addresses of the people in your snaps, the lack of a postal delivery system in Laos means that your pictures will not arrive—unless you take pictures of only the one Lao among the hundred thousand who has a PO Box number.

Different ethnicities react differently to photo-takers. Some hill minorities don't like it but put up with it, perhaps asking for money—and why not? You got something out of them, why should they not get something out of you? The Lao Loum will ask you for the pictures you took at the funeral of granny, the Hmong will be horrified if you take back photos of a Hmong funeral and give them to the relatives.

The one important rule to remember is: never press the shutter until you see the V-sign! As for the rest, people know what a camera is for, and just about everybody has photos on the wall, even if the wall is made of split bamboo. Only if people turn away or say they object is there an ethical commitment not to take a picture. As for sending pictures back: it is really fine if you go back to the same place and give the pictures—that will certainly ensure you can take whatever you want. But the unethical part comes in if you promise to send the pictures and have no way of doing so.

PRACTICALITIES

CHAPTER 5

'Man is born free and is everywhere in chains.'
—Karl Marx

TOUCHDOWN!

Learning to fly with Lao culture is fine, but on first coming to Laos, you are probably more interested in learning your way to the bank and how to open an account there, in learning what schools are available to receive your children, finding accommodation, getting all your documentation in order and making plans for possible negatives, like serious illness.

If you have full-time employment in Laos, your employer should help you overcome all problems... but he or she might not. The truth is that employers vary greatly in the help they can or are willing to give. The shorter term consultancies you might see advertised in the *Vientiane Times* usually require that you already have some sort of residency status in Laos.

If you have a regular job at an embassy or large international organisation, someone will do everything for you. But even embassies are not likely to get you a visa if you are teaching English part-time to their Lao staff. Teachers of English and French can often get jobs that pay by the hour, but provide no official right to live and work in Laos.

Just about all documentation in Laos is time consuming and expensive, and subject to the usual international Catch-22. You need documentation to get a job and you need a job to get documentation. But don't despair. If you really want to stay in Laos much longer than the 30 days permitted as a tourist, help is available…

FIXER

Mister Fixit, or Ms Fixit, is an essential person in the life of many foreigners staying in Vientiane. These Lao make their living through their knowledge of the official and unofficial requirements and regulations. They can save you a lot of time, headaches, and even money—yes, it can cost as much or more to do some things yourself as having a fixer do them for you. There are of course scoundrels around who will say they can do anything for you but most fixers who are really in the business, have a reputation to maintain. They are also likely to have a regular job, perhaps in a government department or with a large foreign company where they work on similar personnel problems for foreigners. Some fixers are better at one thing than another, but usually once you have a relationship with one it does not pay to switch around.

> **Fantastic Four**
> On your first day in town, obtain:
> 1. a mobile phone
> 2. a good map
> 3. temporary transport
> 4. the *Yellow Pages*

A good fixer can get you an official—and legal—ID card, which any foreigner in the country needs, a year-long renewable multi-entry visa, a driving licence, a business licence, an import permit for a ten-wheeler full of your personal effects bought cheaply in Thailand, and even, although this takes a bit of cooperation from you (and a Lao partner), a marriage certificate.

Fixers did not come into being just to serve foreigners, many Lao also use their services to obtain ID cards, passports, move house registration, and many other things that require either endless queuing or somebody who can move behind the scenes and fast-track. Until 2007, any Lao leaving the country with a passport, needed an exit visa which required at least a full day in crowds of people at a special section of Foreign Affairs; and each time they left, apart from the time and agro problem, a passport

How does one find a good fixer? Ask any foreigner living in Laos with a long-term visa not obtained from his employer. Getting a recommendation from somebody who has already used the fixer's services for at least one satisfactory transaction is the best way of keeping costs down and getting good service.

holder had to pay an amount equal to a fistful of dollars. But for US$ 70, a fixer would take a Lao passport and obtain a business multiple-exit visa valid for one year. Such exit visas were abolished in 2007 and Lao now have the same right to international travel as citizens of most other countries. So, you say, that's Lao having problems in Laos, what about me? Well, apart from realising that not only foreigners have documentation problems, it is also worth knowing that where a fixer fits in today, the authorities might tomorrow adjust the regulations to make the fixer's role unnecessary. At the moment, unfortunately, for foreigners with no employer to help them, a fixer is necessary.

Be aware that some of the people who offer to get you a visa, etc, simply take your passport and other documentation and go themselves to a fixer, then add on a cut for themselves; while others simply take your money and do not provide.

How Much Do Things Cost?

A good fixer should be able to tell you precisely the cost of services before you start, and how long things will take. It is normal for you to pay an advance and to entrust the fixer with your passport. Essentially, the fixer's fee covers all payments made to functionaries, most of whom you will never see but almost all of whom need to have their signature on some documentation before you can get what you want.

For some things, you do not need a fixer. And indeed, if you have the time, can speak good Lao and are prepared to stand in queues indefinitely and shell out every time you are asked for an admin fee, and if you are fully entitled to what you need or want, and if you know the current system of constantly-changing procedures, you can do anything yourself... maybe. You decide. Here, I give a quick run-down of some of the main areas of activity where fixers operate, both to give an idea of what they do and to put 'do-it-yourself' in perspective.

Visas

Most foreigners of European, North American or Australian origin have right of entry to Laos for US $ 35, which obtains a one-off 30-day visa at the bridge or airport. Immigration procedures can sometimes change without notice and anybody coming to Laos should first look up the travel advisory website put out by their embassy in Laos or in Bangkok. There is a Lao Embassy in Bangkok, as in every ASEAN country and in Paris, from where the same visa can be had cheaper—for those really on a budget.

For such visas, a fixer is unnecessary, simply costs more and takes longer. Nongkhai, the end of the train line and a short *touk-touk* ride from the bridge, has a string of offices with official-looking Lao-Visa signs outside. If taking a foreigner from town or the rail station, the Thai *touk-touk* driver will usually pull into one of them where for a fee you will be given precisely the same forms that are available free on the Lao side of the bridge at the office where you need to go anyway to get your visa. Such fixers trade on the reputation built up in the past but no longer valid, that Laos is a difficult country to enter. Outside of the Lao Embassy in Bangkok and the Consulate in Khon Kaeng, you cannot get a Lao visa in Thailand, so don't waste your time.

If you plan only to be in Laos 30 days or less—and you can now exit through Vietnam, Cambodia and China at several immigration points (visas for those countries available at the appropriate embassies in Vientiane), a regular tourist visa is all you need, extendable after 30 days for up to 15 days at the in-town Immigration Office on Avenue Lane Xang opposite the entrance to the Morning Market. If you plan to stay for only two or three months, you can still make the run to the bridge every 30 days, do some shopping in Tesco on the Thai side to more than pay for your trip, and return on a new tourist visa.

A sample of a business visa—which comes with a little red book stamped 'Foreign Investor'.

If you plan to stay much longer than the 30 days in Laos, for whatever reason, consider a year-long multiple-entry business visa, which comes with a little red book ID Card gloriously stamped Foreign Investor (valid for 12 months) or the same thing in yellow which is for foreign staff of companies in Laos (valid for either six or 12 months). The red ID gives no right to work in Laos and in spite of being a foreign investor, no legal right to open a bank account. The initial visa and ID will cost US$ 450 to a fixer. It will require a couple of weeks and you have to go out of the country on your B-3 visa (the one you get on arrival), with a little scrap of paper to show on your return, which entitles you to a B-2 visa. The fixer than takes your passport and gets the B-2 visa converted, with no need for you to leave the country or take any part in procedures, into a one-year business visa. You need no money in a Lao bank or proof of income, or letters from your embassy, and the Lao business visa and ID card can be renewed each year thereafter for a similar payment to your fixer, with no need for you to leave the country or hang around in an immigration office. Fixer fees, like all costs, are liable to increase: the same documentation in 2006 cost US$ 400.

If you try to do things yourself, even if married to a Lao and actually working in Laos, you need to obtain documentation confirming your employment in an acceptable occupation in Laos, or submit plans for a foreign business or joint-venture or International NGO through the Foreign Investment Committee at 'KM2' (as the complex of government offices dealing with investment and poverty reduction is known— almost opposite the Novotel). If opening a business in Laos, you need to deposit a large amount in a bank account and leave it there (currently US$ 80,000 but subject to change), and provide evidence from the bank that you have done so, collect various signatures on extensive documentation, all of which will cost money, submit much documentation, and attend meetings to discuss your business plans. You will become a regular visitor to the immigration office (opposite the Morning Market on Avenue Lane Xang), pay to obtain forms, complete them, attach letters in Lao signed and witnessed, and obtain appropriate visas. And repeat this every year.

Certain activities are considered reserved for Lao (guest houses, small trading, forestry, medical practice and so on). Foreigners are to be found in these activities but they have either been resident in Laos since before 1975 (such as the French owners of the apartment block on Sam Sen Thai) or they are married to a Lao and everything is in the name of the Lao spouse. If a foreign company, you will need a Memorandum of Understanding (MOU) before gaining permission to operate in Laos: this will set out what you can and cannot do. Foreign NGOs (there are no Lao NGOs) go through much of the same procedures, with the addition that they have to operate within the oversight and control of a specified ministry. There are no foreign news correspondents in Laos, so don't waste your time applying, and there are no foreign Chambers of Commerce (as there are in Bangkok) to advise and assist.

Business Licences

These are required for all businesses, whether run by a Lao or a foreigner. They specify the name and location of the business, its nature and even the dimensions and wording of the sign you may put above the door or gate. Do not grand-slam by including everything you might possibly want to do one day—keep your operational activity simple. Don't go to the other extreme. For example, my bookshop is called Book-Café and is licenced to sell books. It also has café tables, and I know that coffee, cold drinks and snacks can be sold, but if I expand into a restaurant, I would need to register as both a bookshop and a restaurant, and pay twice the tax.

Large foreign companies will certainly have a comprador-like fixer or fixers regularly employed as permanent staffing fixtures. Such staff will need additional sums over and above their normal salary for such things as licences. Smaller businesses might be well advised that paying a fixer US$ 200 for a business licence is money well spent. A good fixer can advise on what should go on your application to get it through with the minimum of fuss, while fully covering your operational concerns.

Driving Licences

While diplomats and those entitled to diplomatic privileges (the Lao are not tight on this) can show any foreign driving licence through their embassy or office to obtain a Lao licence, ordinary mortals are expected to have an international driving licence, and should strictly be able to show a medical certificate which includes an eye examination and pass a verbal test (at which it is necessary to identify the sign for a train crossing the road!)—the test is very much based on that in France. In reality, most diplomats drive a CD car (recognised in Laos by the letters *sor-tor*—short for *sa-than-thut*, embassy—or *sor-phor-sor*, short for *saha-phasa-saat*, United Nations). The police will never knowingly stop or examine a diplomatic car, so the driver has little need for a licence of any sort, and many diplomats do not bother to obtain one, unless this is required by their office. Some foreigners are 'sort-of' diplomatic and drive *khor-tor*—short for *kheck-tan-phatet*, foreign guest, number plates. These usually are allowed to bring in things from Thailand without being searched at the bridge, but if stopped, the driver will be expected to show a driving licence. Thai registered vehicles, allowed into the country for 28 days at a time, but with no limit to the number of times, can be stopped, and like Lao-registered vehicles, 'fined' on the spot for infringements. Drivers of Thai-registered vehicles must get Lao insurance (this is also a requirement for Lao and foreigners driving in Laos, who can include Thailand on their policies for an extra payment which is well worthwhile, since Thai police in Nongkhai often check Lao vehicles for insurance), but it is accepted that they can drive on Thai licences (even for Europeans).

The fixer will get you an international, valid one-year, for only US$ 30, all included. You do these days need a bona-fide licence of some sort to get your international, otherwise you have to take the full Lao driving test, which takes time and much more money. The international also allows you to drive in Thailand, and if you are driving a Lao-registered car, you can get Thai insurance at the Thai-side of the bridge to cover the period you might need. Lao international driving licenses are stamped in French '*Non-valable au Laos*', but don't worry about that.

Import, Export

Moving goods from Nongkhai into Laos by road, involves you going to the transport office in Nongkhai, even if your goods come from Bangkok, and finding your way between the many parked Lao trucks into the appropriate office and to the appropriate person who handles just what you need. That person will be absent but can talk to you on the phone. She tells you to make out a detailed list, typewritten in Thai, and bring it back to get approval. Many hours or days later you do. The person tells you the list is not correct and offers to do the correct list for you. She is five minutes at a computer and she has a new list for you to sign which looks nothing like the list you gave her. She asks if you would like her to go with you to the bridge and make sure your things go straight across, with no problems leaving Thailand. You have a full ten-wheeler and have already wasted much time, so you ask how much it will cost you—5,000 baht in advance and the truck goes straight through. And it does.

Your Lao fixer is waiting on the other side armed with a letter of import for a company you have never heard of, complete with an attached list of all items on your hired ten-wheeler (and if that gets stuck in Lao customs just watch your costs spiral upwards). The customs man at the bridge says everything has to go into Thanalaeng Customs Warehouse for verification. Quite right, that's the law. So off your huge truck goes under gates that look decidedly one way, to park among a great area of trucks, goods spread around on the mud for verification. Your fixer seems to have disappeared. But he or she hasn't—he or she will be with a customs man armed with bunches of documents. This is not a good time to introduce yourself, but ten minutes later, your truck is backing out and is on its way into town, all papers in order. Total cost to you, not counting hire of vehicle and labour, a fraction over US$ 1,000. Possibly, had you done everything yourself, leaving the goods in the rain and unguarded for one week, the duty alone would have come to that. Fixers can increase productivity and in the end save money.

Smaller amounts, let's say what would fit into the back of a car, do not need fixers, even if they come into the airport as freight. Boxes and cases should clearly be marked 'Personal Effects', carry your name and phone number and not contain any significant electrical goods. Customs officers have a nose for what is acceptable as Personal Effects. 100 books of different titles is okay, 300 is not (so list all items with appropriate quantities). Often such movements are cleared on the spot without inspection and only a very small charge for documentation—although it will need to be signed by 'the boss', this can often be done later at his convenience and without your presence.

Marriage

This is included here not because it is something you are likely to need within days of arrival, but because it fits in with a fixer's other activities. Anyway, best to know from the off that sexual contact or sharing premises with a Lao is illegal unless you are married. This includes homosexual relationships and those with *khatoey*-transvestites.

Marry in haste and repent at leisure simply cannot happen in Laos. This is because the Lao system takes a long and hard effort. Given that you are not likely to be going through this routine too often, it is hardly worth learning the procedures to follow. The fixer fee for handling the marriage is US$ 1,400. This does not include the bride price and feasts, but considering the amount of work involved must be considered a bargain. You will, when all is ready, have the Mayor of Vientiane's permission to marry, and have to cough up another US$ 100 for the foreigner cost of a wedding certificate at a ceremony at the Prefecture.

A good fixer can get it all done with the minimum of disruption to you within three months (a bit longer depending on the time of year—for example, nobody gets married during Buddhist Lent).

Marrying a Lao does not remove the need for a fixer, but it should make life significantly easier—although that depends on the spouse. You also gain a little by putting electricity bills and so on in the name of your spouse (foreigners pay more than Lao for most things).

Fixers and Corruption

Some foreigners get the idea that fixers are an integral part of corruption. This is likely true. Would you need the fixer if there were no corruption? Probably not. But while corruption is against the law, the fixer is not.

CORRUPTION AND THE LAW

Before arriving in the country, or not long after arrival, the expat is certain to hear that corruption is endemic in Laos. Certainly there is corruption, but it was there under the French and almost certainly it has increased with the substantial inflows of aid and investment. Some Lao are to blame, but also some foreigners.

Probably, you are no more responsible for corruption than is the average Lao, who is far more likely to be a victim of it than a beneficiary. But if you have done any of the following, you are, willingly or unwillingly, a partner in corruption.

- Signed two or more contracts for your accommodation, each setting a different price. The law stipulates your landlord should pay 30 per cent of the rent as tax.
- Paid a police officer an on-the-spot fine for a traffic or parking infringement.
- Purchased a bottle of Black Label at less than the duty-free cost.
- Made a large donation inside a plain envelope to a Lao official at his or her home on a social occasion where gifts are common (*basi*, marriage, baby celebration, etc).
- Paid a fee to your local village officials or any government officers for documentation to which you are not entitled by law or for which you pay over the rate set for such documentation.
- Paid an intermediary to negotiate a reduction in tax payable.
- Supported a police sporting venture with cash, food, drink or equipment or made donations, solicited or unsolicited, to the police of your area at New Year or on other occasions.

In recent years, there has been a flood of new legislation from the National Assembly—much of it supported or required by such illustrious bodies as the UNDP (United Nations Development Programme), which has an extensive and expensive 'good governance' programme in Laos. This has had the unintended effect of supporting rather than removing opportunities for corruption, since plenty of individuals and companies are willing to pay to circumvent the law.

Few Lao and fewer foreigners are willing to take civil disputes to court because of the high hidden costs and a lack of confidence in 'justice'. Since the 2003 Amended Constitution, Party members and organisations are accountable to decisions of the courts (Article 85), but if any officials have ever been punished for corruption, this was not publicised.

Laos does not like to publicise its failings. To my knowledge the only disciplinary action taken against a high official for corruption was the demotion of one Politbureau member following the Fifth Party Congress, back in 1991. And, to my knowledge, not a single expatriate investor or aid worker has been in any way punished. The problem is not with the laws, but with enforcing the laws.

HOME

On arrival in Laos, you might be staying at accommodation provided by an employer, but most foreigners stay in a hotel or guest house while looking around for the kind of place they want at the price they can afford and in the correct location—and here you might consider your workplace, your child's daily journey to school and whether it is worth buying a car for the time you are here. These considerations are not as important as in somewhere like Bangkok, where travel is a major source of tension and a huge waste of time, but you should give them some thought.

Of course you may be one of those foreigners living in Luang Prabang or Vang Vieng or elsewhere, but the great majority of foreigners live in Vientiane, so that is where our advice centers. While Vientiane is one of the world's remaining livable cities, it is more expensive than elsewhere in Laos. Generally speaking, if you live in the sticks, you may have some renovation work to pay for but you get a much better deal than in central Vientiane, where, comparatively, property is expensive.

Temporary Accommodation in Vientiane

Presuming that you want somewhere reasonable in price and in quality, and if you have no vehicle, somewhere central. There is one big block of unserviced apartments in the middle of Sam Sen Thai which are cheap (US$ 150 to 300 per month). Prime location, but pending needed renovations which the current owners cannot afford, good to view and see what you get for that money. Most hotels and guest houses will give you a reduction if you stay a week or more, except in the December–February period, when good places are often full.

You can pay up to US$ 1,000 per month for a really nice serviced apartment with pool, or you can pick up a very decent couple of rooms including good bathroom and kitchen for US$ 300 plus, less if further out, more if maid service etc is included. At the cheaper range, your electricity is on meter and you pay the bills, leaving a deposit to make sure you do. Vientiane has seen a lot of building in recent years, but also many more foreigners coming in, so dead central places, where you can walk to the bank and shops, are not so easy to find. Ask as many people as you can; some landlords don't advertise, and some non-landlords are quite happy to let out the upstairs or the whole house, but had never thought of it. Housing agents get many of their properties by sending girls around to ask people if they would like to move out for a year of two and make some money. You can do the same. Lots easier if you speak Lao or have a Lao friend you can trust (it is possible). Be prepared to pay a large chunk of rent in advance—one year or six months. The more you pay, the less you pay. Payment of rent is in US Dollars or Thai Baht.

Keeping in mind that you, as a foreigner, are not personally allowed to own house or land in Laos (although a foreign company may legally own, import and repatriate resources and all profits), and keeping in mind that many properties, even in central Vientiane need substantive renovation and adaptation before they can be used by a modern company, or as a modern home, you might prefer a long-term lease. Leases are double-edged swords: you may want out when you discover the rain pouring through the roof, the doors which no longer close, the wildlife in the kitchen, the electricity system which shorts whenever

The Novotel Hotel has bed-sit offices and a classic architecture.

you turn on the TV, the dribbling tap water; at the same time, if you spend some money and time in making a place comfortable, you don't want to be told that big sister is coming to live in Vientiane next month and you have to get out.

Seeing houses is not a problem in Vientiane: there are far fewer estate agents than in most capital cities, about half a dozen, but they all advertise in the *Vientiane Times* in English. There is also a French-language weekly newspaper *Le Renovateur* that carries personal advertisements. And much of what is available gets publicity on the doors of Pim's minimarts near the fountain and near That Dam, and in the photo shop and Internet shops near Khop Chai Deu, the beer garden on the corner at Fountain Square. This is direct advertising, so you might get things a bit cheaper, and bargaining is definitely in order on three fronts: the monthly cost, the changes to fixtures and furnishings that you would like to see, and the advance rent payment or length of lease. If you don't have transport you can hire a local taxi with driver for US$ 40 or so for the day. The driver himself might know of some places going, but anyway take a map with you and your mobile phone and get him to drive around all areas that you think you might like—not just the riverside.

You will sometimes see 'To Let' signs, sometimes only written in Lao (*hay sao*, 'to let' in the Lao alphabet). There will be a telephone number and you should call it and ask the rent. If the owner cannot speak one of your languages, and you don't speak Lao, pass the phone to your driver or Lao friend. It is often possible to make an appointment to see the inside on the spot—some people even leave the key with a neighbour. Even if you love the place, take matters slowly and do not negotiate at this stage. It is better to come back later and see the owner without the driver or another person accompanying—since the owner will presume he has to factor in some commission for the Lao standing by your side. As a rough rule of thumb, a three-bedroom house, sort of furnished, with small garden and parking would go for US$ 300 as far out as the airport, rather more in town, and at least twice as much dead centre or on the river up to 3 km (2 miles) out.

If you are taking over from other expats leaving the country, there is usually no room for bargaining, but you should get an honest review of the benefits and pitfalls of the place and the extra charges. The outgoing party may also be happy to sell you furniture and electrical items which cost more in Laos than in Thailand, where most come from. Such items rarely make the ads and are usually sold word of mouth.

You will contact a sample of the agents who advertise their services. These agents usually take a one month rent equivalent from the house owner, payable on you signing the lease. In principle, you pay nothing for their services, but in practice of course, the owner factors in what he pays to the agent and the rent goes up accordingly. Even so, some agents can provide useful advice on the location, the house, and even the owner and noise levels, etc.

An agent might negotiate a lower price and even be prepared to cut his profit for a reasonably quick lease. Such agents usually work on the basis of getting an extra month's payment from the owner if you renew your lease. If you want less than a year, this is possible, but then it is normal to pay six months advance, plus the deposit against breakables. Here the agent can be useful. He or she should keep the deposit, so you have a fair chance of getting it back once final electricity bills etc have been paid. An agent can also be useful if you suddenly find yourself with no water or too much of it, and a landlord whose ideas of repair are different to yours. Having seen a house you like with an agent, don't double-cross by renting behind his or her back: Vientiane can be a very small place.

Agents also handle houses for sale. These are not legally available to foreigners, but one Dutch agent who has been in Vientiane for many years advertises 'foreign ownership'— always putting the term in quotes just like that.

What to Look For in a Potential Home?

Do you, and any family members, feel good in it? This may be first reaction syndrome, but if you don't like it from the word 'go', it's no-go.

Noise level

Beautiful *wat* right next door? If you like peace and quiet, consider what the drum sounds like very early in the morning. Notice the loudspeakers? They can go on all day, at a temple fair. Some Abbots like their long *wan pha* sermons to be heard at full volume. Traffic noise is not the problem it is in many towns, but anywhere central along the river looks across the road before you see any water, and that road is one of the noisiest in Vientiane.

Access

Charming little *hom* (lane) but can you get a car in easily and can it get out (and many people drive huge cars in Laos). If unsurfaced, what's it like in the rains?

Water

You are probably on *nam-pa-pa* (the piped water system) but even so, do you have a decent size water tank and pump? And are these uniquely for your house? Is there water pressure in all outlets all day? Is pump noise supportable?

Electricity

Wires are likely to be exposed in the sense of tacked up the walls. That's okay if they are not exposed in other ways or falling out of their holders. Is your meter really yours, or are you paying also for your landlord's house next door (you would not be the first). And sockets: is there more than one per room?

Television

Is the TV set included along with cable TV. The charges for cable are not high, installation charge is. Check that you don't just have Thai and Lao channels, unless of course that's all you want.

Neighbours

This is your chance to talk to them. A hostel or row of rooms can be great fun for young people and very lively—if you like that sort of thing.

Market

All Lao want to live near a market. There is usually one in each village. However, parking can be difficult in all daylight hours and it will be noisy early in the morning.

Security

Bars on all windows? Chances of getting out in case of fire? Can you lock up well and shutter when away? Any fire extinguishers? (The cost of a big one is US$ 15.) Any street security guards?

Air-conditioners

This can be hard to judge on a cold day in January. But check if they are noisy and if the cleaning is included.

Telephone

Not so important now that mobiles are everywhere, but a telephone line can give you cheaper Internet access, although you will probably have to pay installation. If you have no phone line, the Internet costs about US$ 70 per month. It cost less with phone line, but you have to pay phone rental.

Parking

If in the centre of a congested area (near markets), what's it like at the times you will be home? Parking on the street is usually safe from thieves, but not from other cars.

Rain

It can come in not only through the roof but through the tops and bottoms and slats of ill-fitting doors and windows.

Flooding

This is not a problem like Bangkok. But when there is a flood every ten years, it's a big one, often up to second floor level. A few places in town flood into the ground floor at every heavy rain. There is no insurance for flooding in Laos.

Mosquitoes

Is there stagnant water? Mosquito screens? Do they keep the mossies out or keep them in? Although not everybody likes them, screens are useful against the dusk invasion of flying insects.

Contract

Check for the escape clause and make responsibilities clear in both Lao and English. For example, who is responsible for small repairs like the lights, fans, blocked toilets, etc.

Introduction to the office of the nai baan

Your landlord should declare your residence very soon after arrival. The *nai baan* will expect a copy of all your passports. Pay no extra for this service.

TOILETS

It is certainly recommended to use the toilet before leaving home. While many restaurants and shops in Vientiane have some sort of toilet, upcountry many foreigners take Imodium as a preventative rather than wait until it is needed as a cure. That way they can limit use of hole-in-the-floor toilets.

A wad of toilet paper in a handy pocket or handbag is another essential not on the embassy travel advisory. Some traditional toilets have water to wash the backside, but nothing to wipe or dry with, thus the toilet paper in the back pocket is necessary.

In a modern house in Vientiane, you should have a water hose connected to the toilet and hooked on the wall nearby. You unhook, direct and let fly with a nice jet of cleansing water. Toilet paper is then used to dry off (put it into a bin rather than try to flush it away). In the absence of a bidet, women find this easy flush serves the same purpose. Most foreigners get the hang of these very quickly.

Bathrooms

Bathrooms in any rented accommodation are likely to be familiar to you. Older houses often have a large geyser poised over the bath, newer premises are likely to have a more efficient electric instant water heater and a shower, which usually sprays straight onto you and the floor and down the hole or drain in the cement or tiles. More traditional bathrooms often have little but one nail on which to hang your clothes and towel, and a large jar or other form of reservoir containing water with a *khan* (plastic or metal bowl) floating on top. You dip and splash, soap up being careful not to get the soap in the reservoir, and dip and splash again to your heart's content, or to the limits of available water. Take your towel in with you. The more traditional bathrooms dispense with the nail and water jar, and even with the room.

SERVANTS

Any Lao family with any sort of income, has at least one servant. Even some servants have servants. 'Servants' in Lao families will often be distant kin, although the genealogical link may be very distant or fictitious, amounting in reality to no more than coming from the same village of origin (in itself a social tie in Laos). Such servants will not be referred to as servants, and they often sleep in the family's accommodation, and may share a bed with a family member. Under such circumstances, where servants eat and sleep with the family and are referred to only by a nickname, it might be difficult for a foreign visitor to a Lao home to sort family members from servants. You are likely to have no such trouble in richer Lao households, where a servant might open the door for you and serve you a drink—possibly on her knees with a glass of Pepsi on a silver tray raised to the level of her head.

Your relationship with your servants is likely to fall between the extremes you see in Lao homes. Your servant should not share your bed! Indeed, that is against the law if a foreigner is one of the parties. If your servant naturally takes on a demeaning attitude, this is only showing respect. This is far less noticeable today than in the past, but it is still there, and there is not much point in trying to change it.

A few years ago, only vetted servants were allowed to work in the households of foreigners. This has now changed completely and you may pick your servants and negotiate pay and conditions with them. Officially, you should complete a contract obtainable at the Ministry of Labour. This stipulates a 45-day notice period and the payment of an extra month (13th month) after one year, and a bonus of 10 per cent of total salary on completion of contract. You are also legally liable if your servant has an incapacitating accident at the place of work or, and this is very ambiguous, on the way to or from work. Basically, you are expected to pay full wages for six months if incapacitated, perhaps longer. You should produce a

There are laws governing the employment of servants. But no Lao keeps these laws and few know what they are. If you offered the minimum wage as required by law, you would certainly not need to worry about how to treat your servants—you would have none.

medical certificate showing the extent of an injury. With laws like these, it is perhaps small wonder that nobody keeps to the correct procedures.

Insurance is almost unknown outside of the embassies in Vientiane. There is anyway only one insurance company (see the Resource Guide) and its monopoly position means rates are twice those of neighbouring Thailand, with benefits generally less.

Given that a servant in a foreign household has one of the best jobs in Laos, few are going to suggest sticking to the legal requirements. The average salary for a maid working a six-day week in a foreign family is at least US$ 100 per month. Men generally get a bit more than women, with drivers (who are also expected to care for the vehicle) near the top at US$ 150 to 160. To put these into perspective, the maid gets twice what she would get working full time including all overtime in a textile factory; she also gets twice the official salary of a medium-level civil servant.

The highest paid servants are those working for embassy staff, particularly cooks, and particularly those who can cook Japanese and speak some Japanese or English. One Japanese paid US$ 500 to his cook and sent her to language classes; she later went with him back to Japan, with her husband, and earned over US$ 2,000 per month, with everything provided.

If your servant is sick, it certainly is a good idea to send her or him to a clinic or the hospital and pay for the treatment. If you can understand the doctor, he or she will tell you precisely what is wrong with the servant, in their opinion, including if something might be contagious, lead to something serious later on (best treated in Thailand) or just be a case of tiredness or malingering. Be aware that a servant for a foreign family will have her own family coming to her or him for assistance. You are not responsible for every member of that family. If your servant should be seriously sick, it is perhaps a good idea to send or take them to Thailand, where treatment is more reliable, and often cheaper. While operations may be possible in Vientiane, the servant or her employer would have to guarantee such things as the provision of blood to the hospital.

While your relationship with a servant may be formal, you will probably use his or her short name (nickname). It is also acceptable to refer to a Lao by their profession—*than mor* is always used for a medical doctor, *khu* for a teacher, *nai baan* usually for the Village Headman. Your servant is way below any of those statuses, but you can use *mae baan* for a maid, literally 'house mother'; it sounds so much better than *khon say*, which your dictionary will tell you is the correct designation for a servant.

Your relationship with your servant will not stop you being invited to her home when there is a wedding or birth—and if she is the bride or mother, you might ask for a replacement from the same family during time absent. There is nothing stopping you from taking the maid with you to shop in Thailand: you might have to get her a border pass (US$ 20 through a fixer), but it will be a big leg-up for her in terms of her local status. And if she has never seen Thailand's large department stores, lifts and moving staircases, you will enjoy seeing her beautifully naïve reactions.

Time-off for servants is often a difficult point for foreigners. Some insist on giving the weekend. Fine if you prefer to be on your own at that time, but your servant will still expect to take off with pay at Lao New Year (14-16 April, plus a day each end for travel back to the home village if outside Vientiane). Servants will also be socially required to attend funerals, *basi* for various occasions, and to meet distant relatives when they come to town. Occasions for time-off can accumulate if national holidays are thrown in.

Lao servants, like most Lao, are likely to be easy-going and like a social life. If you just have one and she is cut off from other Lao, don't think that a comparatively high salary is recompense. Allow her or him to eat with the servants next door

Do not rush to be generous with giving time-off at the beginning. Staff will inevitably require more days off than those agreed at the negotiating stage. Some have to take time-off to bury at least three mothers (Mother of self, mother of husband, mother who raised them as a child).

or to stand outside the gate in the early evening chatting to whoever goes by while waiting for you to come home. Allow also a snooze after lunch—it pays for itself later in the afternoon.

Whether the lunch itself is provided by you, along with any similar perks, is up to you to decide. It is not a good idea to insist that servants sit and eat with you. This worked with a Mennonite couple, but they spoke Lao and ate Lao food. Realise that most Lao do not like your food, although they would never say so. Apart from the natural honesty of most Lao, it means most things in your fridge are safe.

Telling staff what to do, even if regular routine, requires the same repetition that we have noted takes place in meetings. This I observed taken to extremes by a Swiss housewife who had four servants. She had a Lao speaker write out in Lao on the walls of the servants' quarters (which were no longer used for staying overnight, but for resting) all daily and weekly duties of each staff member. I thought this was going too far, being too Swiss and not at all Lao.

For a start, I knew that two of the girls could not read Lao. I thought it was creating a barrier between foreigner and Lao. I was so wrong. That household had the happiest team of servants I ever met. Even those who could not read were told by the other Lao what their duties were and learnt them. They knew exactly what was required of them and there was no need for the Swiss *hausfrau* to ram it down their throats. The same Swiss house-manager used to make a point when she paid monthly salaries of putting aside for each employee an extra amount, writing this on a notice board—they could withdraw this amount whenever they needed it for any reason, thus she did not have to concern herself with whether the senior maid's father really needed medicine. She still gave a present to each at Lao New Year.

When Toyota opened a service station in Vientiane, I noticed a similar list of imperatives written on the workshop wall as that existing in the Swiss household, for mechanics and customers to see. The Toyota manager told me it had improved service and greatly reduced his need to reprimand his staff, or remind them of their duties.

Trust is an important element with servants and one which most foreigners develop quickly. This does not mean leaving large amounts of money or jewellery lying around, and if you do you might find a maid putting it in a drawer for you. It does mean that when the man calls with the water bill, or the telephone bill, or even the bill for cleaning the street, one servant can be entrusted to pay them from a 'money box' as they come. They are small amounts and a receipt is given; it saves a trip to offices to pay them.

Finding a Maid

So where do you find a maid? It is not a good idea to employ the girl you are having a beer with at a bar. Find accommodation first. Some come with maid service or a maid left over from the last tenant. It is always better, and much safer, to employ somebody living nearby. Find their house and look at it not just to see if it is clean, but where it is—so you can locate her when she doesn't turn up. There are always expats leaving, but if they are diplomats they will have paid top wages and the maid may be spoilt. Usual notice boards and advertising spots are set down in Resources.

If you hang up a sign on your gate saying in Lao 'Maid Wanted', you will get plenty to choose from. Take your time. Ask where they live and go there. To avoid possibilities of problems, men should avoid taking on girls obviously looking for a husband rather than an employer.

There are house agents who also find domestic staff; this can help if you need a particular quality (cooking Swedish or speaking good English), but of course you pay for the service. Think carefully before giving in to requests to live on the premises, and if you do, make sure the house owner and the *nai baan* know and approve. (Some *nai baan* will provide for a small fee such an authorisation, usually handwritten.) Depositing a copy of the maid's ID card at the *nai baan*'s office is good protection for you and for her—if she does not have an ID, suggest she get one.

If you do not want a servant, perhaps because you live alone, work outside and eat out, you can get by. There are places to wash and iron your clothes, some will pick up and deliver if you want them to. The general tiled floor is very easy to clean. Drinking water and cooking gas will come within five minutes of a phone call, and bathrooms are almost self-cleaning.

If you do take on servants and you don't like them (or they don't like you), you split. Just decide quickly if you do not like somebody, and tell her or him not to come again, take back any key and sweeten departure by a small present of money. There is no need to feel embarrassed or go into reasons you think things will not work out.

UTILITIES AND SERVICES
Electricity

Throughout Laos, the electricity supply is 220 volts, as in Thailand, where most electrical products originate, and as in much of the world. Earthing is not always up to standard, so get insulated appliances if you can. Prices are expensive, given that Laos is a net exporter of electricity. Your bills grow as you use air-conditioners and large refrigerators. They come mid-month and are paid at the EDL office (see Resources). Power supply is steadily improving, although blackouts are known, particularly up-country, and some provincial towns have only a limited number of electricity-on hours per day. These can be extended by using the on-hours to recharge car batteries, which may be used for television and electric light, and installing 'emergency' lights that automatically recharge and turn on when the electricity goes off—one set is cheap and can extend your reading time by two hours a day. Some areas have populations too small to benefit from extension of the national grid and buy back electricity from nearby border areas of Thailand, at around double the price Laos sells electricity to Thailand. There are still plenty of project sites in areas without any electricity, where alternative energy like solar panels are gaining ground, but usually a village gets together to send a truck of car batteries to town for weekly recharging.

In Vientiane, you are more likely to be troubled by fluctuations in power supply, including surges, than by occasional blackouts. UPS surge controls may be bought locally, and many expatriates remain convinced that the only sensible computer on which to work is a laptop—as long as you keep it charged.

Foreigners pay more for their electricity than the Lao, although the difference is not so great. Some landlords suggest they pay the bills, which you reimburse. But can you be sure you are not also paying for his mother-in-laws' house next door? Foreigners married to Lao get the Lao price, as long as the name of the Lao spouse is on the bill.

Gas

There are no mainline gas supplies. Getting cooking gas used to be a major headache for expatriates, and still is in areas where most people cook on wood or charcoal. Gas and LPG bottles are imported from Thailand. However, if you are in Vientiane, no need to keep emergency supplies—put the supplier's sticker on the wall near your cooking gas and call the number, in daytime you will be pleasantly surprised at the speed of service.

Telephones, TV and Internet

Telephones (land lines) are installed in a few days (see Resources). Purchase a mobile phone at many outlets for direct use (no registration needed); you can also purchase at around half-price second-hand at the same outlets, but if at the Morning Market, bargain down the price and check that it works. Always change the SIM-card number. If you install a landline, you should get a telephone book; if not buy the *Yellow Pages* (*Na Kham*), officially US$ 9, but cheaper if you can find a recent copy in a second-hand bookshop.

In Vientiane, the introduction of cable TV has changed a lot for foreigners, who no longer need satellite reception. The initial installation costs of cable TV are around US$ 140. This will give two locations in the house

Electrical goods are not guaranteed in Laos, but if you get to know a supplier you will get some sort of service or change in the event of a breakdown within a reasonable time, and a good supplier gives a regular customer a cheaper price than he can get elsewhere. Like so many things Lao, personal factors cannot be ignored. Getting people to like you is an economic as well as a social imperative.

and an initial three months service 'free'. After, prices come down to US$ 45 per year. There is no licence fee for owning a TV as there is in England and a few other countries. The range of programmes is the usual, although unlike Vietnam, pornography channels are not an option. Subtitling on English, French and German films is in Thai, which many Lao can read. Nobody has yet thought of English subtitles for Lao broadcasts and Lao generally prefer the choice of programmes offered by Thai TV (in Thai).

Television sets cost more in the Morning Market than in Nongkhai. However if you bring back a TV from Nongkhai, you might pay more when duty is factored in, and the one-year guarantee is not worth the paper it is written on, unless you are prepared to take the set back to Thailand and go through the import business again on return.

One supplier in Vientiane will provide Internet services without a phone line. The cost is US$ 50 per month plus US$ 20 for monthly rental of equipment. It comes a bit cheaper if you buy the equipment. Compared to other Asian countries, this is expensive and many people who do not need Internet for business, do not install in their homes, preferring to go to a nearby Internet café. Internet cafés or shops charges are pro-rata 5,000 kip per hour and some shops will give you unlimited use any time the shop is open, plus the use of printer, scanner etc, for US$ 50 per month—of course, you do have to get out of bed to go there and all too often you have to guess the letters on the keyboard.

Water

Like most of Asia, water from the tap in Laos is not safe to drink unless it has been boiled. Real purists say boil for 20 minutes. If you do, you really will have no problem, because you really will have no water.

If you live in Vientiane, get a big bottle of drinking water, the kind that is up-ended on a dispenser, for just Kip 3,000 per bottle (30 cents; much cheaper than the cost of boiling). If your landlord gets it for you, it might cost more. When you see a truck carrying water bottles, tell them to come to your house (or call—see Resources). Whether such water is any better than boiled water is debatable. It is not boiled but filtered and possibly x-rayed. At least when you boil water, you can see the bubbles.

Other water, for washing etc, is metered in Vientiane, or may come from a well outside. Like electricity, foreigners pay more than Lao. But it is cheap, so if possible save a trip to the Lao Water Supply Office on Phon Kheng, by paying the man who brings the bill.

Laos has plenty of water, but at times it goes off. That's why sensible people able to afford it have a metal storage tank and a pump. You probably pay more for the electricity powering your pump than you do for the water.

Sewage

Since 2004, most of Vientiane, or the inner bit of it (nobody seems sure where Vientiane stops) has had a centralised sewer system put in. If connected to it, you do not have to pay periodically to have a truck suck the muck out of your septic tank by putting a long tube down your toilet bowl. If you live out in the sticks, you just dig a new hole, using the earth to fill in the old hole and move the toilet and toilet cabin over the new hole. While centralised sewage is an improvement in lots of ways, there is no avoiding the occasional pong coming up from the pipes.

Mail

There are no house-delivery services anywhere in Laos—and never mind the futuristic postman on the stamp!

If in a large town, you hire a PO Box with a number and use that number as your address, adding Vientiane, or Luang Prabang, etc. Because of the limited world view of your postal service back home, it is as well to have your correspondents write out in full, including parenthesis: Lao People's Democratic Republic (Lao PDR/Laos); this should be enough to stop any letters going to Lagos—but some foreigners like to add 'Southeast Asia'. Putting 'near Thailand' will not only make the PO in Vientiane wince, but your letter will probably be sent to Thailand! Letters will generally be put in the box for your collection. Parcels or large envelopes will not be in the box. Instead there will be a slip of paper. In Vientiane General Post Office, take it to counter 16 (at the moment) with some identification like a passport, pay 2,000 kip and eventually it will be found and given to you after you sign for it. PO Boxes cost 111,000 kip to open and 40,000 kip per year—not expensive but not always available. You can pay to go on the waiting list and share another person's with consent. If you do share a box, give out your PO Box address with your name and mobile number beside it—then whoever picks up can call you. If you have a parcel, you will still need to get the slip before going to the PO. No slip, no parcel. Be prepared to open the parcel if it has not already been opened for you.

There are one or two French-style mailing boxes in Vientiane. I have never seen any emptied. If you stay at a reasonable hotel, you can use their PO Box, and might, depending on the owner's policy be allowed to continue using it after leaving the hotel. Embassies and banks will not act as *poste restante*, so don't waste your time in asking.

Vientiane's General Post Office can be an interesting place. It is open Monday to Saturday, 7.30 am to 5 pm. If urgent, you can send EMS from beside the PO, or DHL from their office near the airport. A one-page letter sent to Europe EMS costs around US$ 25! The office closes on Sundays. Normal post can take two to three weeks to arrive, unless it goes to Lagos, when delivery time is two to three years! My international bank (HSBC) in the UK, when informed of movement of my official address from Thailand to the Lao PDR, sent a letter to Thailand to ask which part of Thailand was the Lao PDR in.

All parents of an EU nationality sending their children to school outside the EU (and not just Laos), should be aware that they may be required to pay full fees if their children return to the home country for university education. This is particularly oppressive for English parents working for low salaries with NGOs in Laos. If in any doubt, contact your Embassy or home-based Parliamentary representative. The shock on return could be much greater than any culture shock in Laos.

SCHOOLS

Non-Lao speaking foreigners have little choice other than to send their children to international schools, of which a number exist (see Resources). Main languages of instruction are English and French. Generally, such schools are cheaper than Bangkok and children do not have horrific bus journeys to get to them. Most children in Vientiane are happy and find the schools friendly. Nothing much exists outside Vientiane.

BOOKS

Monument Books, the first shop selling new books (outside of tiny outlets in a few top hotels) opened in 2006. The book scene greatly improved in January 2007, with the opening of the Book-Café Vientiane. This is the only bookshop under foreign management and has a large and varied stock of some new, mostly second-hand, books in English, French, German, Swedish and Italian. The manager speaks English, French and Lao, and lots more besides, and knows his books. The Book-Café has modern lighting, A-Z arrangement, comfortable seating, drinks and snacks, pays best price for good books in good condition, and will exchange your book for another at the price of an ice-coffee. This bookshop is well-frequented by expat residents in Laos, who appreciate that its partnership with Lao Insight Books provides the cheapest prices for new books published and printed in Laos, and that it provides significant support to local charities including those promoting Lao literacy and COPE, which works to rehabilitate victims of bombs left over from the civil war.

There are four other small Lao-run second-hand bookshops in Vientiane and some in Luang Prabang. Northeast Thailand has no significant English bookshops, so stock up in Bangkok or elsewhere. New foreign-language books are expensive and are much cheaper in Australia or the US. (See Resources.)

MONEY

The kip is the only unit of official currency in Laos. This is not, as some wags would have it, divided into forty winks!

You are unlikely to see any one kip notes, unless you ask at a bank or buy a collection of notes as a souvenir. Given that there are around 8,000 kip to one dollar, that is hardly surprising. Recent introductions of 50,000 (the largest note in circulation) and 20,000 kip have greatly eased the situation. Other notes are 10,000, 5,000, 2,000, 1,000 and 500. Numbers are written in Lao and English, All banknotes except the 1,000 and below have a picture of Kaysone, the Father of the Revolution, on one side and a scene of Laos on the other. The 1,000 has women from the three ethnic categories of Lao citizenship against a backdrop of That Luang, the national symbol. The most commonly confused notes are the pinkish 50,000 and the light brownish 20,000; check the English numbers on these notes to avoid expensive mistakes.

The foreigner also confuses the 2,000 with the 10,000. Both are blue and have Kaysone and the National Symbol on one side. Notes below 500 kip and coins (occasionally put into circulation only to be withdrawn quickly) are so rarely evident that the foreigner might safely regard them like the Lao navy—we know it exists but never see it.

Many foreigners find it difficult to think when numbers of kip climb into the millions. It may be some consolation to note that many Lao have the same problem (and a great many more would like to have the problem). For this reason you will find prices of soft drinks and beer and anything up to 20,000 kip, usually written in kip. Prices of cars, houses, and motor-bikes are almost always given in US dollars or Thai baht, as are most things you are likely to buy on the morning market.

Shopping in Laos

Two Australian women examining Lao woven shawls in the market:
Edna: 'Oh, look dear, very cheap, only 25,000. Let's see, that's just three USD.'
Enid: 'Lovely. Let's take ten.'
Shopowner: Two hundred and fifty thousand Baht. Thank you.

Officially, prices should be marked in kip. Restaurants and foreign language bookshops must now put prices only in Kip, following a Bank of Lao PDR decision. But both will inform you of the $ equivalent if asked, and this is sometimes on the bill or on a convenient chart setting down equivalents on the payment counter. The kip has been stable since the year 2000, but reputations die hard. It is not a convertible currency, so you cannot get any before arrival. Since dollars and baht are acceptable, this poses no problem to new arrivals, although change may be given in unfamiliar kip. Do not take Lao currency out of the country with you except for a few souvenirs. For some reason, that is against the law.

The black market, which for the years following the change of regime made foreign salaries in Laos very attractive to expats working here (even the Soviets were paid in dollars), has been dead for years. Many shops will still change your money into kip but at the official rate or just below it. The official rate is available in banks and at official change offices, of which there are plenty. Avoid changing at hotels, where you lose. Tatty notes of any currency are usually acceptable, but not tatty or old US dollars, which will be refused even in banks.

Bank Accounts

Foreigners may open US dollar, Thai baht and Lao kip accounts, but only if they are working in Laos and have correct documentation. The majority of banks are Thai and offer good service to foreigners, but don't presume that with an account in a Thai bank in Vientiane, you can easily withdraw money in Thailand; or vice-versa. You can't. For this reason, some foreigners travelling frequently to Thailand, where ATMs are everywhere, keep a Thai baht account in Thailand (unless you are also resident in Thailand, it will pay no interest, but is convenient). There are no controls or onerous bank charges. But if carrying large amounts across to Thailand, remember that there are varying amounts that may be imported or exported on both sides. The legend of one Australian woman caught crossing the bridge with over US$ 70,000 in her knickers lives on—she kept her knickers but lost her dollars. It is not, by the way, a habit of Lao officials to search women's knickers.

Banking hours vary slightly, but are generally 8:30 am to 3:30 pm. Thai banks keep Thai and Lao holidays, so you may ask for a list of the year's bank holidays when opening an account.

Tax

In practice, you are not likely to be taxed if you work for a foreign company—at least not in Laos. Collecting public revenues in Laos has always been problematic. The IMF noted that many big Lao companies paid little or no tax, and that small foreign companies paid more tax than they should pay. Lao shop owners and service providers will generally be visited by a team of tax collectors who discuss with the owner and decide on the tax to be paid on the spot; the owner pays three months or more in advance. Some anomalies are evident, but the tax system is not oppressive. VAT was officially introduced at the rate of 10 % on 1 January 2010, but is currently applied at the wholesale supply level rather than small outlets and services, to which it is to be gradually introduced along with appropriate training and explanation. Since prices of many basic items imported from Thailand are 20 per cent or more higher than in Nongkhai supermarkets, there is still some work to do on supply chains before VAT becomes a part of daily life. The introduction has served simply to increase incentives to buy in Thailand, possibly decreasing revenues to Laos yet further.

SHOPPING

You can get most basics in Vientiane and in the three other major towns. Most come from Thailand and are more expensive for it. The Lao continue to buy and sell on markets and most *baan* (villages) in Vientiane have one or are near one. The biggest are the market at That Luang and the well known one at Talaat Sao (Morning Market), so named not because of the gold and handicraft sections at the front, where most tourists go and which are open until 5:00 pm. and beyond, but because of the very large food and furniture etc market some way behind that, off Khou Vieng. The food market kicks in with deliveries around 3:00 am. and does most trade in the early hours—hence the name.

There is also an 'evening market' now also referred to as 'Talaat Chin' (Chinese Market) because most of the items sold there are from China—cheaper, but no guarantees.

Meat is best bought early because of lack of refrigeration. There are also plenty of people who invest in a handcart and a pig or two a day, who walk around streets selling direct at prices nominally above those on the market. Fish is usually alive in tubs when purchased and will be weighed alive and a price given before it is cut up for you. Chickens must be dead when sold. Considering 80 per cent of the population works on the land and food is not scarce, prices are not really cheap, although they might appear so compared to European markets. Eggs, for example are 1,000 kip each, limes are 2,000 kip each, a fish that can feed two-three people is 15,000 kip (US$ 1.50). All prices are more expensive than in Thailand's air-conditioned supermarkets across the bridge.

Most things can be had at a market, if you know where to look. Parking can be problematic, and you pay (about 3,000 kip) the person who directs you into a lot and gives you a ticket—not anybody else. If you want refrigerated products like fresh milk (now made in Laos), fresh Cheddar cheese (imported from Vietnam) and ham in nice slices, together with butter, you will find small selections in the minimarts, at a price.

The attempt to create a 'domestic' supermarket at ITEC, out on the 'new road', succeeded only in creating many empty shelves, expensive imported products, and few customers. In mid-2007, a shopping mall with a spiraling (and frightening) car park opened right next to the Morning Market. There will be some air-conditioned shops, and the plan is for those currently in the Morning Market to move into much more expensive

Laos also produces the same cheap textiles made throughout Southeast Asia. Transport of this clothing to market in Europe is more expensive than similar products made in Thailand, but the EU does not levy duty because of the position of Laos in the Least Developed Countries (LDC) category. Some large sizes are available at Lao Cotton, which suffers from a quality-control problem, but for most things bigger than average, you will have to go to Thailand.

accommodation. But still no supermarket; so the big money will continue to go to Thailand.

There are of course some products in which Laos excels and in which foreigners are most interested. Chief among these are the traditionally woven or machine-made *sin* (the long tubular skirts) and accompanying shawls from the northeast. Wood products are beginning to make a presence and some beautiful hardwood lamps and tables can be purchased or ordered. Quality of joints and seasoning of wood is far from perfect, but some things available are attracting foreign exporters.

TRANSPORT

You will not be long in Laos before you discover the delights of the *touk-touk* and the jumbo. These are two different vehicles, although many Lao as well as foreigners confuse the two. The *touk-touk* is a small motor-cycle adapted to pull a small, open backed carriage that can carry four Europeans at a pinch or eight Lao. The jumbo, as the name suggests, is bigger and more powerful and can carry more people. If you want a vehicle to yourself or something that has a reasonable chance of going direct to your destination rather than give you a tour of the lanes of Vientiane first, go for a *touk-touk*. This will be smaller, noisier and slower, but makes up for it by being a bit more expensive. You might hear the indiscriminate term *song-thao* used to describe either: it simply means 'two rows' and refers to the seating arrangements.

Some jumbo ply almost regular routes, i.e. from the area near the airport (Wattay Nyai) to the Morning Market, but you can get on or off anywhere. You can stop any jumbo anywhere by raising your hand in a languid flip-flop. Tell the driver where you want to go before getting on. If he wants to go there too, which depends on the destinations of the other passengers, he will nod. Best to tell him the price, for confirmation, if you know it, ask him only as a last resort. Currently nothing is under 5,000 kip, or for foreigners 10,000 kip, if you are within town. If you want to go as far as the bridge think in terms of 200 baht or more, although at that price you can get a regular taxi. Note that such transports of delight maintain the general rule: lower prices are quoted in kip, higher in baht. If you don't have a computer as a brain, note down the baht and kip equivalents on a card and carry it in your top pocket for easy reference.

It is possible, depending on your location, to have a regular vehicle service to your place of work—but ask at the office first since a colleague might pick you up on his or her way in, or sometimes it is cheaper and more comfortable to use the office driver.

Motorcycles

Some foreigners go for motorcycles, either rented or purchased. These can be made in China (legality doubtful) and go for 17,000 Baht new in Vientiane (unwritten guarantee three months). A legal Korean import will cost 27,000 Baht (guarantee 18 months), and a Thailand-made job, 36,000 Baht. The fact that Lao who can afford it go for the Thailand machine is a good indicator of relative qualities.

Advantages of motorcycles are the price and cheap running and repair costs. Disadvantages are that a new law makes it compulsory to wear a helmet, and you have to decide what to do with it when you get to where you are going—a Lao just leaves it in the bike basket and none seem to get stolen. This law is enforced sporadically—whenever the police need the money. Motor-cycles are easy to buy and the shop will complete registration for you. But very few motor-cyclists in Laos have a licence, and although the test could not be easier, it takes a long time to get a licence. The majority of Lao don't bother and pay the small fine if stopped by the police. While a bike might seem fine in the dry months, it takes on a new perspective in the rain. And foreigners will be singled out if not wearing a helmet or holding a licence.

Cars

Cars are expensive. Figure US$ 13,000 for a five-year old Toyota pick-up, with no mileage indicator—suggesting the steering wheel might have changed sides on an illegal import from Thailand. Cheapest new cars are Chinese, but few people buy them. A new small Korean car can be had for as low as US$ 16,000, but if you are above six-foot, make sure you can see out. Cars are much cheaper in Thailand, but tax to bring any into Laos makes them more expensive than buying in Laos. For example, tax on a seven-year-old Land Cruiser brought in is US$ 5,000.

Cars are advertised (see Resources) for sale duty paid or duty not paid. Because of the great number of project vehicles and embassy cars, there are many cars advertised duty-free. That means you have to do the paper work, or get somebody to do it (US$ 100) and pay the tax. Second-hand car-sale outlets are dotted around Vientiane and people come from all over the country to buy in Vientiane, because price and choice is said to be better than elsewhere in Laos. However, many cars have new instrument panels, suggesting they may have originated in Thailand (which drives on the left), and few have a realistic indication of mileage. Most cars now use diesel, available all over but at a price some 20 per cent higher than in Thailand, so once more, weekend shoppers fill up in Nongkhai, giving revenues to Thailand rather than to Laos.

Theoretically, all cars should have a road worthiness certificate after a check every six months. In practice, many people do not know this and few bother. Obtaining a license is easy if you have diplomatic privileges (and therefore don't need one!), for others, you can get a short-term license at the Office of Vehicle and Driving Licence Control in The Ministry of Telecommunications (near the Australian Embassy and the Monument), you need a valid license from any country, not necessarily your country. After a few months you get a longer-term licence, or your fixer may go straight for an indefinite (life-long). Alternatively, you can get an International (which also qualifies you to drive in Thailand), which should be

Lao driving is non-aggressive and slow. You might never hear a car horn—a blessing if you come in from Nepal. However, accidents are frequent, especially accidents involving motorcycles, and if you spend much time driving around Vientiane, you will see at least one accident a day.

converted to a Lao within one year (but some foreigners just get a new one-year International one instead).

Few Lao drivers have compulsory car insurance and no motorcycles have it. In the case of accident, both parties agree on who pays or go to the police station near Wat Sisaket for arbitration, which can take weeks or months. There is an unwritten law that cars pay for damaged motorcycles and bicycles. There is only one monopoly insurer in Laos, so rates are high (see Resources). Foreigners buying one of the 30-50 year old jeeps for US$ 2,000–3,000 often decide to cover repair and accident costs themselves, calculating it is cheaper to write off their vehicle in the case of a serious accident.

Police are present at traffic lights and most accident spots. They act immediately if you pass a red light—and the flash from green to red has been noted as the quickest thing in Laos—or take a wrong turn (even if there is no sign to indicate). They almost always accept an amount that would be less than the official fine, US$ 3–5 is normal, but don't expect change. Some days are definitely worse (or better) in terms of police 'control' than others. End of the month and before Lao New Year, some drivers decide they cannot afford to take to the road!

Motorcycles going the wrong way up a one-way street seem to be immune to police control—unless driven by a non-Asian. This is less a cause of accidents then riding in pairs, to chat to your friend, using mobile phones while driving, being drunk, and not looking before turning. Death toll in Vientiane municipality alone is around 2,000 per year—mostly motorcyclists.

In 2010 it became legal to turn right at any traffic light set on red, if in the right-hand lane. This is indicated by a sign on the light written in Lao with Free Right Turn in English below it. At the same time it became illegal to use a phone when driving. As yet, there is no requirement to use seat belts.

Transportation Rentals

There are very few places offering self-drive car rental with insurance (see Resources). All require a deposit returnable if the renter can find nothing wrong when you get back. All are expensive: US$ 55 per day plus petrol, as a guide. Private deals are possible for around US$ 30 per day, with no insurance. For US$ 40-50 a day you can hire a taxi with driver. The real problem is finding a taxi. Nowhere can you hire in one place and deposit in another.

Many places offer motorcycle rent for US$ 6–10 a day, plus fuel, depending on the bike. Legally, you have to stay within Vientiane Municipality (which is a very large area but not always clearly demarcated). If you want to go to Nam Ngeun or Vong Vieng, it is possible, but tell the person renting the bike. Small (100 cc) motor-bikes can have problems in the mountains.

Planes, Trains and Buses

Until very recently, foreigners were much worried by the safety record of Lao Airlines. This has greatly improved with the purchase of new aircraft used on the main tourist routes, some aircraft hired from Singapore and a government decision to contract French engineers for maintenance. Main airports now have facilities to assist landing in difficult weather conditions, but local flights to places like Bokeo and Luang Nam Tha are subject to cancellation throughout February and March, when the burning of mountain fields combines with mist to make landing by sight dangerous. Flights to remote locations often have to turn around during these times because they cannot land. Luang Prabang is certainly as safe as any other international airport and plans exist to upgrade other airports to similar standard and increase the number. Tickets are roughly twice the price for a foreigner as for a Lao. You need to show your passport on domestic flights and pay a small domestic airport tax.

Three kilometres of train line and one station was opened in 2009 to extend the line Bangkok-Nongkhai into Laos. Plans exist to continue this line over six years to Savannakhet and across to join up with Vietnam's network. As for busses, VIP busses now go to the main Mekong towns, but not to places off the main roads. Thus, even if you go through a major urban centre, like Pakse, you will need to get down and find a local bus to carry you on to areas further south or east, or hire a *touk-touk* at a high price. Given this fact, most Lao and some foreigners take an ordinary bus from Vientiane for rides that can take over 24 hours but go to the destination without changing. Buses stop frequently—in fact anytime anybody asks to relieve themselves (no toilets on board). They also frequently break down—even if just going the 25 km (16 miles) to the bridge. Such busses are not air-conditioned and are crowded with passengers and their baggage. Sickness pills are a good idea, but can you get your fellow passengers to take them?

Boats are not regularly used as transport, although there are some wonderful tourist experiences to be had in the later part of the year (when waters run deep) and you can travel from the west of Laos (Houay Xai) to Luang Phrabang on a luxury cruise. Similar cruises are beginning in the south of the country.

In 2010, Laos surprisingly introduced the VIP Sleeping Bus. Air-conditioned, two passengers share each double bed welded to the floor. These go between main towns. Beds are designated female or male, and any foreigner wanting to share one with a Lao of the opposite sex may be asked to produce evidence of marriage. In a short time such buses have proven extremely popular with Lao and foreigners alike. Unlike domestic flights, foreigners pay the same fare as Lao on the bus.

DEATH AND BIRTH IN LAOS

According to Lao law, you should always carry your passport or identity card with you. Some foreigners also make out a will in English and Lao, particularly if a Lao partner is to benefit. The Lao authorities should contact your embassy or consulate in Vientiane or Bangkok, or the embassy that handles things for your country. If you want a Lao temple cremation, say so, or your body may be shipped to Thailand, embalmed and repatriated, at great cost to whoever gets your money.

If married to a Lao or you have a child in Laos for whom you accept responsibility, you will have Lao documentation provided at the hospital. Make sure all names are correctly written, as on passports. If your baby is born in Thailand, you can get a Thai birth certificate at the amphur office that should list names and nationalities of parents. You will need this to get a passport for your child from your embassy.

Even with a fully correct birth certificate, a child born in Laos may find it difficult to obtain citizenship if you have not registered everybody as dependents, and registered any marriage at the embassy responsible for your welfare. If you pass on or are otherwise not around, this difficulty is compounded, so a will, legally witnessed at your embassy, is a reasonable precaution. A full list of the 25 embassies in Vientiane is in the *Yellow Pages* of the Lao phone book, but this does not inform you of which embassy is responsible for nationalities not represented (e.g. British are represented in consular matters by the Australian Embassy). If you have no Embassy in Laos, chances are Laos is covered by your embassy in Bangkok, sometimes Hanoi. A search under your country name on the Internet will inform you.

LEGAL ADVICE

All significant trials of foreigners in Laos in recent years (Australians, Americans and French) have involved legal representatives from the defendant's home country, working alongside a Lao lawyer and through the embassy. This is expensive, but without somebody rooting for you, you could be held a couple of years before coming to trial, tried in a morning and given a long jail term in the afternoon. In all recent cases involving foreigners with legal representation and country support, trials have been within a reasonable time, and conviction (anybody brought to trial is convicted) has resulted in long sentences—such sentences were not appealed or quashed, but deportation took place within days or weeks.

EATING IN LAOS

CHAPTER 6

'*Gin khao phuu di-o, bo sehp.*'
'Eat alone and the food is not tasty.'
—Lao proverb

LAO FOOD

Just as Laos has been described in tourist promotion literature as the "Land of the Undiscovered", with tourists prompted to "See Laos before the tourists come", so we might describe Lao cuisine as one of the undiscovered cuisines of Asia and urge you to try it "before the gourmets come".

There might well be understandable reasons for the world's failure to take note of Lao food. Lao cuisine stands very much in the shadow of Thai cuisine, which has been promoted throughout the western world. Laos has suffered the isolation of a long civil war and a government policy that for a decade after the change in regimes was hostile to tourism. The Lao do not flaunt themselves or their culture, rather thinking that they are the junior partners in an arena of Asian tigers. One thing for sure: it has nothing to do with finding ant eggs. You no longer have to climb mango trees, knock down the ant-nests into tubs of water and skim off the ants to collect the eggs. Ant-eggs now come in nice convenient frozen packages, even in Asian supermarkets in the West.

LAO RESTAURANTS

"If there is anything much to Lao cuisine, how come there are no Lao restaurants in Laos?" This amazing comment came from a foreigner resident in Laos for some 10 years —one who would, as he said, rather starve than eat anything Lao. There are in fact several large restaurants that advertise themselves specifically as Lao. One of these is the big and beautiful converted colonial building on Sam Sen Thai near the junction with the Avenue Lane Xang—the Kua Lao (Lao Kitchen); although this one caters mostly for tourists, who also get a cultural show and can order French wine to go with their Lao food, it is perhaps the best introduction to Lao cuisine, and one that will not frighten the foreigner. A special menu means a visitor can order one of several combinations and try a little of many Lao foods, something difficult for the individual to do in a normal Lao restaurant.

Another, far more Lao eatery in its modesty is tucked away in a *hom* near That Dam. This one has real Lao home cooking in a homely décor but has few customers. The Lao tell me, "Why go out and pay good money for food that my wife can make at home?" Understandable—the Lao want Lao food, but something more special. There are another three specifically Lao restaurants which advertise regularly, have beautiful surroundings but are expensive and rather too sophisticated to provide a Lao atmosphere. It must unfortunately be stated that many Lao themselves do not appreciate the value of traditional Lao cuisine and what both Lao and foreigners want in a Lao restaurant. The single Lao restaurant mentioned in all guides, including the first edition of this cultural guide, is no more. It was unwittingly torpedoed by its Lao owners. The Bounmala on Khouvieng Road served the best barbecued chicken in Vientiane, with sticky rice, various fish dishes, various forms of laap, and of course Beer Lao on draft. All in a wonderfully ramshackle and open wooden environment big enough for parties to dance Lao lamvong after dinner. It was full every day and a goldmine. Until the owners knocked it down and built in its place an airconditioned concrete monstrosity that now serves only Korean food and Singapore beer, and where the empty tables stand as monuments to misunderstanding. A great loss to its owners and a great loss to affordable and enjoyable Lao cuisine.

Khaay luuk (eggs with chicks inside) is a popular Lao cuisine commonly sold at roadside markets.

Do not expect good Lao food to come cheaper than French, and there are probably more upper-range restaurants openly claiming to be French in Vientiane than claiming to be Lao. Of course, it all depends on what you mean by Lao and by restaurant. If we count the small shops and houses that might have a small sign saying *khay laap* (we sell *laap*), probably written on cardboard, only in Lao and propped up on the fence (avoiding tax rather than evading it), or that might have no sign at all, just a couple of tables and an open door, i.e. places that sell genuine Lao home cooking, we are talking of hundreds rather than handfuls. And don't forget the Lao food to take away—like *khaay luuk* (eggs with chicks inside) and *khao nio ping* (roast sticky rice on sticks). And the delicious snacks to go along with an ice-cold Beer Lao, like *sin savan* (heavenly beef), which will be sold in many restaurants as an appetiser to equal any.

Go a bit deeper into the real Vientiane and you can find some real specialities that are perhaps not for everybody: fried termites, scorpion claws and snake stews. I realise not everybody is likely to go for the type of Lao *laap* which is raw and swimming in blood. Why, you might be thinking, have blood for breakfast in Vientiane when you can have *jambon de Paris* and a nicely buttered baguette? East and West don't always meet on the dining table. Khop Chai Deu, the very well-known restaurant on the corner of Fountain Square, still has fried insects on the menu. Since the evening clientele of that open-air popular meeting place is mostly foreign (whereas the upstairs buffet lunch is almost entirely Lao), they sell far more pizzas than plates of insects. Mind you, when it comes to getting protein for your money, insects win over pizza every time, and fried termites go great with Beer Lao.

GOING OUT TO EAT

Lao may be poor, but they love to go out to eat. The two most popular restaurant foods in Laos are undeniably *pho* and *sin dad*, neither of which is Lao in origin, but both of which have been 'Lao-ised'. *Pho*, a cheap noodle soup, is Vietnamese in origin and even in name. For several years after 1975, when it was difficult to find food in Vientiane, let alone restaurants, *pho* was always there, any time, and at that time was heavily laced with marijuana, which gave it a character far more Lao than Vietnamese. (Now illegal, marijuana has been replaced with monosodium glutamate [msg]—that's progress). *Sin dad* restaurants must account for a large percentage of the non-western restaurants in Vientiane. Between town and the airport, it is difficult to find a restaurant not serving *sin dad*.

Lao currently say that the very best is the garden *sin dad* restaurant on T2 Road (pronounced Tay-song) near the airport, although if taking into account ambience, environment and good value, I would go for the Sindad Sailom, a large garden restaurant at the end of the long lane that starts almost opposite Settha Palace Hotel on Sai Lom Road. The name *sin dad* is Lao for 'barbecued' meat—Lao distinguishes barbecue or roast over naked coals (*ping*) and thin slithers cooked quickly on a thin metal plate over naked charcoal (*dat/dad*).

While *sin dad* is undeniably Korean in origin, the metal plate is shaped like a very large orange squeezer set over a clay bucket of charcoal which is set in a hole in a normal size table, not a Korean one. The 'orange squeezer' has gutters running all round to catch the juices of the meat slithers (pork, beef, chicken or seafood) placed with chopsticks on the metal above the charcoals. This gutter or small trough is filled with flavoured water and gives a salty soup. The essential difference with the Korean version is that the Lao throw into the water lots of vegetables and noodles. So *sin dad* is something of a Lao variant-combination of Korean barbecue and Chinese Suki, served with a superb dip-sauce for the meat. Foreigners who work out how to eat it, really love it.

Sin dad is near impossible to eat if you are alone, but perfect if you are inviting a group of Lao out. They all love the food and can eat together while picking what they prefer; it is a slow meal, with almost a ritual setting up of the charcoal stove. For social cuisine at a reasonable price, nothing is better.

Both *pho* and *sin dad* are favourites with most Lao, but both have a noodle base and neither is eaten with the *khao nio* (sticky rice) which is the most characteristically Lao aspect of Lao cuisine distinguishing it from Thai. Both are also eaten with chopsticks, while traditional Lao foods are eaten with the fingers or Thai-style, with spoon and fork.

Sticky Rice and Laap

Sticky and non-sticky are two distinct types of rice. *Khao nio* is more starchy and while the Lao often eat *khao chao* in restaurants, *khao nio* is the diet of the home. Many Lao say they simply do not feel full if they do not eat *khao nio*.

Khao nio is served in woven baskets and eaten with the fingers. A small amount is dug from the basket and kneaded between fingers and the base of the thumb. The small flattened wad thus formed may be pressed into the most usual accompaniment of *laap* (minced pork, fish or chicken) and popped into the mouth, or dipped into a prepared sauce before being eaten. Apart from accompanying the many types of *laap*, *khao nio* is traditionally eaten with roast or barbecued chicken or fish (*ping gay* or *ping pa*).

Khao nio cooking requires a different set of instruments to *khao chao*. After soaking in water for at least two hours, *khao nio* is placed in a funnelled basket into the open top of a metal pot full of water: this simple cooking may be done over wood or charcoal fires.

Khao nio is best eaten fresh and soft, but it has the quality of keeping much longer than non-glutinous rice. Once cooked it is packed hot into a basket (individual size or large for a family), and may be carried to the fields and eaten throughout the day, meaning further cooking at midday is not essential.

PA DEK

What it means to be Lao has been defined by a Lao organisation that started as a group of Lao concerned that development in Laos did not always follow Lao ways, and for that reason many projects fell by the wayside. They call their organisation *pa dek*, which is the name of the specifically Lao all-purpose

Ginger Money

The Lao spirit world uses ginger as money. The ginger slices look just like coins.

sauce. Their definition of a Lao, only half in jest, was proclaimed as they received the UN prize for indigenous self-development back in 2003. It is beautifully simple: a Lao is someone who uses *pa dek*.

Pa dek is to Lao, what *nam pla* is to Thai and *nuoc mam* is to Vietnamese. It is a fish sauce but much 'rougher' than that of its neighbours, and certainly more pungent. The smell is unmistakable, and some foreigners think the smell off-putting enough. It is, one might say, an acquired taste. Often made up in advance to ensure availability, it is stored in an earthenware pot (often outside the house) and its use as an ingredient in Lao recipes certainly makes them distinctive.

You are unlikely to find salt and pepper on the table or eating mat in a Lao house or restaurant. But there will be various sauce 'dips' for meat and vegetables. Vegetables and leaves are usually served raw in a large basket. Some may be cooked at the time of eating, or pre-cooked in a soup, and many should be familiar from salads in the west. Lao use more fresh mint than Thais, either chopping it up with the *laap*, or serving it in the basket. They also use more garlic and ginger, both as an ingredient and as a condiment—you will often find somewhere within your many plates of food a small tray containing separate but generous portions of chopped garlic and chopped chilies; this will usually be put by you into your individual sauce bowl, according to taste.

FISH

The fact that most Lao Loum live on the sides of a river means that fish forms a major source of protein in the Lao diet. Many rural Lao catch the fish themselves, usually with nets; others buy at open air markets along river banks at prices unimaginably cheap in Europe, or for that matter in Vientiane, where prices are two or three times the cost at source.

There are many ways to cook fish—and it can also be marinated and eaten raw. Foreigners generally prefer the barbecued fish, which are sold equally by the side of the road in Vientiane and in markets throughout the country.

Fresh fish sold at a Lao market.

Most places in Laos are not far from a market, where fresh vegetables, fruits and meats are readily available.

You can eat it either with a basket of *khao nio* or a plate of *khao chao*, either with fingers or spoons and forks.

To try the Lao way of eating it, ask for *phan pa* and you will get a huge basket of leaves, mint, coriander, basil and lettuce or cabbage. Use the lettuce or cabbage leaves like Vietnamese use rice paper, place fish on the leaf, add onions, garlic, mint and whatever else you fancy, roll the leaf around the ingredients and dip it into the sauce of choice before dipping it into your mouth.

MEALS
Breakfast

In general the daily fare of the Lao consists of some or all of the following. Sticky rice can be eaten at any time. Cooking is still mostly on charcoal, available at every market. In towns, many people make do with strong Lao coffee (originally planted by the French in the perfect conditions of the Boloven Plateau), well-laced with sweet sticky condensed milk, into which *ba-tan-go* (a sort of deep-fried doughnut), or freshly baked baguette are dipped. Others will make a quick breakfast out of the night before's left overs, but with fresh rice.

Those in a hurry to get to work—yes, it has been known—stop on the way and take a bowl of *khao phiak* (rice 'macaroni' used as a vehicle for chilies, in hot water), *khao tom* (called *johk* in China and Thailand), or the famous noodle soup, *pho*. Many Lao, even in rural areas, must have their strong morning coffee, another difference with their Thai neighbours. In Vientiane there are many shops and stalls which cater only for this morning trade, where individuals order individual portions and coffee, to partake in the first of the day's many social encounters. There is a predominance of men in the morning coffee shops, and many have been faithfully going to the same shop all their adult lives—rather like the English male fixes on his pub.

> ## Nutrition
> While up to 40 per cent of under-five-year-olds are considered to be underweight, the diet of the Lao Loum (but not of all Lao) is considered good in terms of vitamins and proteins. This is largely thanks to the reliance on fish and vegetables.

Lunch and Dinner

Lao daily lunch or dinner is not as sophisticated as you might see in a Thai or Lao restaurant. Nobody takes the time to carve vegetables or fruits. Meals generally consist of the following:

- A basket of *khao nio*
- A soup. This can be the plain and mild *gheng jurt*; no spices, just some vegetables and *thao hu*, similar to that in Thailand, or it can be the Lao ant egg soup. If time allows, boiled chicken soup can serve many people for a small amount of chicken.
- A meat dish. Sour pork (fermented), served with cucumber slices. Or river catfish grilled or fried.
- A cooked vegetable dish such as stir-fried water spinach.
- Uncooked vegetables and leaves in a basket.
- One or two sauce dips for meat and vegetables.
- Simple fruits such as the sweet Lao finger bananas.

On small occasions, there will also be a chicken dish, egg omelette, crispy frogs, and in the rainy season, mushroom and bamboo shoots.

Desserts are not usually part of a Lao meal. Most involve sticky rice and coconut milk and can be seen as Thai rather than Lao. There are a couple of shops serving only such desserts in Vientiane, one on the river road near the minimart.

Soul Food

Food is also evident in the *basi* ceremony. Very often, a bowl of chicken or a simple banana is placed in the outstretched palm of the person receiving the *mat khen* to sustain his *khwan*. After the *basi*, the food is eaten. Similarly, when feeding monks in the home or temple, what is left by the monks has spiritual value and is eaten by laymen to strengthen the soul rather than the body. Household spirits are also given food and drink. Such is the importance of food in the Lao sense of well-being.

Sample Recipes

Here are two simple recipes, of guaranteed Lao authenticity, that you might like to have a go at:

Sin Savanh/ Heavenly meat

This beef dish can be the perfect appetiser to go with your Beer Lao, or it can be a substantial snack if combined with sticky-rice.

Ingredients (Serves 4)

- Half-kilogramme flank beef steak
- 10 cloves garlic, minced
- 2 tablespoons lao-lao or cooking wine/wine vinegar
- 1 tablespoon soy sauce
- 1 teaspoon salt
- 1 tablespoon sugar
- 1 teaspoon ground black pepper
- 2 tablespoons sesame seeds
- 4 cups cooking oil

Continued on next page

Continued from previous page

Preparation

Cut steak into the thinnest strips you can manage. Thoroughly mix all ingredients except the cooking oil in a large bowl. Add beef strips and mix well. Marinate for 2–3 hours or overnight. Remove strips from the marinade, place on tray, dry in the full sun all day. (If no sun dry in the oven set on lowest for 3–4 hours.) Check that beef does not dry so much it crumbles. Heat oil in a wok over medium heat until very hot. Deep-fry the dried beef until crispy. Drain well and serve.

* * * * * * *

Gaeng Khai Moht/ Ant Egg Soup

This soup is best known in northern Laos. The best ant eggs are said to be found in nests of ants who live on mango trees. The nests are built on the underside of branches, allowing the Lao to knock them off with a long stick and catch them in a bucket of water. Only the eggs are eaten, so discard any hatched ants. In the West (or Singapore) you should find frozen ant eggs in oriental supermarkets.

Ingredients (Serves 4)
- 3 cups chicken stock
- 1 stalk lemon grass, cut in half and smashed
- 1 teaspoon salt
- 1.5 tablespoons fish sauce
- 4 fresh chillies broken in half
- 1 bunch young tamarind tips (or 2 tablespoons tamarind juice)
- 1 shallot cut in two
- 2 cups ant eggs
- 1 spring onion, cut into one-inch lengths

Preparation

Boil chicken stock in a pot. Add lemon grass, salt, fish sauce, chilies, shallot, tamarind. Boil for 15 minutes. Add ant eggs and spring onion pieces. Remove from heat and serve.

SEVEN FOR HEAVEN:
POPULAR AND TRADITIONAL DISHES
Khao Nio Ping

When grilling fish or other meats, a few skewers of sticky rice kebabs add to the Lao flavour of your barbecue. Rice-on-a-stick can then be eaten lollipop-style without need to handle a separate basket or plate. Cooked sticky rice is combined with salt, moulded around half a skewer (leaving room to hold), coated with beaten egg and grilled for two minutes. When ready to eat, brush lightly with oil and grill for another two minutes until crisp on the outside. Best served with peanut sauce.

Som Muu

Uncooked pork is ground and kneaded along with chillies, fresh ginger, diced pork skin, salt and minced garlic. Wrapped tightly in banana leaf it is tied up and kept in a cool place to cure (not the fridge—'cool' in the Lao sense) for two to three days. Served on a bed of lettuce. To taste, top with fresh ginger and more chilies.

Cheo Pa Duk

This nutritious dip is made with grilled catfish fillets. These are added, along with eggplants, to a well-pounded mix of chillies, garlic, shallots and shrimp paste, and pounded again. Soup stock is mixed in and the serving bowl is placed among various vegetables to be dipped. Sticky rice can also be dipped in the same preparation.

Gaeng Kao Lao

This soup is said to have originated in the parts of Laos so heavily bombed and defoliated that vegetables were hard to find. Some small shops in Lao towns serve only this. The soup is made from beef or buffalo (originally, those who were bombed in the fields). Add onions and garlic, plus salt and soy sauce if available. The thin-sliced beef is boiled and served in a soup tureen, sprinkled with black pepper and fried garlic.

Laap Pa

This is made with minced Mekong fish, with plenty of garlic, onions and chilies. It tastes good even without the chilies, which are indeed very spicy. Best eaten with mint leaves and pressed into sticky rice well-kneaded in the hand. The fish can be replaced by chicken and this is a very basic and popular finger food in Laos.

Ping Pa

This is found almost everywhere near the Mekong. It can be eaten at any time of day. Grilled fish is stuffed with lemon grass, garlic, shallots, onions and salt. It is grilled on both sides until golden brown, and the meat is normally taken off the bone with the fingers and eaten with sticky rice. Alternatively, *Ping Pa* comes with a basket of leafy ingredients and mint plant and fish pieces can be wrapped in lettuce or cabbage together with sauce.

Ping Gaiy/ Thort Gaiy

Essentially, this is simple grilled or fried chicken, eaten with sticky rice.

DRINKING ALCOHOL

Lao do not drink alcohol at every meal. Here the Lao differ from their neighbours in parts of northern Vietnam. However, alcohol is a normal part of any event, and there are plenty of events, and it is normal for 'community meals' involving people from outside the family, to contain some sort of alcohol. In the country as a whole, *lao-lao* (which literally means Lao alcohol) is the cheapest and most common. This usually involves a low-key degree of ritual, the host with a bottle pouring shot glasses for each guest in turn. Variants include the delicious (but sometimes dangerous) *lao-hai*, which comes in a large clay pot with two straws poking up through a rice-husk 'stopper'. The alcohol is drunk through the two straws, usually by two people at the same time, and the liquid is then replenished with water poured through the rice-husk stopper.

Today, apart from a funeral or an ordination, there is no Lao gathering where a foreigner would not be especially welcome if he orders in a crate or two of Beer Lao. This is also likely to be drunk in a traditional way: using only one glass, drinks are poured by the host (as things develop, by anybody) for each guest in turn. The use of a single glass emphasises the social aspect of drinking while tending to lengthen the time required for inebriation. Whereas the Lao have taken to the French habit of drinking coffee, it is rare to find wine at a Lao occasion. This perhaps has to do with the cost of a bottle of wine compared to cheap beer and very cheap *lao-lao*.

EATING HABITS

The most important thing about etiquette associated with eating is that it is a social habit. Only very rarely will you see a Lao eating alone. More likely is that a group of people will come together, in a home or restaurant, for an occasion or just for a get-together. Table manners are minimal. Things come in any order and all can be served at once, providing a variety of choice throughout. If at a large feast in somebody's home, expect refills to come along from time to time.

There are very few taboos and much variation, making etiquette almost a non-Lao concept. You may eat the same foods with your fingers or a spoon, and sometimes chopsticks. Sticky rice and the general use of 'dips' to flavour the generous supply of vegetables tend to favour fingers, but anything goes. Even using the left hand, while on the list of taboos for just about every Asian country, is not going to raise any eyebrows—quite a few Lao are left-handed, and it is natural that they eat with the left hand.

Because everything is cut up or chopped up in the kitchen, knives are not at the dining area, which may be a table or

The Lao know that many foreigners cannot eat very spicy food. Thus, there will always be something among the foods set out that is less 'hot', or not spicy at all, so don't be afraid to ask. If you really cannot eat Lao food at all, it's okay to say that it disagrees with you. Afterall, there are plenty of Lao who will tell you straight out that they cannot eat European food. You will not offend them by saying the food is too spicy—it's just like saying the sun is too hot. People will understand.

may be a mat on the floor, or may indeed be both: a table on the veranda for the important guests and mats on the floor inside the house for the rest—don't think of this as segregation, although it is to an extent, as there will always be too many guests to all sit together in the same place. When eating daily fare among the household family, it is usual to sit on the floor in the kitchen, or near the kitchen if there is only a traditional 'kitchen', which is barely a kitchen at all, being a charcoal-burning stove outside. Meals may last some time, lapse into drinking sessions, and become meals again as replenishments arrive. There is no obligation for you to remain in one place and, if you pass somebody you know, or would like to know, on the way back from a trip to the toilet, and want to sit down with some new people for awhile, there is no problem.

A person inviting provides the food. If in the home, provision is literal. If in the restaurant, the same norm applies and the host or inviter pays. This is not always the case in the West. But if you invite a Lao to a restaurant and leave him to pay, or pay his share, he will feel insulted.

Lao going out to eat do sometimes share the costs. A restaurant meal for ten people can amount to a person's salary for a month, and such groups or larger are by no means uncommon. The fact that you will frequently see women paying in restaurants simply means that women manage the household finances, and generally they do not leave a tip, or only a small one.

ENJOYING THE CULTURE

CHAPTER 7

'Fly me to the moon and let me play among the stars.
Let me know what life is like on Jupiter and Mars.'
—Frank Sinatra.

CEREMONIES AND FESTIVALS
Boun and boun

Lao use the same word for religious merit (*boun*) to mean a festival, a temple fair or any of the many public holidays that involve some party. It is almost impossible to conceptualise an important event without some religious significance, either Buddhist merit making or traditional religion in the form of the *basi*. Usually, both activities are present, although kept distinct enough that they do not readily get confused.

All of the major ceremonies will involve some movement of the individual out of the private world of family home into community and society, and the opposite movement from society and community into the private world. Often this movement takes the form of *tak bat*, when individuals perform merit in the public domain by providing for monks and honouring the Buddha, in the street or in the temple. The reverse movement is evident when monks go to private homes, and communities and relatives gather in private homes for *basi*, which has a central focus of the community coming together to protect and strengthen the *khwan* of one or more individuals. Such movements of the public world into the private and individual, and of the individual out into the greater society, are evident in all those ceremonies and festivals—calendar and life-cycle—which have a distinctly Lao substance; indeed they can be seen as a material manifestation of being Lao.

CALENDAR
January
International New Year
On 1 January. While there is nothing specifically Lao about this occasion, the Lao make it so by using the day's holiday to *het boun* (make Buddhist merit at the *wat*) and to invite for *basi* at home (strengthening the *khwan* of individual participants), and generally party like people of most countries.

These three elements are found to varying degrees in many of the festivals and ceremonies of Laos. In Laos, unlike Thailand, the Gregorian year is generally used in everyday conversation; the Buddhist year clicks over on 15 April (Lao New Year).

Boun Khun Khao
Mid-January, date moveable. A harvest festival to thank the land spirits for the last harvest and request a good year ahead.

February
Makha Puja/ Busa
This is a combination of ceremonies held on the full moon of the third lunar month. It celebrates the first great teaching of the Buddha, when 1,250 monks spontaneously visited him to hear his message. Each *wat* has an evening sermon, which is followed by a triple circumambulation of the *sim*, the central chapel holding the main Buddha image. Circumambulations (*vientien*) are always clockwise, except at funerals. This walk around the most sacred part of the *wat* is in silence, no dancing, no drum playing, no drinking. Members of the community carry candles, the Buddhist symbol of learning and enlightenment. Celebrated in Vientiane and throughout the country, most spectacularly in the Khmer ruins of Wat Phu in the southern province of Champassak.

Chinese and Vietnamese New Year (Tut Jiin and Tet)
Both New Years are the same, a fact that stems from China's long presence in Vietnam. This can be early in February

or as late as March. There are lion dances and usually some fireworks. The Lao Loum play no role except that of spectators, although many will visit their Chinese and Vietnamese friends or bosses during this time. Some business closures, but this is nothing like Lao New Year.

Boun Wat Pu
Son et lumiere at the famous ruins of the Khmer temple in Champassak. Coincides with *Makha Busa*.

March
Lao Women's Day
On 8 March. Women get the day off and men should wait on them. However, there are always some waitresses on duty. Many men buy their wife a present rather than do the housework or washing.

Boun Pha Wet
Temple fairs held in various temples at different times. Monks teach on the Buddha's penultimate life.

April
Pi Mai (Songkran)
This used to be a moveable feast, but some time ago the Lao set it for the three days, 14th–16th April inclusive. (At the same time the Thais set the same occasion at 13th–15th April.) The first day is actually the last day of the old year. It is the 15th which is the first day of the New Year. In Laos this is also the first day of the Buddhist year—thus 2550 began on 15 April 2007. Note that this is different to Thailand, where the Buddhist year is much more used but begins on 1 January.

House cleaning takes place, new clothes are worn, Buddha images are lustrated, offerings are made in every temple; many Lao say they go to nine different temples on the same day—others pay children to go on their behalf. (Nine is a lucky number in Laos. The sound of the number is the same as the word for 'advance'. Like the number 3, the number 9 also has significance in the Buddhist religion.)

Sand *chedis* (small stupas) are built in temple grounds (later the sand is used to renovate the temple). Foreigners often only notice the drenching of all passers-by with water, intended to bring on the rain at the end of the hot, dry season (it always seems to work and there will usually be some rain at this time). Water used may or may not be clean, so a shower before dinner is a good idea. Unlike in Thailand, the water throwing does not get out of hand or last too long. The authorities tolerate a certain amount of water fights from the backs of pick-ups, but do not allow the throwing of water in temples or shops or anywhere after 7.00 pm, so you can eat outside without fear. Water-throwing stops after the last day.

Where *Songkran* includes a Sunday, an extra day's holiday is declared. Since Lao final consonants are pronounced very softly, many foreigners mispronounce *Songkran* as *songkram*, which means war. This may be avoided by sticking to *pi mai*. The greeting at this time is *sok-dii-pi-may* (good luck in the new year). *Pi Mai* is more picturesque and boisterous in Luang Prabang and those who have never seen one often decamp from Vientiane at this time; on the other hand, those who have perhaps seen too many often lock themselves away for the duration. Vientiane tends to be quieter than usual at night, with many restaurants and services closed. Be aware that your maid or other staff are unlikely to work at this time.

May
International Labour Day
1st May. Some small parades in Vientiane. Most Lao take occasion of the national holiday to go out to one of the popular restaurants outside Vientiane (Tha Ngon, Ban Hom, Nam Ngeun reservoir or some other place near water).

Vissaka Busa/ Puja
The 15th day of the 6th lunar month. The day of the Buddha's birth, enlightenment and death. Serious *wat* activity with sermons and much chanting, as on *Makha Busa*.

Boun Bung Fai

A specifically Lao, pre-Buddhist festival. This can coincide with *Visakha Busa*, but has nothing to do with Buddhism. Different places can carry out this festival at different times. Giant rockets are fired from bamboo platforms into the heavens to prompt rain (even if it is raining hard at this time).

The festival can take place in any open space, most often in the fields that need the rain. As the rockets are fired, usually in the afternoon, there is much drinking and dancing and banging on long-drums. Evenings see *mor lum* performances which may go on all night. The *mor lum* is a traditional singer, often a woman, who improvises calypso-style; the best are well-known and often risqué. If the rains have not come, there will be successive *Bung Fai*—in a land where most rice terraces are rain-fed, prosperity and life itself depends on the rain falling.

July

Boun Khao Phansa

The precise date is announced in July, but is inevitably one day later than the beginning of 'Buddhist Lent' in Thailand. In Laos, some men decide to forego the drinking of alcohol for the three month period (or part of it). If late, this day can fall at the beginning of August. Monks should 'retreat' during this period, remaining within the wat to study and teach. Some lay people also take this time to reflect on life and Buddhist teachings. The rice has been planted and the Lao can reflect on the sound of it growing.

On *Khao Phansa* day, or just before, many unmarried men, at least 20 years of age, enter the monkhood temporarily—some for the full three months, others for a week. The merit they make is ritually transferred to their mothers and unknown ancestors to help a favourable rebirth. During the three months of Lent, there are traditionally no executions or marriages. In fact, while people are sentenced to death for serious offences in Laos, executions never seem to take place (another difference with Thailand). Men who become monks during this period are considered adult in the fullest sense and often marry at the end of the Lenten period.

August
Ho Khao Padap Din
The first new moon of the month (sometimes in September). During this time, merit is made at most *wat* for the dead and their eventual rebirth.

October
Boun Ock Phansa
Date dependent on that of *Khao Phansa*. Again, usually one day after the same event in Thailand. In Laos, many people float the small round boats cut from banana stems and carrying incense and candles, known as *khatong*. This is similar to the Loy Khratong festival in November in Thailand, but does not achieve the same magnitude. After *Ock Phansa* (leaving Lent), many marriages, held up during the three months, take place.

Following *Ock Phansa* many boat races (*suang heua*) are organised, sometimes between Laos and Thailand, each facing province taking responsibility in turn for inviting across the Mekong.

November
Boun That Luang
After early morning alms-giving to monks at the temple associated with the national emblem of *That Luang*, the country's largest trade fair is opened on the grounds outside the *wat*. It lasts one week and is very crowded, with Lao buying cheap Thai products, very loud evening music (and coming from several sources), plus some drunkenness. At some point a procession takes place from the symbolic *That Luang* stupa to *Wat Si Meuang*, the guardian temple of Vientiane and one of the oldest. All Lao go to *Boun That Luang*, although many foreigners living in Vientiane find it too crowded and noisy for comfort.

Hmong New Year (pay jau/ Peb Caug in Hmong)
This takes place at the end of the Hmong rice harvest and times vary almost from village to village (although each year the Government sets a specific date). It may be in

November or as late as December. The fact that it takes place in different locations at different times means you might miss it in one place, or go to it several times in different places. The most noted and known of its activities is the ball-game, where soft cloth balls are gently tossed back and forth between men and unmarried girls. For dates: try asking one of the Hmong working behind the Post Office in Vientiane. The largely Hmong town of KM52 is the nearest large population of Hmong—on the road to Luang Prabang, look for the KM52 milestone.

December
National Day
2nd December. Commemorates the 1975 coming to power of the Lao People's Revolutionary Party.

LIFE-CYCLE CEREMONIES
In Laos, there is a distinction between festivals and ceremonies, but one often contains elements of the other. This is to ensure that any event has some element of *muan* —which I translate as 'comfortable shared fun'.

Life-cycle ceremonies are home-based and often focus on assisting an individual rather than his or her community. Most involve a *basi*, usually in the home, and go on from an activity associated with the spirit world to a secular party, or move physically from the private world of home to the public world of the community wat or to a restaurant, where a party may be private in the sense of invite-only (almost) but often includes so many people who are not family or neighbours that it may be considered within the public domain.

Some elements are common to all life-cycle events in Laos, and the most important of these is the *basi*, which can take place at any time, and does. Because of its omnipresence, the *basi* will be considered first, without reference to any particular occasion. It is a ceremony and therefore has a format, but the format can expand or contract to fit the occasion and space available.

Similar to the Hmong, some other minorities in Laos have their own New Years, in addition to the official Lao New Year.

Basi

The *basi* (also known as *su khwan*—strengthening of the *khwan*) functions to repair and sustain individual *khwan* (souls) within a Lao community and thereby maintains community harmony. It is very difficult to be disagreeable to somebody when you are constantly tying strings on each other's wrists and wishing them well, and of course eating and drinking together following the *basi*. While essentially Lao and involving Lao pre-Buddhist beliefs, foreigners are most welcome to a *basi*, and you might even find yourself the guest of honour at one.

The ceremony always takes the same basic form. A *phakhoun* offering to the spirit world is set up in the middle of a room or other space—a bit like a Christmas tree in the West, even to the point of having candles at its peak (although the *phakhoun* has money in place of the fairy!). This is bedecked with flowers and pieces of white thread, cut to length and looped over long sprigs that 'grow' from the tree. As guests take their place around the 'tree' and take in the palms of both hands held in a *nop* one of the long white threads that are looped around the *phakhoun*, a master of ceremonies begins without much formality to chant blessings in Pali and Lao. He calls on any of the 32 *khwan* of any of those present who have in any way become lost or displaced to return to their homes. (Whether there is one *khwan* divided into 32 parts or 32 *khwan* united in one is not a question of any value to Lao metaphysics.)

When all *khwan* are in their place or back in their place, it is time to tie them down. The master of ceremonies ties the first threads on the principal focus-person of the ceremony, possibly a baby, possibly an adult arriving or departing, possibly the new leader of a project, possibly anything at all. As he ties, he makes a wish in Lao. Others follow his lead, sometimes tying a rolled up bank note onto the wrist of the focal point. Others present reach out a hand to touch elbows or shoulders to switch into the good vibrations. This is one time you can touch across the sex line—within reason. Then it is *mat khen* time for all, and anybody can exchange wishes and threads with anybody else, with no special significance except for the person who is subject of the ceremony, who gets the most threads and wishes.

As threads are tied the wish is made and it is thereby tied to the *khwan*; if you can't verbalise your wish in Lao, any other language will do. There might be a certain amount of playfulness and smiles, but don't try to be too clever— remember the *khwan* are listening, and so are the people. If somebody ties your right wrist, hold your left hand in a half-nop, if your left wrist is tied, raise your right hand. If both wrists are being tied at the same time, it means only that you are popular.

Sometimes a bowl of food or a banana or an egg is placed in the hand before the wrist of that hand is tied. This association of food and welfare is significant, and the ritual pieces of chicken and eggs may be eaten afterwards—but not immediately by you. They might pass around several hands before the *basi* is over.

A *basi* can vary in time depending on importance and the number of guests. When it is over, all guests are fed.

Chanting prayers while gathered around the *phakhoun* decked with flowers, white threads and money.

Threads are kept on the wrists for at least three days, unless they drop off of their own accord, which has no sinister meaning. At any event involving a *basi*, it is important that harmony be evident. So if you find your deadly enemy present, there is no obligation to mat him or her, but do not show your emotions.

Naming a Soul

Lao children are born with the components of the soul, but the parts can be somewhat mixed up and need sorting out. Thus, a child will be the subject of a specific *basi* when it is 30 days old. This hopefully marks the time when the child

Mat khen involves tying the white threads to someone's wrist and wishing him or her well.

is free of the worst conditions that give Laos such a high infant mortality rate. It is also the time when the mother is freed from her 'roasting' beside a smoky fire intended to purify her. During this time the new mother eats no chilies and exists on boiled chicken. Such mothers and babies may be visited during this period, but the baby's first *basi* marks its introduction to the community and ensures its 32 *khwan* are in place, at the same time strengthening the *khwan* of the mother. This seclusion of mother and child for 30 days is still widely practiced in Laos.

In this as in other important ceremonies, participants may hedge their bets and invite 9 monks (or any odd number) to visit the house in the morning. The baby will be presented to the senior monk, usually the abbot, whether boy or girl, and receive his blessing in the form of the line of monks chanting, and a thread, similar to that in the *basi*, tied onto the wrist. In spite of the prohibition related to touching women or receiving anything directly from a female, monks say that tying is not touching, so no special precautions have to follow blessing a girl child.

On such occasions the abbot may also perform the first haircut, which is also significant, snipping a piece of the child's hair symbolically. The first hair cut can be spiritually dangerous, so better have a monk do it. Following this the monks are fed and leave the house before midday. Then it is time for the *basi* to address more directly the child's *khwan*. From this day onwards the child may be known by its real name, which is not mentioned in his or her presence during the first 30 days, because the baby's soul is so fragile during this formative period that the spirits might focus on it before it has the strength to resist their advances. During the first 30 days, the child is only referred to by its nickname, often something unattractive to spirits, like 'fatty' or 'fertiliser' or the ubiquitous 'tiny' (Noy, or even smaller, Ten). In practice, a person usually maintains use of the nickname in the family and outside throughout life. Nicknames and official names are sometimes changed following a period of bad luck or on the advice of a learned monk or elder.

Birthdays

The Lao do not make a big thing out of birthdays unless it is one of the important ones, which come in multiples of 12 (12, 24, 36, etc). Getting presents is not traditional. It is considered more blessed to give than to receive, so a Lao may make merit on the morning of the birthday and have a *basi* followed by an invitation to eat. Things are changing, even in Laos, and presents may be given today—particularly by a foreigner! Young Lao may give each other presents of a token nature or nothing at all. If nobody gives a birthday cake, the birthday person may provide one. Sometimes this is eaten, sometimes it is smeared on the faces of those present, sometimes a bit of each. Birthdays, especially of the young, are really for friendship groups. The exception is a 60th birthday, which is the fifth cycle, marking a retreat from a more active life into a more contemplative one.

Ordination (*buat*)

Any man of 20 years plus may ordain as long as he meets the basic requirement of being free of family obligations and debt. In Laos, it is also considered inappropriate for men to ordain (or for women to ordain as nuns) unless they can read the Lao language, required to study Buddhist literature.

Before ordination, a man's head will be shaved and he will be the subject of a *basi*. Monks do not attend this or any other *basi*. Lao Buddhist monks are taught, as part of the political element in their teaching, that spirit worship and magic are not allowed to monks. While monks should not dabble in such things, some do. In practice, however, there is no conflict between formal Buddhism and the lay belief in the *khwan* and how to care for it: Lao consider the two sets of beliefs to be complementary, not contradictory.

Marriage and Divorce

Traditionally, marriage in a rural setting was little more than a *basi*, or two *basi*, one at the *mun* (engagement) and one at the *tengan* (marriage). Traditionally, villagers would witness the union. This is still the case (even if a European is involved), although more often than not, marriages today will also be witnessed officially by the *nai baan* (village headman) involved.

All Lao dress up for the marriage, particularly the bride, and particularly her hair—in spite of almost every Lao woman having beautiful long hair, it is skimmed back and curled away out of sight under a roll of false hair.

The marriage *basi* also serves the function of welcoming a male stranger into what is essentially a matrifocal household. The *basi* is preceded by the groom and his family being prevented by a closed gate from entry into the bride's compound. The passage of money opens the gate, in all senses of the term. For many Lao, the *basi* and the feast that follows is the only legitimisation of their marriage and wedding certificates are comparatively new (required for foreigners marrying Lao, and expensive!).

For divorce, there is no specific *basi* held and often no official legitimisation of change of status. This possibly accounts for the fact that statistically, Laos has a comparatively low rate of divorce. Since partners who cannot live together simply split, there is often no registration of divorce. Those Lao who marry foreigners overseas usually do not bother to register either marriage or divorce in Laos.

A bride and groom in traditional wedding attire. The bride's elder sister is at the left.

Death

His or her *ngan sop* (funeral) is the most important set of rites a Lao attends. There is obviously no question of the focus of attention having the *khwan* reordered and repaired. That will have been tried and finally failed before coming to this point. The pre-Buddhist *basi* is not therefore appropriate for the deceased; on the other hand all Buddhist aspects of merit-making are not only appropriate but essential.

Variants may be observed in funerals as in all ceremony, and many of those variants in Laos point to traditional practices in the area of origin within Laos or in the neighbouring countries, the deceased's ethnicity, and the wealth of the family. For example, the picture of the coffin leaving the house is taken at a Chinese-Lao house. However, the family was at least as Lao as Chinese and cremation, not burial followed, with all Lao Buddhist cremation procedures observed. The Hmong have similar procedures on leaving the house but go on to bury their dead (usually). But not all Chinese do things this way, and not all Lao. Thus, even in this most important of ceremonies in Laos, culture is a mosaic of traditions.

Some corpses may be kept at the *wat* before cremation takes place, others will be kept in the house, with daily chanting by invited monks, until the coffin is carried out feet-first on the morning of the cremation. Guests will have been provided a simple breakfast and will not eat again until the cremation has taken place. Family members lead the procession, carrying a portrait of the deceased, and a jar in which the remains will later be collected. Behind them come monks, each with a hand on the sacred white thread which is fastened behind the monks to the foot of the coffin. The coffin is carried on a handcart or a truck. Behind the monks walk the men of the village and invited guests, and behind them come the women.

Female family members may be dressed in white (white and black are not regarded as colours and bright colours should be avoided at funerals—except for monks), and some of them may have ordained as nuns for the occasion.

The coffin is carried out of the house, foot first, over the bent backs of the female family members.

The only covered crematorium in Vientiane is that in the centre of town, a gift from Thailand. Most Lao cremations take place on an open funeral pyre set in the grounds of the *wat*. On arriving inside the temple grounds, the funeral procession passes three times in counter-clockwise circumambulation (funerals are the reversal of the normal) around the prepared funeral pyre. The white thread is untied from the foot of the coffin and fastened to its head. Monks chant, telling of the inevitability of suffering and death, as the coffin is lifted onto the pyre. The family and guests then climb the short steps provided and pour coconut water onto the face of the corpse or onto the coffin. This takes some time, so if many people are present, mobile tents have to be erected and chairs provided underneath.

Monks sit in the front rows nearest the pyre, but not in the very front row, guests sit behind them. Cold drinks are served and guests are free to talk and take photographs. The funeral pyre is usually lit by a small rocket and as the flames reach up to the sky, guests file off.

Pouring coconut water onto the coffin as part of the funeral rites.

That evening and for the following two evenings, monks come to the house of the deceased's family to chant and bless the departed and the living. Guests turn up uninvited and are fed. The survivors should not be left alone, and although this is not an occasion for a lively party, there is no need to be morbid. The Lao do not believe in Tibetan-style instant reincarnation—it might come soon, or it might wait for a long, long time until the personality has been forgotten as anything other than an abstract ancestor.

GAMES LAO PLAY

There is no national game in Laos and the comparatively small and diverse population has yet to shine in any international games. Boat races are as popular in Laos as in the other Mekong countries. Also popular is the Asian game of *tokror*, known in Laos as *kataw*, in which a rattan ball is kicked back and forth over a net, and Lao men sometimes play *tee kee*, a rough type of hockey using a rattan ball. However, none of these games is specifically Lao.

The Lao are realistic about their limitations. The Vice-President of the Lao Football Federation explained the decision not to enter the 2010 World Cup competition as follows: "This is due to the low level of our footballers."

Laos hosted the SEA Games in 2009, an event which greatly increased sports facilities within the country, particularly those near the one university, some 20 km (12.43 miles) outside Vientiane. The national stadium is right in the centre of town on prime land that will no doubt find alternative use in the near future. Currently, it provides a convenient location for football matches, with some other activities (e.g. rifle shooting) taking place in the same place (but not at the same time!) In the cooler months, the stadium attracts a reasonable crowd, but probably rather less than in the air-conditioned bowling alley and snooker hall just across the road.

There are some swimming pools around, and several of the bigger hotels allow paid entry, but the only one of decent size, well-enough maintained, and cheap enough for Lao to afford is at Sok Paluang, not far from the German

Men playing *tee kee* at the Boun That Luang.

Embassy. Golf courses and ranges cater exclusively for foreigners and those Lao at the top of the middle class. Some Lao take tennis seriously and there is a tennis club, sometimes combined with badminton, in most urban centres. *Petanque* (the French version of bowls) is also played by some people: it is debatable whether this is a hangover from French colonialism or came through Thailand, where it was introduced by Thai royalty formerly resident in Switzerland.

Lao games perhaps focus more on entertainment than competitive sport, and most places where games are played will have a bar and some sort of restaurant. Entertainment tends to be more home and neighbourhood based. Dancing, in the form of the *lamvong* is perhaps specifically Lao in form—and when watching it look for the triple circles (each dancer turns in a circle, circles are turned by each couple and the circle of participating couples makes one large circumambulation before the dance finishes). But *lamvong* never reaches competitive levels. There is *muay-Lao*, as there is *muay-Thai*, a form of kick-boxing, but it attracts a comparatively small following.

Forms of sport which come closest to belonging to Lao culture are usually associated with some form of gambling, which is illegal outside of licensed casinos. On days of leisure, there are cock-fights in every village. No spurs are attached and fighting is rarely to the death, and owners of fighting cocks can be seen petting and caring for their animals before and after a fight. Cocks usually surrender when they realise they cannot win and it is at this point that bets are collected. Cock-fighting is not against the law, but the associated gambling is—although the law is rarely enforced in a neighbourhood setting, where the village police (*thamnuat baan*, often translated as 'militia') are part of the community. Another 'fighting' pursuit is that involving stag-beetles, although this is usually at the level of English schoolboys playing conkers.

There is no ministry of sports in Laos and comparatively few associations promoting individual games. Limited funding and the small size of the population have a lot to do with this. Laos does enjoy sporting competitions with regional neighbours, where costs are lower and skill-levels more comparable, but sport is generally not presented as an important part of Lao culture.

Within the confines of the home, neighbours may come together to participate in fish fighting. Such fish are kept in separate bottles, usually separated by opaque cards, until the time of the fight, when each will contest territorial waters by locking mouths in a sometimes deadly kiss and wrestling their adversaries in the hope of making them flee.

Some of the ethnic minorities have occasional games, usually also based on animals fighting rather than men fighting. The Hmong sometimes come together to watch two bulls fighting, although this is not a regular occurrence. Perhaps the most common game throughout Laos is simple cards. This is almost always accompanied by gambling and takes place behind closed doors. Some Lao addicted to gambling enter serious debt, even to the point of selling their house and daughter. This may be only a minority but there is nearly always a money-lender cum debt-collector within walking distance. It is against the law to borrow from them and those caught will usually be locked away in a police cell until someone pays their fine, which adds to their debt. The tolerance of the Lao and respect for family members means there is very little social pressure to control gambling, which is also a major source of police corruption.

Board games are sometimes played but never involve arranged competition or championships. Most popular is perhaps *dame(s)*, the Lao using the French word for drafts or checkers. *Maklouk*, or chess, is also played by some Lao.

THE ARTS

It comes as a surprise to many foreign visitors to learn that Laos has a school of performing arts. It is actually a full school, teaching all subjects plus classical dancing and music: students have to be selected to it. Most of the students seem to be from middle-class backgrounds with family associations in the army. Some of the students perform most nights at the traditional dancing show near the river, or in one of the big hotels or restaurants.

The National University has a Department of Art, in town, where exhibitions are occasionally arranged. There are also a few 'art galleries' around Vientiane and Luang Prabang, where paintings and sculpture in wood are exhibited for sale. The art scene is not large—when a group of Thai art students visited Vientiane they made a bee-line for Le Silapa (the name means 'Art' in both Thai and Lao), only to find it was a French restaurant, not an art museum.

Laos is best known for the architecture of its many temples in Luang Prabang (the town is a UNESCO World Heritage site), and for its weaving, particularly the shawls and *sin* of Sam

Students from the amateur National Dance Troupe perform at the Cultural Hall, Vientiane.

Thousands of megalithic stone jars throughout Xieng Khouang Province's Plain of Jars. Thought likely to relate to prehistoric burial practices, the jars remain one of the most enduring enigmas of Southeast Asia's earliest prehistoric civilisations.

Touk touks along a street in Luang Prabang. These small motor-cycles with open backed carriages are a popular means of getting around in Laos.

That Luang, the Golden Stupa in Vientiane. Built in the 16th century on the ruins of an earlier temple, this national symbol is said to contain relics of Buddha.

The Patuxai (Victory Gate) is known to Lao as *Anusawali – the Monument*. Begun in the 1950s by the Royal Lao Government and clearly inspired by the French prototype, the structure was completed after 1975. Lao Buddhist detail has been added to the façade.

Hill tribes such as the Hmong, Mien and Akha (pictured here) are collectively known as Lao Soung, and make up perhaps 15 per cent of Lao.

A *wat* in Luang Prabang—famous for its beautiful and unique architecture.

Neua, in the north. There are still many Lao houses in the countryside which have a loom erected between the sturdy stilts, and many women who know how to form the special patterns of their region. Old weavings employing vegetable dies are in places coming back into fashion. Many of the hill minorities weave their own clothing, and one division of Hmong (Njua) batiks the skirts of the women and appliqués the jackets of men and women.

Specialists are rarely employed in the realm of art unless it is art for religion. The many cast and carved Buddha images attest to the skills of these specialists. However, perhaps the most acclaimed art is that of the Mien (Yao) minority. The Mien artist, when in a state of complete purity will make a set of 17 large paintings, which will completely cover the inside walls during important ceremonies. He also paints a long spirit bridge and 'masks' of gods that novitiates wear when entering the ranks of 'master'. All

The famous caves at Pak Ou, near Luang Prabang, with thousands of hand-carved Buddha images.

of these fantastic works of art are rolled up and kept out of sight until they are required to represent the pantheon of gods in the Mien religion. While exhibition of such work is against the ethic of their production, the skills of each artist are now so internationally acclaimed that foreign museums will bid very highly for the few surviving full sets.

In Laos, folk art is decoration or design added to objects serving a functional or religious purpose. Examples are the old high-wheeled buffalo carts, woven baskets and mats, low rattan tables, and most significantly the wooden Buddhas, sometimes lovingly but crudely carved by farmers and placed as acts of merit in wat or in caves or other places of spiritual significance. In the famous caves at Pak Ou near Luang Prabang, thousands of hand-carved Buddha images have been placed over centuries of merit-making.

LEARNING LAO

CHAPTER 8

'Those who know do not speak.
Those who speak do not know.'
—Zen Buddhist reflection

STARTING UP AND TAKING OFF

If you intend to stay around in Vientiane and want to meet Lao, and maybe work here or do business, you will find that speaking Lao pays great social and practical dividends. Lao is also the basis of a family of languages that stretch from the *Sip-song-phan-na* (12,000 fields—the words are Lao) in China, through Lao-Thai enclaves in northern Vietnam, through Thailand and into northern Malaysia. Nobody knows how many people speak a Lao-Thai language, but it is a great deal more than the three million or so ethnic Lao in Laos. A conservative estimate places the figure at over 120 million people—twice the population of the United Kingdom. If you want to meet Lao on Lao terms, it means learning at least some of their language.

If you were in Thailand before coming to Laos, you may know some Central-Thai. This is a double-edged sword—you can get by from your first day, but be aware that there are foreigners (including Thais) living in Laos for ten years or more who speak and understand practically no Lao— precisely because they can get by in Thai. So natural is it for a Lao to speak to a Thai-speaker in Thai, that you will need to make it clear that you want to understand and speak Lao, not Thai, and periodically remind them of this—nevermind that they are watching Thai TV at the time.

You might be quite determined to learn Lao. Even so, your initial contacts are likely to be with those Lao who speak English, or the minority who speak French, Vietnamese, Chinese, Japanese, Russian, German, Polish or another language associated with the former 'eastern bloc' (presuming, of course, that you speak one of those languages). The colonial and soviet eras in twentieth-century Lao history have left behind a kaleidoscope of languages in the country; but quantity is by no means matched in terms of quality.

Apart from those Lao who have spent years studying or working overseas, the general level of English is not high. While this might be frustrating for the tourist, look upon it as a positive factor. Although Lao is not an easy language for most Europeans to learn, it takes really only a small effort to get your spoken Lao up above the spoken English of most Lao. And once you get to that point, you begin to take off. But start while the enthusiasm is hot; the more you delay, the more you will learn to get by without Lao, and the more likely you are to remain a foreigner in the fullest sense of the term.

LAO DIALECTS

An early word of advice: Vientiane Lao is understood almost everywhere, and you are strongly advised to make sure you are learning that dialect of Lao. If your main Lao 'teacher' is from Champassak in the south, your Ds and Ls will be inverted quite naturally. Thus 'Lao child' will come out *lek dao*, instead of *dek lao*. This is carried over into English, so 'dog' becomes 'log', 'law' becomes 'door'. There are also vowel differences—*nom* (milk/breast) becomes *num*—and some vocabulary differences—bread is not *khao chi* but *khenumpan*, which comes perhaps from a Thai word and perhaps a Lao-French word: *khenom-pain*. Differences in Lao dialect are just as varied in other parts of the country.

Many Lao can live in Vientiane for many years, but continue to speak their own dialect. They understand other dialects, so there is no felt need to make efforts at adjustment, and they

The difference between a language and a dialect is a political border. The Lao language in Laos is called Lao; on the other side of the Mekong River, it is called Northeastern Thai or Thai-Isaan.

will spend much time with relatives and people from their place of origin, reinforcing their dialect.

Education is, at least theoretically, in Vientiane Lao, as are all government pronouncements and the Lao TV channel, but there is no attempt to promote use of Vientiane Lao over the Lao of other regions. There may be good political reasons for this softly-softly approach to standardisation. There are also pragmatic reasons—many teachers come from the areas in which they teach and naturally use dialect with the children under their charge. It is also extremely difficult to change pronunciation habits.

Are you now thinking that maybe you should stick to Thai, or even learn central-Thai which, because of the ubiquitous nature of Thai TV, is understood throughout Laos almost as much as Vientiane Lao? Some Thais and foreigners (the two are not the same in Lao thinking) definitely feel this to be logical. But if you plan to spend some time in Laos, you will want to understand what people say to each other, not just have them understand the Thai you speak to them.

CULTURE THROUGH LANGUAGE

It is accepted all over the world that learning a culture fully implies learning the culture's language. But even if you become reasonably proficient in Lao, do not expect many Lao to be able to explain their culture. Culture is a natural thing and putting it into words requires an original thinking exercise and linguistic practice that few Lao have ever been called on to do. To appreciate this, just try explaining in your language how you tie your shoelaces or put on a neck-tie (while keeping your hands behind your back!), and if you manage that, go on to explain the Christian God, Father, Son and Holy Ghost. Bet you can't!

Help Available

No language school could get by just teaching Lao to foreigners. But there are several English-language schools that in addition to teaching English to Lao, have some classes or can arrange for private tuition in the Lao language to foreigners. Most of the 'Lao courses' use their own duplicated materials and cover conversation rather than teaching to read, transliterating Lao into English. Such courses rarely go much beyond beginner's level and will not take you to the point where you can have an official meeting, or even a reasonable conversation, entirely in Lao. There are very few material aids available. To my knowledge there is not a single language laboratory in Laos teaching Lao—but several teaching English, French and Japanese. The US Foreign Services Language Institute has a very complete set of tapes and books for around US$ 300, but you have to order on the Internet, you will not find it on sale in Laos. If you are determined to get to a reasonably advanced level, you must be prepared to learn the alphabet and how letters go together to make the various sounds of Lao. This is not really learning to read—there is anyway very little to read in Lao—but a short cut to knowing how words should be pronounced and building vocabulary.

Being married to a Lao or having a close Lao friend does not always help. If the relationship starts in English or another language, it inevitably continues in that language. Even when the common language is Lao, the foreigner may be perfectly well understood by just one Lao; other Lao may not understand a word he says.

How Long Does it Take to Learn Lao?

With a reasonable teacher providing a short intensive course (3 hours a day for 4–6 weeks), you should learn the tones and basic sounds of Lao and have enough vocabulary to tell people how much you love their country, shop without great problems, tell the masseuse where it hurts and order a beer. If you are looking at more serious language learning, one to two years should get you almost there. The younger you are the quicker you learn, and women and children learn quicker than old men. Spoken language learning ability has nothing to do with intelligence or formal education—in fact, a linguist suggests there is an inverse relationship (that's just to make you feel good when you have to cope with failure). See Resources for some language schools.

Is Lao Beyond Me?

Lao is not beyond anyone, even you. You learnt your mother tongue at a time when you could not add 2 and 2. To some extent, you must be prepared to become a child again. (And not be afraid to make mistakes at first).

Another big plus, perhaps the biggest, is that the Lao will like you more for speaking their language, rather than mock your abuse of their language—which is unfortunately too often the experience of language-learning foreigners in England or France. Also very much on the plus side, once Lao people realise that you speak some Lao they will use the language with you—so while a good Lao teacher might be hard to find, you can have language lessons free just about everywhere you go.

The habit of repetition, which has been mentioned several times in this book and will be mentioned again… and again, helps a lot, so do not complain that all Lao say the same things over and over. Lao do not speak fast, although at first it may seem they do. And while the written language rarely leaves any gaps between words, the spoken language does: words are not run together, French-style. The spoken language includes several spoken punctuation marks. And best of all, its grammar could hardly be simpler.

CHARACTERISTICS OF THE LANGUAGE

Lao is not a phonetic language to the extent of, say, Malay or Spanish, but it is nearly so. You might not catch a Lao nickname when first heard, but ask a Lao to write it in Lao and, if you can read what he or she has written, you will pronounce it correctly—and watch the amazement on the face when you do. Many Lao still cannot read their own language; the shortest step to admiration and status is for you to be able to do so (even if you do not understand what you are reading!). Written Lao is easier than written Thai. The two alphabets are close but different enough; however, if you learn one, you will not find it difficult to learn the other.

Lao has 33 written consonants and a massive 39 written vowels. Don't let that put you off! It actually makes learning the language easier for you.

"What! English has only 19 consonants and 5 vowels, how can Lao be easier?" Quite true: English has 'A' as in bat, bath, band, can, can't, saw, teach, table; 'E' as in bet, be, eye; 'I' as in live, alive, pie; 'O' as in on, done, ode; 'U' as in uterus, bus, urchin; 'C' as in cat, church, nice; 'G' as in get, age, plough. Get the point? Feeling some sympathy with the poor Lao student of English? In Lao, each vowel has a symbol or combination of symbols and you can more or less see them and pronounce them. And while the Lao alphabet might look long, it contains separate symbols for aspirated and unaspirated consonants and long and short vowels.

All Lao vowels can be long or short, and vowel length, like tones, carries meaning.

Lao Grammar

I have said that Lao grammar is easy, and so it is:

- Adjectives follow nouns (as in French) except when they don't as in expressions like *ping pa* (grilled fish).
- Lao gets by without classifying nouns as masculine, feminine or neutral, with no declensions of nouns or verbs, and, most marvellous of all, with no tenses.
- Lao also has no plurals, although when counting it does use classifiers more than is done in English—'one loaf of bread' not just 'one bread'.

Lao cannot pronounce two consonants without putting a vowel in between. The problem is that the vowel so put may be written or simply understood.

There is also a smaller problem with final consonants on syllables. Lao write them, but pronounce them only in a few ways. This is no problem for the foreigner learning Lao, since a final 'L' will always be pronounced 'N', and so on. Lao learning English have a much greater problem, as they have never learnt finals such as 'football', which becomes 'fut-bon'. A greater problem for the foreigner is that finals are pronounced very softly, you simply might not hear them. There is a great difference between *songkran* (New Year) and *songkram* (war), but first you have to hear the difference, then remember it. Again, Lao have the same problem with English using finals they are not used to: 'can' and 'can't' tend to sound the same, and the Internet shop across the street has a sign on the door written in English—*Clo* (closed).

As in all languages, Lao as 'she is spoke' differs to Lao as 'she should be spoke'. (Now, why did I just write 'she'? Should I not have written, 'it'? And 'spoke' not 'spoken'?) Lao pronounce the syllables of all the words in their language, except when they don't. So, *pa-tu* is the correct word for door, but you must be prepared for the fact that many people when speaking familiarly will contract this word to '*tu*'. *Tu* alone is the correct word for cupboard. Foreigners unused to tonal systems, may open the cupboard (closet) instead of the door. Lao would not—the door *tu* is low tone, the closet *tu* is high-falling tone. This explanation might not do a lot to encourage you, but language learning takes time, and the learner must at some stage relate what he hears to both situation and familiarity.

For Europeans, Japanese, and other speakers of non-tonal languages, the biggest hurdle is one which must be tackled right at the beginning of learning Lao: the tones.

Tones

Written standard Lao has six tones. These are determined by the initial consonant, the vowel length and the final consonant if there is one (and the tone thus formed can be changed by tone marks). The rules are nicely set out inside the front cover of Russell Marcus' *English-Lao-English Dictionary*, which is recommended for that reason (plus you actually can put it in a pocket). If you have tried learning Thai (which has five tones), be aware that Lao uses the same tone marks but not in the same way.

But do not worry about tones. Certainly moving your head around as you say a word will not produce them. And they have nothing to do with the tongue or the lips. Tones are formed in the throat. And the easiest way to learn them is to learn the pronunciation of each word as you learn it. To Lao, tones are integral 'sounds' of words—indeed, if asking what tone a word is, you ask for its *siang* (sound). Of course, not a single Lao you will meet will be able to tell you that a certain word is 'high', 'mid', 'low', 'rising', 'high falling', 'low falling'. Only foreigners learning Lao use such terms. A Lao will simply repeat the word, trying to make it sound standard—but don't be surprised if you get different sounds from different Lao.

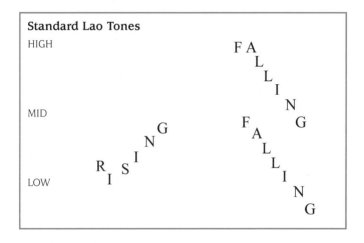

Standard Lao Tones

HIGH

MID

LOW

Lao are used to differences in spoken language that clearly place a person in his locality of origin, but unlike English, there is no status or snobbism attached to regional differences. Lao is not a single language confined to the borders of the country. It is well known that there are many more Lao speakers in northeast Thailand than in Laos. Lao can also communicate with 'Thai' groups in northern Vietnam and China. Lao is a family of languages. With time and patience, which are certainly not lacking, Lao could communicate with more than 120 million 'Lao or Thai' speakers throughout the world—that's a lot more people speaking some form of Lao than naturally speak some form of German or Italian. Anyway, you have over 3 million mother-tongue speakers in Laos. That should be enough to begin with.

Phrase books and dictionaries that try to write Lao using English have an obvious problem with the tones and vowels. Usually they introduce tone markers which have nothing to do with markers in Lao writing. In doubling vowels to show long as opposed to short, the reader will often be faced with a very familiar if very different vowel in English. So, lists of 'useful words and expressions' are really not so very useful. (This, however, does not stop this book from producing some in a Glossary at the end.)

FREEDOM OF EXPRESSION

Not to put you off (any further!), but some people function better in Laos without speaking Lao. If coping through interpreters or slowly and simply to poor speakers of English, some kind of filter or muzzle is placed on the visitor. Once you speak good enough Lao, the muzzle can come off your lips but must go onto your mind. You are not censored; you are expected to exercise self-censorship. Speaking Lao carries with it no freedom to speak your mind. A Lao will assume that a foreigner speaking Lao should conform to all speech patterns and taboos. Thus, some foreigners are better off not being understood.

LAO BUSINESS

CHAPTER 9

'*Weyla pen ngeun, pen kham* (time is silver and gold).'
'Time is money.'
Lao and English sayings

THE BACKGROUND

Opportunities for expatriate managers and foreign investors to learn much about Laos before coming to the country are extremely few. This, plus the fact that most investment in Laos since the change of regimes in 1975, has been a result of extension of business activities already established in Thailand (and to a lesser extent in Vietnam), has often meant postings to Laos get filled by people formerly in Thailand. Those coming in from overseas are likely to have a period in Bangkok for briefing, and if they get any language instruction at all, it is likely to be in Thai rather than Lao.

The same can be said of many embassies, who handle Lao-related activities from Bangkok, for UN agencies, and for the larger international non-governmental organisations. Regional offices are likely to be in Thailand, conferences and training is likely to be in Thailand, and Thailand is the place expatriates (and Lao) are most likely to go to shop, holiday and relax. This focus on Thailand, and particularly on Bangkok, has economic advantages, particularly if a company in Laos is represented in Thailand and therefore has better access to ports and international connections, but it also in some ways relegates Laos to playing the roll of a branch office.

Opportunities for promotion and profit are far fewer in Laos than in Thailand, a place that the whole world has heard of and where many expatriates, before they became expatriates, have been to on holiday. Thailand is seen as the world's playground—it has excellent communications, huge import/export facilities, a developed middle-class skilled in all areas, a developed consumer-oriented domestic market, and now, an internationally exchangeable currency. Nevermind that recent years have seen the temporary devastation of a tsunami and political unrest leading to yet another military coup, Thailand is the safe-haven, Laos is marginal in most meanings of the term and at best, the location of a few dramatic gains by venture capital. Laos is the place where investors like to be sure all their capital will be amortised, with interest, within five years.

Nobody looks at Laos more as a 'little brother' than Thailand itself. Thailand is the biggest export partner of Laos. Thailand controls the practical banking system within Thailand and Laos. Thailand controls Laos' access to the sea (Danang Port in Vietnam cannot compete with Bangkok). Thailand is by far the biggest import partner of Laos. Without Thailand, Laos would definitely not be the same.

Laos Imports and Exports (2010 estimates)

Exports (f.o.b.) — Total US$ 620 million
Export Partners (places exports went to)
    Thailand 21 per cent, Vietnam 12 per cent,
    France 8 per cent, Germany 4.8 per cent, UK 4.5 per cent

Imports (f.o.b.) — Total US$ 900 million
Import Partners (places imports came from)
    Thailand 68.3 per cent, China 10.4 per cent,
    Vietnam 5.8 per cent

INDUSTRIES

Contrary to the opinion of many foreign visitors to Laos, Beer Lao is not the premier industry of the country. The major industries are as follows: mining (copper, tin, gypsum, gems and gold), timber, electric power, garments, tourism, cement and handicrafts.

The major agricultural products (remember that 80 per cent of Lao live in a rural environment) are as follows: sweet potatoes, maize, vegetables, coffee, sugarcane, tobacco, cotton, tea, peanuts, buffalo, pigs, cattle, poultry. Of these only coffee and cotton are cash crops at more than domestic level. Coffee is of recognised high quality but has been burdened with very low prices for a number of years, although picking up in 2007, and cotton is made into clothing locally which has suffered from poor quality control (a general problem in developing countries).

Opportunities exist in several agricultural product areas but have not been taken up. Buffalo and cattle hides, and even horn, is sold to Thailand in a part-cured state. Full curing and use in leather products takes place in Thailand.

Electric power has suffered at times by the largest investors (particularly EDF, French Electricity) pursuing very much stop-go policies, even to the point of changing their mind on the morning of signing the Agreement and changing it back again a few months later. It looks very much like electricity will become a mainstay of the Lao economy, with guaranteed power available for the development of other industries; at the moment however, Laos imports half the amount of electricity that it exports. The reason for this strange state of affairs is that it is simply not economic to connect some areas with the national grid; to service those areas Laos therefore imports (or reimports) electricity from Thailand (at a much higher price than it sells to Thailand).

Proposals for smaller hydro-power projects to provide for these areas and to increase electricity exports have so far raised no interest among investors. Some very remote villages have recently benefited from micro-loans to install solar power panels on an individual household basis; but this provides only for domestic consumption.

With the huge Nam Theun 2 (NT2) hydro-power facility in full production and exporting to Thailand, it is estimated that an extra US$ 333/year per Lao man, woman and child enters the economy for use by guaranteed agreement with investors for poverty reduction in Laos. In 2020 this amount will increase significantly as initial costs amortise.

Cattle and pigs have potential but only if meat products can be improved and economies of scale introduced to what is essentially a small-holding subsistence economy.

Laos has some of the best hardwood forests of Southeast Asia: opportunities for a well-sustained furniture industry are obvious, but depend on availability of skills, quality control, and transport to export markets.

Industry is certainly moving ahead, and the industrial production growth rate in 2005 was 13 per cent. This is very high, but it is easier to achieve such high growth rates from a low starting point.

Overall, the prospects look realistic for Laos to achieve its goal of leaving the ranks of the Least Developed Countries by 2020. The economy has been growing at a rate above the 7 per cent needed to achieve that goal for several years (2006—7.5 per cent). In 2009, the real growth rate was 6.4 % and in 2010, with Thailand again in political turmoil and the world economic turndown continuing, the Lao economy was set to achieve 6 % +.

Currently the economy of Laos suffers from the fact that most of the population is of school age— skilled university graduates are few, and many in the productive age-range leave to take up higher-paid work in Thailand. All of these factors are set to change significantly and it is by no means over-optimistic to imagine Laos by the year 2020 being a nation of productive, fairly skilled and reasonably-educated workers in expanding industries fuelled by domestic hydro-power.

> This is the backdrop against which business is conducted in Laos: prospects, optimism and plans, good relations with all neighbours and ASEAN partners, some significant success stories, principally in mining and hydro-power, and some opportunities awaiting investment and profitable exploitation.

FOREIGN COMPANIES

Foreign companies, at least on paper, get as good a deal or better in Laos than in many other Southeast Asian countries. They can enter joint ventures with Lao, or they can fully own their companies, and transfer all assets. They can lease land but not own it, and can sell their leases. Of course they must abide by taxation and employment laws, even if they see that some Lao do not, but larger investors can negotiate tax holidays and favourable terms.

Larger investors are welcome, but the individual who wants to open a guest house, small retail outlet or restaurant may find himself in areas considered reserved for Lao. Joint ventures have an uninspiring history in Laos, and some have failed, with the Lao partner appearing to benefit. Foreign business managers complain that it is sometimes difficult to know what the law is, how far it will be enforced, what degree of corruption is acceptable and how to get round such traditional factors as nepotism. While foreign investment advice is available at the offices which deal with it, in town at 'KM2', and while foreign companies may join the Lao Chamber of Commerce, there are no foreign Chambers of Commerce (as, for example, exist in Bangkok). Many foreign businessmen feel therefore that there is nobody to look after their interests—and company law in Laos is very much in its infancy, with no really independent lawyers to take the foreigner's side in litigation.

The Foreign Investment Code allows that foreign investors and their Lao partners should settle differences through consultation, but does not specify channels of mediation specifically enough for many foreign managers on the scene. Things can and do go wrong, and one angry outburst by a foreign manager directed at his Lao partner or competitor can be enough to demolish any further chances of cooperation. In this scenario, some foreign managers do very little. This would seem to be preferable to rocking the boat, but is head office, or even the regional office, likely to try to understand? Probably not. The manager of a foreign company in Laos must therefore be first and foremost a diplomat. And diplomats do not get angry in public (unless ordered to do so), and at the same time a good diplomat always keeps something up his sleeve—he or she knows that he or she cannot fully trust either Lao partners or the home office which pays his or her salary.

LAO WORKING IN THAILAND

It may surprise some expatriates to discover that many Lao prefer to work for other Lao or Thais than for foreigners.

In 2007, Thailand officially requested thousands of workers from Laos, but obtained only a small fraction of requirements. This appears a paradox, given the official poverty and unemployment figures. But official statistics are hardly more indicative of the real situation than an expatriate's first impressions of Laos. Many thousands of Lao simply see no need for 'legality' and go across the bridge or take a boat across the river without passing through any immigration control on either side. In the northeast of Thailand, Lao are almost identical to northeastern Thai in language and physiognomy. They can remain in that huge area and do menial work for higher pay than in Laos, or they can hop on a train or bus to Bangkok or other locations. They can obtain work in Bangkok-Pattaya within locations known to employ Thais from the northeast; mostly textile factories, bars and massage-prostitution parlours and restaurants. Plenty of Lao in such situations marry Thais within Thailand. To be recognised within Laos all such overseas marriages should be registered in Laos, but few people bother, since the prohibition on European foreigners living with Lao outside of a recognised marriage is never applied to Thais in Laos or Lao in Thailand.

Thus, the foreign employer in Laos is competing not only with the low wages paid in Laos but with unofficial opportunities for Lao in Thailand.

WORKING WITH LAO
Ambition
Any expatriate businessman or manager in Laos needs to understand and work with the Lao character. Even Lao staff born in Vientiane, graduating from Dong Dok University, and fluent in English, will retain traditional priorities of family and traditional values that make up Lao character and qualify ambition.

Lack of driving ambition can be useful to the foreigner. It is possible to return for a second period of duty in Laos and find the same person behind the same desk as ten years previously, doing the same job.

While just about all Lao will want the material props of middle-class existence as on daily display at the flick of a switch on Thai TV, very few will do much to realise such wants. The Lao knows his or her place, which is within his or her family. High achievement, in the form of education, occupation, a nice house and car, and lots of money, is fine. Why? Because it will help the family no end.

Real ambition remains within the family. The person who stays with mother and father until their end, pays the bills, ensures all within the household have enough to eat, cares for those less-lucky family members who get themselves in a mess, pays for granny's trips to the doctor, sends the children to school, meets the costs associated with the boys entering the monkhood, and provides elaborate funerals that will help *pho* and *mae* into a favourable rebirth; that person shall inherit the earth, or that part of it in the hands of mum when she goes up in smoke and her ashes are thoughtfully enshrined in a little *chedi* in the temple next door to the house where your staff member grew up.

Compared to this natural ambition, jobs like senior buyer, warehouse supervisor or even senior accountant at a foreign company cannot hope to compete unless they complement. Nothing can compete with a houseful of siblings, children, children's spouses and grandchildren and great grandchildren. On the other hand, one can earn a lot more money with the foreigners, to build up family security back home.

Ambition for the average Lao is couched in terms of enough. *Phor yuu phor gin.* Enough to maintain life. Enough to allow some accumulation of merit. And if there is anything left over, well, fine, we'll have more of what we have already, a bigger house to hold more nephews and nieces, a bigger TV, a fridge, an overhead fan, and just maybe an air-conditioner.

Striving to be better and to gain ever more is not terribly Lao. If more comes by, okay, it won't be refused. But it takes a non-Lao mindset to think that reading books in isolation and studying for exams all alone and spending lonely years to get to the top, has any intrinsic value in itself and can really lead onto a top job. It certainly takes a different way of thinking

So, what is the point of ambition? All that striving isn't really Buddhist and isn't really Lao. It is much easier and safer to accept one's lot in life—much less to think about, fewer headaches, and less strain on the *khwan*.

when even the compensatory salary is missing. The salary of a ministry official, who has made it if anybody has, is nowhere near enough to buy the house he lives in or the car he drives; if they involve ambition, it is not ambition to rise through study, effort and hard work. Even an orphan with no family can become a traffic policeman and earn more in one day stopping motorcyclists than an under-manager at the textile factory.

Violence

Ambition and competition come a little too close for comfort to the violence that characterised Laos during the decades of conflict for political control. Violence in any form, physical, verbal or psychological, is one thing the Lao cannot tolerate. Faced with it, they very sensibly withdraw before somebody gets hurt.

The fact that a visitor is most unlikely to witness any violence between Lao, and can feel safer walking around Vientiane at any hour than in most capital cities of the world, does not mean that violence is unknown to the Lao. The Lao backed into a corner with no escape, or the Lao insulted, can lash out as wildly as any other. As long as superficial respect and harmony is maintained, passivity is the dominant characteristic of the Lao personality. This passivity can be pleasantly contagious and many foreigners find it so attractive that they discover themselves almost sub-consciously fitting into the pattern. Others do not and cannot restrain themselves from telling the Lao they will always be poor unless they apply themselves more directly and dynamically to pulling themselves into the 21st century. Lao passivity can be frustrating to those with goals to meet and for whom time is money. When such comments attach to an individual Lao or his family, they can not be ignored.

The foreigner in Laos should be aware that the threshold between *bo pen nyang* and *jai rohn* can be easily stepped over, usually with very few if any warning signs. This is known to many residents who live close to Lao, perhaps married or in business partnership, or both, where destinies and profits are so intertwined that a Lao cannot resort to conflict avoidance or flee the scene. Many a foreigner discovers to his chagrin that the pretty little Lao woman that he found so docile and pleasant has a capacity for violence. And many joint ventures have foundered only because of personality conflict between directors.

Typically, when relations break down to the point of open dispute, there is little time for arbitration involving families or the Foreign Investment Committee or the Lao Chamber of Commerce. There are also no standard procedures to follow. There is now a written penal code, although custom remains important in any legal settlement of disputes, as laws do not cover all eventualities, and publicly disputing people, whether husband and wife, or two drivers involved in a car accident, or two contenders for a lady, or two landowners claiming the same property, may both be ordered, along with any witnesses to appear before police officers or the *Nai Baan*, where, if no serious hurt has been done, both sides will be interviewed and given the chance to resolve differences in a protected area.

The Lao way much prefers that people agree to a solution and only if this is impossible, or if a law has been too obviously broken, will a third party decision be made, usually requiring one of the parties to pay compensation to the other by a set date. A police report is made of such agreed or required settlements and all parties sign; if one does not keep to the agreement, he or she could be brought from home and detained in a police cell for an indefinite period. Understandably, most Lao prefer to avoid police involvement.

When the cool surface of social relations is seriously broken—and sometimes one word is enough to completely reverse the peaceful world—a Lao feels injury to his or her *khwan*. And if the 32 parts of an individual's *khwan* get out of order or if even one part feels itself in danger, an individual in charge of his *khwan* can suddenly lose control. The violence that follows is in no way governed by an 'eye for an eye' formula, violence in its nature is seen as outside of reason. It therefore knows no limits and does not burn itself out easily.

Both foreigner and Lao might seek to avoid such a situation developing. The European is more likely to say, "Let's talk about this." The Lao is more likely to go into a silent avoidance until *jai hohn* (hot hearts) cool down. Talking about differences with a Lao may not resolve a problem. However careful the talk, there is always the assumption that one or both of the parties is wrong. And Lao can be very, very sensitive on this score. Admitting fault and asking forgiveness is not completely unheard of, but if an apology is expected or required, it is not likely to come and differences could become more inflamed.

Withdrawal into temporary silence is perhaps not such a bad way of quarantining disputes until a solution finds itself, particularly if there is no real cause other than getting on each other's nerves. A Lao wife behaving in this way may physically retreat to her family. There is absolutely no point in a foreigner husband trying to convince his wife's family that he is right and she is wrong—a family member can do no wrong. If physical violence has taken place, even if provoked by torrents of verbal abuse, the husband is always wrong.

In a traditional Lao family milieu, there are always people around and disputes, if they occur, are less likely to be manifested in anything more than the silent treatment, which everybody can ignore. On the other hand, when a Lao is estranged from the natural social environment and living with a foreigner in comparative isolation, familial constraints are off and real violence is possible. What is perhaps surprising is just how many couples survive together for years with periods of extreme violence interspaced with mutual coexistence.

It is hard not to make a parallel with Lao history, in which periods of violence were interspersed with coalitions during which contending factions superficially lived at peace. This domestic pattern is not appropriate for the workplace: be aware that disputes can simmer for years. You are here to do a job. Your Lao adversary has all the time in the world and a lot more friends than you. You must practice prevention rather than seek a cure to problems. You cannot afford to antagonise.

Conflict-avoidance is a principle of daily interaction throughout much of East Asia. Perhaps the long years of civil strife make it particularly appropriate to the contemporary personality of the Lao population, most of which has only known peace and only wants peace.

Being Wrong

Never expect a Lao to apologise. And even if you, on reflection, decide that maybe you were wrong, saying so with words won't do much to help the situation. Saying so with gifts, social visits and even flowers, is a much better idea.

In the event of a dispute, show willingness to compromise. Blame yourself not for being wrong but for failing to understand the alternative, and ask for it to be repeated, and repeated again if necessary. Consensus must be the final goal, not humiliation of your adversary—no matter how much you think he deserves it. Throughout you must be *jai yen*. This is vital. Any ranting and anger can come from your opponent. It is as 100 per cent as anything can be in Laos, that the person who loses his cool loses his face.

Don't try to prod your opponent into *jai hohn* reactions, you do not have the skill. At the same time be aware that he or she might goad you into behaviour that will cause you to lose face and lose the battle. Let each skirmish end on neutrality until a consensus is reached, then make sure everybody signs, shakes hands and has a drink.

THE WORK ETHIC

The Lao are quite capable of working hard and long hours when the rewards for doing so are evident. Thus at the traditional rice transplant and at the rice harvests everybody who can do so will be in the fields; if they are not, the family's granary will be empty. In cash crop areas like coffee plantations, farmers sometimes travel great distances and live in simple field houses on cold plateaus for up to two weeks at a time so that they can complete harvests. Until the opium elimination campaign in very recent years, many Lao Soung did the same in the mountains, because without an intensive and sustained input of labour for a couple of weeks, the opium would be lost.

However, modern life and a degree of urbanisation has qualified the regard for hard work. The same farmers can compare the fruits of hard work with the seeming manna from heaven that falls partly to them in the form of remissions from kin in America, but mostly to those who live in new large villas with Mercedes cars parked behind the gates. Far more grand buildings have gone up in the past five years than in the previous 30 years of people's democracy. Adding insult to injury, many poor labourers with no land titles have had their shacks bulldozed to provide land for the villas, on the construction of which they might get a job if they are lucky. The workers in factories and the labourers on new roads see their own supervisors living in comparative comfort but spending their time sitting drinking coffee in meetings. And of course, everybody sees the foreign managers and aid-workers living in luxury without any visible evidence relating that luxury to hard work.

The large proportion of the Lao population below the poverty line (almost 40 per cent) is composed of people without work, people growing crops on poor lands and a large number who are incapable of any real work because of mental or physical handicap. In this scenario, with barely mention of the easy payoffs of corruption, the work ethic is not seen as central to an improvement of livelihood. The expatriate manager should be aware that he or she is part of the problem and if he or she wants staff to work hard, he or she should be able to demonstrate that doing so will bring rewards.

A Good Comprador

One thing is for sure, an expatriate alone wishing to set up a company in Laos will have a very difficult time. Official sanction is required and you don't get what you want by dropping into the 'one-stop shop'. I have already gone into the functions of a 'fixer'. A foreign company wishing to set up in Laos will need to submit all details of what it will do, attend meetings and interviews at which goals and means are the subject of much repetition. Whatever you do in Laos, whether you want a business licence or a marriage licence, be prepared to repeat repeatedly. Fine if you get on with everyone you meet. But it is in the nature of things that you will get on better with some people than with others.

It is every bit as important in Laos as in your home country to get on with those people who matter—and get them to like you if you can, it helps, it really does. But how do you know who is important? And how do you get people to like you? The answer, in one word, is comprador.

You need someone to hold your hand—and maybe even to hold your tongue. You need someone who can swim with the sharks, keep them well-enough fed, and leave you to bask in the pleasures of a morning's golf with an important man, a visit to somebody's new grandchild, a well-filled envelope at a daughter's marriage, and of course ensuring that the Lao who work for you and for your company have a reason to work well and enjoy being part of your team. Try to do it all yourself and you will find that in this supposedly relaxed and laid back country, there is simply too much for one man to do, particularly a foreigner.

Managing Your Staff

Just as you will need to manage, gently of course, those people who are managing you, so you will need to be nice, but not obsequiously nice, to those who do the work for you—your staff. Under the reality or pretext of transparency, cooperation, planning, transfer of skills, whatever, you will have regular meetings with as many of your staff as you can get around a large table. Rules are—you control but do not criticise or complain, you praise what can be praised and you repeat as many times as is necessary what is important. Repeat, repeat, repeat. That is not the same as insistence or moaning, in fact it is the opposite of both.

If there is some bad news to put across, for example if you have to reduce the staff by 10 per cent, make sure you (and your comprador) are not to blame personally. As far as you can, give decisions the appearance of consensus. You, of course, are trying your best to make the cuts as painless as possible, keep them to the minimum, and sweeten all departures with written recommendations, public praise at the farewell parties and cash. The most important of these is probably the last. Make sure your company fully meets compensation requirements, otherwise you will have legal problems to sort out.

The Importance of Repetition

The foreign manager may be concerned to get a job done within a set time and up to a standard quality. Both of these imperatives, if really important, should be repeated many times. And repeated again.

The same repetition of what is important will occur in your business meetings with Lao, whatever language they are conducted in. The important points being made will not be in the introductory remarks, and given the softness with which Lao politely speak in meetings and given the background noise often present, you might miss what is important if you rely on your interlocutors saying, 'Now, the point is...', or rely on technical means of emphasis like slide shows, flip charts, and graphical highlighting through flow charts etc. Even your Lao interpreter might skip the repetitions, unaware of their significance, or thinking he has already interpreted that once—you should brief any interpreter that you need a full interpretation.

Meetings might be longer than you are used to, but once you have noted the same thing repeated three times, perhaps more, you can safely assume that you have grasped the important point. If you have important points to raise, use the same technique, repeating the same thing, maybe using slightly different words. Your partner in dialogue might repeat what you have been repeating, and you might repeat

Once you get used to repetition as a management tool, you should feel much less the need to raise your voice or criticise. You'll also have a better chance of remembering what you said. And if you get just one thing from this book, it should be recognition of the importance of repetition.

what he has been saying. This is confirmation. On the other hand, if you disagree, you might choose not to confirm through repetition your understanding, which will give you the chance to study any proposals and gain some other opinions before the next meeting. It is important to understand that emphasis is demonstrated by repetition rather than raising the voice or an almost confrontational statement that this is important. Afterall, what may be important to you might not be important to others and vice versa. For really important matters, count on more than one meeting, even if you repeat exactly the same dialogue twice (or more). And always leave a meeting, however short or long, with a friendly action and statement, to ensure a return meeting will be possible.

Use the same approach in your workplace. Repeat what is important. Asking for confirmation that what you have said has been understood is fairly pointless, as even if a person has no idea what you are talking about, he will say he understands perfectly. If you have regular meetings of your team (recommended), allow those responsible to repeat what you have already told them in a round the table planning session. If people get the idea that your idea is their idea, so much the better.

Emphasising the need for quality—or of a certain quality that can be realistically met in the time and resources available—is not always possible by use of words alone. A physical example of the required quality, along with the lecture on its importance, is much more likely to produce what you want. If in a new area, where no reference models are available, or if your work doesn't actually produce anything that you can place prominently on inspirational show (training, accountancy and so on), you make a point of praising work well done and the individuals who did the right thing and the importance of what they did. Again, repetition is appropriate and if you have weekly, or even daily, meetings of your staff, they should be able to count on a praise section. If it's missing, they will have the first inclination that something is wrong.

Lao were used to repetition in their lives long before the change of regime. The seminars reinforced this method, consisted of repetition of what the strata of decision makers above had already agreed upon and said. The same process is used in Laos today. The central authorities decide something by consensus, this is repeated through the system down to the *nai baan*, the *nai baan* calls a village meeting, every household sends a member who gets the message. Before any such meeting finishes, several villagers will have repeated the important points. After such meetings, the theory is that those household members present carry the message back to their household and tell those who did not attend; they remember the bits that were repeated a few times.

This point about repetition has been deliberately laboured because it is of prime importance in any business or working environment. Remember that some 80 per cent of Lao are villagers, doing much what their parents did before them, learning by copying their elders and betters. Remember that most of those who go to town work in factories or do other repetitive labour and learn on the job by repeatedly copying what others do. Remember that just about all Lao learning to read or going to school learn by rote repetition and learn by heart rather than by analysis and dialectical debate.

Repetition is not wasting time, it is saving time. Getting things right is quicker and cheaper than putting things right. Quiet, respectful, repetition is far more effective than any form of criticism. Just make sure that what you are saying is correct—repeat the wrong thing a hundred times and you would have created a problem. Even then, the solution lies in repeating the right thing as many times or more. This is known in business and management as building change into the system. It is also an established tool of politics.

Nepotism and Trust

The practice of favouring a relative or somebody you grew up with in the same village, speak the same dialect and call by a kinship term, has very deep roots in Lao society. Laos has always had an agricultural system more marked by family small-holding and cooperation between individual households than by feudalism (one reason attempts to introduce collectives post 1975 failed badly). On the family farm, people cooperating together are related—either direct kin, or people who are so much a part of the household they are automatically distinguished as kin. These are the people who can really be trusted. Moving into the world of commerce and industry, it made infinite sense to continue the practice of hiring and promoting relatives above strangers.

Than along came foreign companies and advisers on business culture, with rules that employment and competition must be competitive and that any relatives of management personnel must declare their relationship and, in some cases, would be automatically barred from applying. These rules were to be enforced by an expatriate manager who, unless he had married a Lao, had no kin of his own in the country and therefore would be perfectly objective.

If you are an expat manager in Laos, your job is to enforce the home company's rules, not to argue with them. But be aware that if you deny a branch-manager the right to have his nephew employed as his assistant, do not expect the branch-manager to get along with you in any way more than verbal acquiescence. Were he to do so, he would be denying the relationship of trust within the kinship unit. So, if you have to select or promote a stranger over the nephew, make sure that the uncle understands that this is only because the nephew does not meet the basic qualifications for the job. Better still, have the decision come from the home-office. If you simply reject a person because he or she is not as good as a stranger, and if you are silly enough to say so, you might have missed the opportunity to create a team that could really work well together, and you might have created a situation where trust between you and your branch-manager requires very regular monitoring—at which point you have already denied trust, limited the possibilities of delegation, and given yourself yet more work. On the other hand, and there is always another hand in the practice of management, if you do employ the branch-manager's nephew and you later have some problem with either the branch-manager or the nephew, you will have problems with both. Relatives tend to stick to each other like glue.

Nepotism can be complicated by other factors. Political affiliation means a person may move in circles of decision and power that you dare not risk antagonising. It's all much like a duffer in England getting a job because of family and school links, which may count as much or more than ability. You will no doubt employ this person, and may even profit from the connections; of course you will never be able to sack this person. Perhaps the sad thing in an under-developed country is that the less well-connected but far more able is then likely to be employed as the assistant to somebody you don't really need. But this is not a problem unique to Laos, to some degree it is a problem experienced in all organisations everywhere.

Counting to One Hundred

As to practical advice for the expatriate. If you feel at any time anger, brooding violence, frustration, impatience or hatred, do not count to ten. Count to one hundred—and do it in Lao. And if you still feel the tensions, count another hundred. And if you are still not sure what to do for the best, remember this: "If in doubt, do naught."

And know that even in this conflict-avoidance society, there are Lao who will deliberately push you to the point of public anger, precisely because they know it is the easiest and quickest way of destroying the credibility of a foreigner. So, as a preventative, give no reason to be disliked. But if provoked publicly, keep your cool and you turn the loss of face tables on the agent provocateur.

FAST FACTS AT YOUR FINGERTIPS

CHAPTER 10

'Make Haste Slowly.'
—English saying

Official Name of Country
English: Lao People's Democratic Republic (Lao PDR)
Lao: Sathalanalat Paxathipatai Paxaxon Lao (Sor Por Por Lao)

Capital
Vientiane

Administration
16 provinces (*khoueng*) and Vientiane Municipality. Divided into districts (*meuang*). Sub-divided, including the capital, into villages (*baan*)

Nationals
Lao or Laotian

Official Language
Lao

Area
236,800 sq km (91,429 sq miles)—a little smaller than UK

Time
Greenwich Mean Time plus 7 hours (or 6 hours in summer time)

National Seal
The Party symbol, the hammer and sickle, was quietly removed in 1991, leaving the symbols of agriculture (rice fields), forestry (trees), Buddhism (That Luang stupa), hydroelectricity (a dam), roads and industry (cog wheels).

Telephone Country Code
856 (+21 for Vientiane)

Earliest Known Facts
Mekong areas inhabited over 10,000 years ago. Possibly the world's first rice cultivators (3–4,000 years ago) and metal workers.

Climate
Tropical in south. Temperate in north. Monsoonal. June-October wet. November-May dry. Hottest March-June. Max temperatures 42 degrees. Humidity average 66–82 per cent.

Terrain
Vientiane and Champassak plains, plateaus in northeast and south, west mountains. Elevations: Lower Mekong 70 m (230 feet), Phu Bia 2,817 m (9,242 feet). Landlocked. Arable land 4 per cent of total.

Population
6.9 million people. 41.6 per cent under the age of 15. 20 per cent urban. 60–68 per cent ethnic Lao. Many minorities, each with distinct language: largest groups Khmu, Hmong, Mien (Yao), Akha. Significant Vietnamese and Chinese presence in towns. Growth rate: 2.2 per cent. Life expectancy: 53 years (males), 57 years (females).

Religion
Buddhist 60 per cent, Christian 1.5 per cent, Muslim 0.8 per cent, animist 37 per cent

Currency
Kip (non-convertible)

Credit/Debit Cards and Getting Cash
Cards acceptable only in top hotels or restaurants and a few expensive shops geared to export. Credit and debit cards can be used at most banks and ATMs to withdraw money. Western Union money transfer facilities at some banks and Vientiane Post Office. ATMs are currently few—one on Samsenthai opposite Lao Plaza, one near Lane Xang Hotel (sometimes closed), one in Morning Market.

Cheques
Very rarely used.

Bank Accounts
Resident expatriates may open US$, Thai Baht, Kip accounts. No restrictions on withdrawal.

Water
Only bottled or boiled is safe to drink. An estimate of 55 per cent Lao with no access to clean water.

Gross Domestic Product (GDP)
US$ 15 billion — 48.6 per cent agriculture, 25.9 per cent industry, 25.5 per cent services. Real growth rate 6.4 per cent (2009)

Industries
Mining (copper, tin, gypsum, gems), hydro-electric power, garments, tourism, cement, handicrafts

Exports
Electricity, copper, gems, timber products, garments, handicrafts, hides, coffee, beer.

Imports
Foodstuffs, building materials, vehicles, electricity, fossil fuels, electrical goods.

Education
Literacy (above age 15): 68.7 per cent—77.4 per cent males, 55 per cent females.
Enrolment: (primary) 85 per cent, (secondary) 35 per cent, (all levels); 67 per cent males and 55 per cent females.

Health
Notified numbers with malaria: 759 per 100,000, tuberculosis: 327 per 100,000. Infant mortality: 82 per 1,000 live births. Physicians per 100,000 people: 59

Military Structure
Institutions: Lao People's Army, Air Force, Riverine Force, Village Police (militia). Conscription: 18 months for males under 49. Estimated numbers in service (2005): 110,000.

SYSTEM OF GOVERNMENT
After a long fight for Independence that achieved its goal on 19 July 1949, Laos along with most of Indochina fell into a civil war that was a proxy for the conflict between the United States and the Soviet Union. After many attempts at forming coalition governments of the main factions, the Lao People's Revolutionary Party took full power and renamed the country the Lao PDR on 2 December 1975, under the Premiership of Kaysone Phomvihane. Party structure, Congresses, and decision making procedures are very clearly inspired by those of the Soviet Union, which was the principal ally and donor of aid during the first decade following the change of regime. During that time, offices carried portraits of Karl Marx along with the heroes of the Lao Revolution.

Surprisingly, no mention is to be found, either in any government documentation, or the Constitution, promulgated after much discussion and delay on 14 August 1991, of the word 'Communism'. The 'Hammer and sickle' red flag is seen less in Laos as the years go by. It

The poorly-paid Lao army is loyal to the President, and such military adventures that marked Laos before 1975, and continue in Thailand, have no parallel in Laos. Continuity is valued at least as much as change and in 2006 the Vice-President moved up to the Presidency and the First Deputy Prime Minister moved up to become Premier.

is the flag of the Party; the flag of the country is two red strips separated by one blue with a white 'full moon' in the centre.

The system is presidential. The President is not popularly elected but elected by the National Assembly for five years (last change was in 2006). The President proposes the Prime Minister, who must be approved in position by the National Assembly, and serves a five-year term. The Council of Ministers is appointed by the President and approved by the National Assembly, which is elected nation-wide, with the electorate casting their votes in the constituency of their residence.

Political elections to the National Assembly, the Legislative arm of the Government, are marked by peace and order. There are no big rallies, no threats, no scandals, no bribes, no imprisonments, no trials and no assassinations. Candidates may hold meetings, but there is little if any socialist or communist rhetoric and practically no reference to communist goals—apart from the global Millennium goal of eradicating poverty. Each Lao candidate is allowed one sheet about A4 size on which to list his personal data, including ethnicity, attach a photo and indicate his accomplishments. These are not distributed but posted in the office of the Nai Baan (Village Headman), where elections take place on a specified date. It is mostly on the basis of these information sheets that voters decide between the many candidates. Recent elections to the National Assembly have shown some surprises, with many Representatives losing their seats to relative newcomers, but only one elected N.A. member is currently independent of the Party. Currently women hold 22.9 per cent of seats in the National Assembly, among the highest proportion of women in any parliament in the world.

Voting is compulsory for all aged 18 and above, and unless they have officially changed their place of residence, which many migrants to urban areas do not do, a large proportion of the urban workforce moves back to the village of origin to cast their votes. At such election times, something of the atmosphere of Lao New Year is felt as extra buses carry voters great distances. Turnout at the vote is as close to 100 per cent as it can be, with Lao queuing early at polling stations, dressed in their best traditional clothes. After the voting, most people take the opportunity to visit relatives and attend *basi* and the accompanying feasts. Thus, voting may be compulsory, but the Lao do not lose the chance to make it *muan*.

If you wish to know the relative Party status of the many Lao in the Central Committee, a handy chart is available from the Government printing office in Vientiane. Each member holds a ranking number that might go up or down, or disappear completely, with the following Party Congress, usually held every four years. At the very top of this Committee is the Politbureau, currently 11 members. Number one is the President, but number eleven is not only a woman but also a Hmong.

CULTURE QUIZ

14 SITUATIONS TO SET YOU THINKING.

The expatriate will not spend all his or her time in situations where Lao culture predominates. The advice I have given for eating Lao food in Lao homes cannot be applied to a diplomatic function at Lao Plaza Hotel, where the culture of international diplomacy will predominate. Advice on appropriate behaviour to Lao monks cannot be applied to visiting monks from China or Vietnam. Situations, people and places are all different. I can advise you to drive on the right hand side of the road, but cross the bridge to Thailand and you might be stopped by the police for doing just that.

I make the point about not thinking too much in situations that should come naturally, like tying your shoelaces or driving your car. The same is true of any action in any cultural setting. If you know what to do and how to do it, there should be no great thought process involved. If you have to be constantly on your guard, life is no fun. You are, I presume, a reasonable person, and reasonable people do not go out of their way to cause discomfort to others. At the same time, there is no reason you should bend over backwards in order to please the Lao, and they won't expect you to. Thus, for most foreigners in a Lao cultural environment, respecting Lao ways is not going to be a problem. Much of it is common sense.

In most situations, Lao will act pretty much as you do, but not in all situations. Sometimes your natural behaviour will not be the natural behaviour of a Lao. Thus, this little situationist quiz. There are no answers that are 100 per cent right and few that are 100 per cent wrong. The objective of this section is to give you a "dry run". Commit a real *faux pas* and nobody need know. It's a bit like crashing in a link-trainer rather than in a jumbo-jet with a thousand people on board. So don't worry about right or wrong, just try to set yourself in the interactionist situation.

SITUATION 1

You have invited your Lao secretary to dinner and agreed to meet at Sindad Sailom. She turns up with three other girls who do not work with you. When it comes to the time to pay the bill, what do you say?

Comment

You say to the waiter, *"Check Bin"*. And when the bill comes, you pay it. You invited your secretary alone, but you should have known she would bring at least one friend. You didn't bargain on paying for four guests, but there is no way out. So accept gracefully. At least you now know that your secretary might be a good girl! If they suggest going on to listen to hard rock at the music centre or to the Suradit Disco, it's okay to plead you are tired. Next time, you might try a buffet lunch.

SITUATION 2

You agree on a price and climb into a *touk-touk*. The driver keeps turning round and asking if you want a girl, a boy or marijuana. Do you ask how much? Do you direct him to the nearest police station? Do you say "No, thank you, I've given them up for Buddhist Lent?" Do you shake your head and say nothing?

Comment

If you do want any of the things on offer, no need to use a *touk-touk* driver to obtain them. There is always the chance that if you do use his services, the police may be involved somewhere along the line. The driver is out of line and tempting you to break the law. Either a firm and unfriendly "No" is required, or shake your head and say nothing. Most *touk-touk* drivers are like this, particularly after dark. That's their problem, not your's. No attempt at conversation is appropriate, and no smile.

SITUATION 3

Walking along the street, you meet a Lao man you were recently introduced to, together with his wife. You can't remember their names. Do you shake hands with the man and *nop* the woman, just say hello, smile and walk past, *nop* both of them, shake hands with both of them, stop a few minutes and ask where they are going, talk about the weather? Use "you" or "*chao*" throughout or ask their names?

Comment

Whatever you do doesn't matter very much, unless you snub them and walk past as if you haven't seen them. It really depends on whether this is a social relationship you want to expand or to drop. If the latter, you don't need to know their names and a smile suffices. If the former, say hello and where are you going. That gives them a chance to react. If they are not interested in developing any sort of relationship with you, they will give a non-committal reply—*talaat* (to the market) or *nyang seu-seu* (just walking) something that doesn't invite further questions. A smile or a *sok dii* in such circumstances is enough of a goodbye. If, on the other hand, they greet you enthusiastically and initiate a handshake or a *nop,* don't shrink from it. And feel free to ask their names and to tell yours—it shows some sort of interest. Nothing is right or wrong in such situations. You just have to be reasonably polite and play it by ear.

SITUATION 4

You are a foreign woman walking alone in the early evening, going to meet some friends in a restaurant. A motor-cycle pulls up and two young men on it say in English, "Hello beautiful girl, where you go?" Do you give a non-committal reply? Smile and say nothing? Walk on as if you have not seen or heard them? Reply in fluent Lao that you have no idea what they are saying and can't they speak Lao?

Comment

A Lao girl, even a good girl, would probably not worry too much about this and might well have some sort of conversation with the young men, who are paying her attention and thereby complimenting her. But you are not a Lao girl and neither you nor the men are going to be able to distinguish between clever playfulness and sexual interest. So, presuming you do not know the two men, the safest thing is to walk on as if you have not heard them. They may pursue and continue to talk to the limits of their English, but do not provide any encouragement by smiling or saying anything in any language. Without you doing a thing, they both lose face by failing to attract you. The more they persist, the more face they lose. As long as you are not dressed outrageously or being in any way provocative, quietly enjoy your superior moral position. Even so, don't turn into any dark little dead-end lanes. If things look at all menacing, which would be very rare, reach for your mobile and call your friends and ask them to come to where you are walking, giving perhaps the number of the motor-bike. For an unaccompanied woman it is a good idea to keep some numbers of friends (foreign and/or Lao) on the top of your telephone name list, so you can call them easily if there should appear to be any need.

SITUATION 5

You agree on a fare for quite a long distance in a *touk-touk*. On the way, you have to take a detour because a road is closed. On arrival, the driver asks for more money as he did not know they were going to close the road. What is your response?

Comment

You have been inconvenienced as much as the driver, so no real reason to pay. Roads do get closed and opened in Vientiane quite regularly, either for repairs or because important people are passing. This is all part of a driver's lot. Only if you like this driver and use him a lot should you consider paying a bit extra—but if you do, give the extra before he can ask for it. "And here's 5,000 extra because we took so long." Believe it or not but I have been with Lao who have done just this. Since there is no question of tipping on agreed fares, this should make both you and the driver feel good, and get you better service next time. But if you want to stick to the agreed fair, that's okay too. It is always a good idea to have plenty of small change, and to hand over the exact fare without need to calculate and count change. You will notice the personal element here: if you have taken this driver before or if you like him, you pay, if you don't like him you do not.

SITUATION 6: LITTLE THINGS

You are off to Xieng Khouang for a few days. You tell the maid to come into the house everyday to make sure all is okay and to feed the cat. You have a strictly professional relationship with this maid, no hanky panky. She asks you to bring her back a souvenir. Do you tell her you are going to work not shop? Ask her what she would like? Or say "of course" when you have no intention of doing any such thing.

Comment

If you return with no souvenir for the maid, it will not break her heart. No need to explain that you didn't have time or that there were only two-ton jars and unexploded ordnance as souvenirs. So a flippant agreement to a request is no real agreement at all, and the safest. On the other hand, it is so normal for Lao to bring back little gifts for their workmates and friends and to request them, that you are doing Lao if you do bring back some little thing. Wherever you go in Laos, it is always interesting to visit the local market: that is where you see the ethnic groups of the region in interaction, and where you get an idea of the local domestic economy and the comparative wealth of the area.

During such a trip, it is no trouble at all to pick up some small gifts for your maid, the secretary, the girl who makes your tea and does the cleaning. No obligation. (Although obligations grow along with relationships.) Nothing expensive (unless you have other motives) just a hair clip, a Vietnamese or Hmong souvenir, a small cheap Chinese figure or some local fruits. No doubt you could find the same in Vientiane, but bringing it back is the thing. Shows you were thinking of somebody, even if only very cheaply and briefly.

Do not get a present that suits your tastes. The giving is important. You might be amazed to find it on the shelf in your maid's room or on your secretary's desk. In the end, it's a cheap way of getting people to like you. A lot cheaper than taking her out to dinner with three friends.

SITUATION 7: THE BIRTHDAY PARTY

You have been invited to the birthday party of a quite poor unmarried girl. You ask the time and get the answer 5:00 pm in the evening. What time do you go? What do you take as a present?

Comment

Ask if there is to be a *basi*. If not 5:00 pm sounds a bit early and you could be the only guest. Most Lao eat quite early, but not before six, so around that time might be more appropriate—earlier and they will still be preparing the food. What to take as a present is important because it will indicate how you see the relationship developing. Any romantic hopes? Take along flowers—red roses, not white (although white are okay between friends, if that is your intension), preferably a dozen and set in a sponge-basket with other foliage so the receiver can put them on show immediately and not have to clean them and find a vase, which she probably does not have.

If you are interested enough to get red roses, something more should accompany them. A fairly respectable, but nothing too prim, shirt with a nice colour is perfect. Try to make sure it is not too small! No gold bracelets—not at this stage. But if there is a *basi* here is your chance to really lay it on the line—but only if you think your interest is reciprocated. A US$ 10 note tied publicly on the wrist is obvious enough, along with a few wishes for finding love and happiness. If, on the other hand, the girl has a boyfriend or husband, or you have no deep interest, a few cakes would do fine and skip the rest. Even if there are several cakes it doesn't matter. Don't go expensive, quantity not quality. And if you are invited to a boy's birthday? A crate or two of Beer Lao, of course.

SITUATION 8: FRIENDSHIP AND GRATITUDE

You drop in uninvited on a family living upcountry. They invite you in and sit you down with a glass of water. While chatting, others passing by climb up the steps and join in. Soon somebody opens a bottle of *lao-lao* and the one glass is passed around. More people come in and you are enjoying being the centre of attention. Some food is brought out and whatever the family was doing they have stopped and the women are now busy cooking up a meal, which you presume will be carried up and served to the group of mainly men. You ask a boy to go off and get some beer delivered, giving him money enough for two crates. The *nai baan* drops in along with some of the *thamnuat baan* still dressed in their camouflage uniforms. The women bring in the food and soon the small house is packed with people eating and drinking. There is no occasion apart from the fact that you dropped in.

After several hours as it gets dark, you decide you had best head back. You take leave slowly with plenty of last drinks and with everybody sending you off, climb down the steps and go behind the house to where you left your car. As you start your 4x4, you notice you don't seem to be going anywhere. You climb out and see that during the several hours you were in the house, the vehicle sank into the soft earth up to the axles. While you stand by helplessly, the villagers dig down and under your car and place under it several long and thick bamboo poles; after a lot of drunken effort and laughing, they lift your vehicle out of the mud, and you regain terra firma. You get out again, feeling very grateful. Do you reach into your pocket and hand around whatever bank notes remain?

Comment

If you had got stuck on a strange road and unknown villagers had come to your help in the same way, it would be most appropriate to pay for the service and say thank you. But in this situation, you practically became one of the family and one of the village for a few hours, and relatives do not pay for such help. More appreciated than money (YES, more appreciated than money!) would be for you to shake each hand, thank them and say you look forward to seeing them all again very soon. They will wave goodbye with a genuine feeling of friendship (or maybe it's just the glow of the beer).

SITUATION 9: THE LIFE-SAVING OPERATION

You are puzzled by the fact that somebody keeps calling your mobile and ringing off before you can answer. You have read this book and suspect this is somebody too mean to pay for a call. However, after several days of this, you get fed up and return a call. The caller claims to have met you two months ago when you were so kind and bought beer for everybody in the village. The caller goes on to say that mother is in need of an operation and without it mother will die within two weeks. Could you pay the US$ 500? Do you hang up? Say don't call again? Say the caller has the wrong number? Tell her to call back in two weeks?

Comment

While a lot of Lao do need life-saving operations, the family is the first line of social security. You can't even remember this person, so there is no strong link to justify asking you for money. And why call now after two months? And if it's so urgent, why not pay for a call? In the circumstances, telling her to call back in two weeks is justified. She probably will, still saying her mother has two weeks to live. Now why do I slip into the feminine?

SITUATION 10: THE CULTURAL SHOW

You go to a Lao dancing show at the Cultural Centre. It is totally crowded, except for the front row of seats. Behind those empty seats is a line of monks. You squeeze down to the front and see there are no reserved notices on the seats. You have your Lao friend by the hand but your friend says you cannot sit in front of the monks. There is nowhere else to sit and you cannot stand in the packed aisles. You go out the side door, taking your friend with you. Who was right, you or your friend?

Comment

Your friend. You went to a cultural show. You got a cultural lesson.

SITUATION 11: THE BRAIN-STORMER

The home office is sending you a high-ranking trainer to train your staff in new techniques of management and financial monitoring. You have attended sessions with this trainer in the home country and know that she favours open discussion of issues, a think-tank approach to problem resolution, and innovation over continuity. She is very much a star of your organisation and you cannot risk antagonising her. At the same time, you doubt very much that your staff will enter into "brain-storming" sessions. You want her to go home with a good impression of you and your staff, and you want to minimise damage she might do to your harmonious and productive management style, which favours continuity and introduces change cautiously. How do you prepare your staff?

Comment

Call a meeting of all staff who will be involved in the training sessions. If your personnel officer and main driver are not to attend training, include them in your meeting. Inform everybody that the home office is very pleased with their performance in Laos, and that therefore a very important person will be coming to listen to what they have to say, to note their input, and to learn lessons that might be applied elsewhere.

HERE'S THE PLAN, SELL TO THAILAND FOR X KIP AND BUY IT BACK AT XX KIP.

You stress (by repetition) that this is a chance for the Laos office as a whole to burnish its already shining image at HQ and to suggest future interaction HQ-Laos, which might eventually include sending some staff members for regional training and perhaps even on missions to HQ itself. You go through all the routine preparations for the visit—Who is to go with you to meet at airport. Accommodation. Training venue and equipment. The office *basi* for the visitor (essential). The venues for an official dinner and who should be invited from outside the office. Any visits outside the office for familiarisation with operations in Laos and for recreation. And having gone through the procedural aspects and made it clear who does what, and having several times noted how important this visitor is at HQ, you go through all sectors of operations, having the responsible staff member state out loud what s/he does and how things in her/his section work. Each should try to think of a problem encountered during the last 12 months and be able to say how the problem was solved. If necessary, have several subsequent meetings, not necessarily of all staff, before your visitor arrives.

You will prepare a briefing paper for your visitor, drawing attention to your star staff. And unless the trainer determines otherwise, you will attend as many sessions as possible and take notes. You will, of course, make sure that things are as the rules require them during the visit—so take the sticking plaster off of the safe combination and make sure the driver completes the driver's log as driving takes place, not at the end of the month by imagination, and if appropriate that he request the visitor to sign after every journey. After the trainer has gone, have another meeting to go through what the staff learnt and any changes that HQ requires be introduced. Training is too important to be left up to trainers. Don't forget the thank you memo saying how much your staff appreciated the sessions.

SITUATION 12: THIEVES AND GOSSIPS

Worst-scenario time. Your secretary does not like your driver and takes every chance she can to discredit him in your eyes, reporting whenever he is five minutes late, hasn't washed the car and other minor matters that do not seriously affect the office. You let things be because the driver is behaving much like anybody else. Then one day the secretary says the driver who collects office supplies along with all mail from your PO Box, is stealing part of them and his wife is selling them in her stationery shop on the market. You go quietly to the driver's wife's shop in the Morning Market but can find nothing incriminating. This is not something you can ignore. You have either to sack the driver or the secretary. How do you handle the situation?

Comment

Tackle things immediately. You think it unlikely your secretary is deliberately lying about such a matter, but everybody takes a paper clip or pencil at some stage and perhaps she is exaggerating or mistaken.

You may know enough about Laos to realise that calling in the police could destroy office harmony and is unlikely to unveil the guilty party, particularly if he or she has any clout with the police. But do you know enough about your staff? Not just their qualifications and functions, but who is related to whom, and who are close friends or distant enemies? These are important things for a manager to know. Have you taken the trouble and time to get to know the people on whom your own welfare and reputation depend? Maybe not, but this is not the day to start.

Have all stationery stock that should be in the office checked. If the clerk responsible says it is all there, check enough items yourself to convince you that there has been no major theft. If convinced, say so in private to your secretary and tell her you intend to take no action against the driver. If she retracts (don't expect a full retraction and certainly not an apology) say that's okay, the matter ends there. If she resigns, accept. If she holds to her story and gives some sort of evidence—she saw him taking things to the market or somebody saw him and told her—then you are in for a longer haul. Make sure she remains in the office.

Call in the driver, alone. For once you can indulge in some straight talking. Tell him the accusation against him—he has the right to know—but not who made it. If he resigns, accept. If he maintains innocence, note whatever he says—literally, write it down in front of him. Tell him to remain on standby outside your office while you examine the accusation (but not sitting next to the secretary). Reluctantly, call all staff to a brief meeting. Inform them that there might have been theft in the office. Do not be specific, just say theft and might, and that everybody is to remain in the office for the rest of the day.

Start your enquiries with the clerk responsible for ordering stationery. Inside your office, alone, with all order books and records of use. And if current office supplies are more or less as they should be, what about past orders, even past years? It is the clerk's responsibility. How does he get on with the driver and secretary? Is he related to either? You have a third person to investigate. Call in the staff one by one. Even if they have nothing to say, keep them for ten minutes and take the time to find out how they are, how's the family? Pity you didn't take more time with them before this. Ask any with the right to request stationery if they have checked stationery requisitions against what has been supplied to them by the clerk. How does this tally with the clerk's account?

The driver has by this time been sitting a couple of hours in the office and you can bet he knows what's going on. If all requisitions and supplies add up, you have no reason to sack the driver and every reason to change your secretary. If they do not add up, and the discrepancy cannot be explained, then both the driver and the clerk and you may be in trouble. If they do add up, tell your secretary and ask what explanation she has for what appear to be false accusations. If there is nothing more substantive to her story, tell her that since she is unhappy in the office, she may resign and keep any benefits.

If you have some evidence against the driver, giving him the chance to resign on the spot saves a long drawn out conflict situation and take the keys to your Benz before paying him off! You have, of course, made an enemy for life.

Whether you have the power to sack somebody depends on your HQ, but it also depends on Lao law. Sacking in Laos can mean that you go to court to defend against an action brought by a Lao. Don't expect sympathy from HQ, after all you are responsible for any losses in the office and for maintaining inter-personnel harmony; maybe you will be the one for the sack. Had there been harmony and had you done your job, this mess might not have arisen. So you see... it's all your fault. That's what expatriate managers are for. In some situations, there is no win-win possibility. Go for damage control.

SITUATION 13: THE UNGRATEFUL WIFE

After several years in the country and many ups and downs, you marry a Lao. You buy a house, in her name, open a business, in her name, put your money into a joint account, meet all your obligations to her family and more, and behave yourself much better than any of the male members of her family. Then, one day without consulting you, she empties your joint account and gives all the money to her elder sister. You complain you should have been consulted, she says she has done nothing wrong.

Rather than risk a real confrontation you go out for a few beers up the road to give her time to cool down; you have learned to avoid confrontation—so you think. By this time, half her family is living in what you thought of as your house. You come home at 8:00 pm and find the doors locked and bolted against you. It is pouring in rain and you have nowhere to go. You force the door and enter. Your wife attacks you with a meat cleaver. You manage to grab her hand. The rest of the family is looking on. As you make her drop the meat cleaver, the rest of the family—those you are supporting at school, those you took to Udon for good medical attention, those you supported in business, those same people who called you son, and brother and uncle—they all fall on you, hold you down and tell you will have to go, leave the house immediately, never want to see you again.

You protest that it is your wife not you who is at fault. They reply almost in chorus that you had no right to force the door of their house, you are a foreigner who abused the Lao who took you in, you are wrong, your wife, soon to be your ex-wife, is right. What do you do?

Comment

You go. You made a mistake. Wrong wife, wrong family. You have no rights. Probably by now you also have no money. Better go while you can.

OR

You stay. Under Lao law such as it is, with all its faults and changing all the time, your wife can divorce you. But if she does, she gets nothing. The party seeking divorce, man or woman, gets nothing. If this is explained to them by the *nai baan*, they may take a fresh view of the situation. But don't crow. Get angry and hit her and they have evidence enough to get you out. A lot of *jai yen* is needed. Maybe some valium too! Maybe some sessions with the *nai baan*, who is responsible for maintaining peace in his village, and with the government officials who married you, and would have to go to the trouble of un-marrying you. If your spouse insists on divorce without showing good cause—and the occasional tiff or argument with a relative is not good cause if there was no violence—the person seeking divorce gets nothing. Stay put, be on your guard, but know that you have the law on your side—unless of course you married a rich and influential person, or unless you kill your wife.

SITUATION 14: THE INTIMATE CONFIDANT

Khimpheng, your valuable Head of Personnel, is a woman in her mid-fifties currently on her third husband. You have been to her house many times and like her husband and children, most of them grown up. You know or think you know that Lao avoid confrontation and saying bad things about others in public. She often comes into your office and talks on a level you find a bit troubling, often complaining about other staff members. One day she starts to complain about her husband and his behaviour with the children, particularly the youngest adopted girl, of whom the husband is both too fond and sometimes too disciplinarian. You think this is going outside of normal work or social relations. What do you do?

Comment

You listen. For once you must have been doing something right. Do not look upon discussion between Khimpheng and yourself as in the public world, for her they are an extension of her private world and she expects what she says to be held in confidence. It is fairly normal for a staff member to go to a boss she respects and tell him about her problems: these could be with other staff or they could be so completely personnel you feel like telling her or him to shut up and get back to work (but don't!). There is obviously a limit on this type of thing, and if all your staff begin to come in with their personal problems, you would have no time for anything else and would have to take a step back in social interaction. This is unlikely to happen.

The avoidance of confrontation in Lao society does not mean an absence of potential confrontation. Khimpheng's gripes about her husband may perform a cathartic function. She needs to unload, however much you think that is not a Lao characteristic, and finds that you, a foreigner and her superior, are a safe choice of confidant. If she asks for advice be neutral when you give it, sympathise even if you don't believe what she says, and take the line that you hope it will all work itself out. And give yourself a pat on the back. In private of course.

DO'S AND DON'TS

DO's

- Do repeat whatever is important and look for repetition in meetings as an indicator of importance
- Do flatter at every opportunity
- Do hold something in reserve, at least your bank account
- Do get to know your staff
- Do make payment after eating or services, unless required to pay in advance (as for example in the main sandwich bars)
- Do be as clean as you can reasonably be
- Do open wrapped gifts only in private unless requested to do otherwise
- Do remove shoes or sandals when entering the central *sim* of a temple, any home unless told otherwise, and anywhere you see a sign telling you to do so (some shops)
- Do get name cards made, if necessary with a map
- Do use first names or nicknames, adding a prefix for a VIP
- Do keep your head when all around are losing their heads
- Do keep your temper, counting to one hundred or one thousand if necessary
- Do provide food if inviting people to your home
- Do pay if inviting to a restaurant
- Do treat monks with the utmost respect
- Do beckon waiters or anybody with the hand and fingers downwards
- Do speak softly but loud enough to be heard
- Do smile unless you are at a funeral or a serious meeting
- Do take your time and allow time
- Do be reasonably generous without responding to unreasonable requests
- Do tell people what they want to hear rather than the truth
- Do remember that the Lao is always right, you are always wrong

DON'Ts

- Don't lie around in a temple
- Don't walk barefoot in the streets
- Don't rush to *nop* anybody except monks
- Don't worry about details of etiquette, most things go
- Don't say bad things about anybody
- Don't rush or expect others to rush
- Don't feel obliged to tip unless in a western restaurant, but don't pick up small change offered
- Don't trust words at face value
- Don't let people know when you disapprove of something
- Don't be mean with your money
- Don't expect people to like you if you behave badly
- Don't ever believe that you really know the Lao
- Don't have high expectations and you may not be disappointed
- Don't blame little people with no education and few modern skills for creating problems. Help them, don't damn them

GLOSSARY

baan	village
basi	soul support ceremony
bo	not/no
bo pen nyang	never mind
boun	merit/festival
buat	ordain
chao	you/lord
check-bin	bill (restaurant)
dames	drafts/checkers
dayyin	to hear
dek	child
dii/bo dii	good/bad
doy	first person (humble)
erh/urh	yes
falang	French/westerner
fan	boy or girl friend
fur	noodle dish
gaiy	chicken
gheng jurt	non-spicy soup
gin	to eat
gin khao	eat (rice)
gin layo	eaten already
het boun	make merit
het hai	slash and burn
heuan	house
hom	nice smell
hom	lane/small road
hong mor	hospital
jai hon	angry
jai yen	cool-tempered

jot	stop
jumbo	transport
jup hom	sniff-kiss
kataw	ball game
kengjai	respect to elder
khanom	cake
kha-noy	little slave
khao chee	bread
khao jao	non-sticky rice
khao nio	sticky rice
khao phiak	rice noodles
khao tom	rice soup
khao/ock	begin/leave
khatoey	male transvestite
khay	eggs
khay	sell
khay luuk	egg with chick
khay mot	ant egg soup
kheck	guest
khop chai (deu)	thank you
khor tang	make way
khor thort	excuse me
khu	teacher
khu-bha/nya-pho	monk
khwai	buffalo
khwai lek	plough etc.
khwam lap	secret
khwan	soul
kit hot	miss/think of
laap	minced meat dish
laay	a lot/many
lamvong	Lao dance
lao hai	rice alcohol
lao lao	Lao alcohol

Lao Loum/Soung/Theung	categories of Lao
leu	or
luang	royal
mae	mother
mae baan	maid
mae-sii	nun
mak	like
maklouk	chess
mat khen	tie thread
men	bad smell
meu theu	mobile
mia	wife
mor	doctor
mor lum	traditional singer
mor nuat	masseuse
mor phii	spirit doctor
mu baan	village
muan	enjoyable
muay-Lao	Lao boxing
mun	engagement
na kham	yellow pages
nai baan	village headman
nam	water
nam jai/chai	kindness
nang	mrs/miss
napteu	respect (general)
nenh	novice monks
nom	milk
nop	palms-together hello
noy	little
nyay	big
pa dek Lao	sauce
patu	door
Pha	Excellency/title

pha phum	land spirits
phan pa	fish and vegetables
Phansa	Buddhist Lent
phii	spirits
phii heuan	house spirits
pho/mae	parents
phor	enough
phuu-dio	alone
pi mai/songkran	New Year
ping/dat	barbecue/roast
pua	husband
pui	fertiliser
sa ha phasa saat	United Nations
sa than thout	embassy
sabai-dii	hello
sai gop	sausages
Sangha	order of monks
sao	girl
savan	heaven
say	boy
sehp	tasty
seu lin	nickname
siang	sound/tone
silapa	art
sim	temple chapel
sin	Lao skirt
sin deuan	end of month
sindad	barbecued meat
sukhwan	see *basi*
tak bat	give to monks
talaat sao	morning market
tee kee	hockey
tengan	marriage
thamnuat baan	militia

than	mr (respectful)
than phatet	abroad/foreign
thao daiy	how much
thao ni	that's all
thaohu	soya-bean cake
that	stupa
thi-hak	darling
thio	trip/outing
thoh pit	wrong number
tom	female transvestite
tuk-tuk	transport
wan pha	Buddhist holy day
wat	Buddhist temple
wow-lin	joking
yuu	location/live

RESOURCE GUIDE

TELEPHONES (LANDLINES)

To call in to Laos, you will need to dial: 00 + 856 + area code + number

Province	Area Code
VTE Capital	21
VTE Province	23
Champassak	31
Saravanh	34
Attapeu	36
Xekong	38
Savannakhet	41
Khammouane	51
Bolikhamxay	54
Xiengkhouang	61
Houaphan	64
Luang Phabang	71
Xayaboury	74
Oudomxay	81
Bokeo	84
Luang Namtha	86
Phongsaly	88

Calls to Xaysomboun Special Zone: access code is 21 2900 Xaysomboun numbers have 3 digits instead of 4.

Calls within Laos:

Land line to mobile: prefix 020-
Mobile to land line: prefix 021-

EMERGENCY

As English on emergency numbers might be limited, have a Lao or Thai-speaking friend make your call if it is possible.

- Fire 190
- Ambulance 195
- Police 191

Yellow Pages

The *Na Kham* ("Golden Pages" but translated as "yellow") contains not only numbers and addresses of shops, tradesmen, car repair, etc., but also the private telephone numbers of anybody in Laos who has put their name in the book and has a land line. There is no other telephone book. Even if you only have a mobile, this is a useful reference source. Do not assume everything is in there, assume many things are not. New bilingual editions should appear every January. Cost US$ 9 a copy, or look in a second hand bookshop. Many advertisers have hyperlinks from the *Yellow Pages* website, in English: http://www.laoyp.com

HOSPITALS

Health problems are one of the biggest concerns of foreigners spending some time in the country. Hospitals and clinics exist but are poor in terms of hygiene, trained doctors, supplies, equipment and medicines.

If you have no choice, or only a minor complaint, Mahasot Hospital is a large establishment. Various foreign aid-agencies and governments have attempted to assist Laos in terms of building and stocking hospitals and clinics, but are hampered by laws that make it difficult for foreign medical staff to practice in Laos. There has been some success in foreign-funded malaria programmes, but one of the most notable successes was the provision of a machine to Mahasot which identified fake drugs. Huge quantities of medicines were found to be fake.

Given that doctors in the hospital have little access to drugs, and that the hospital has a limited budget to build stocks, many in-patients are simply given a slip of paper with a drug name written on it. They send a relative or friend to get the drug from the only two reasonably stocked pharmacies in Vientiane, next to each other at the back of the hospital, near the river road. Alternatively, the relative can try to obtain the drug from the general market or from Thailand (although new controls in Thailand make it difficult to buy many drugs at pharmacies).

Foreigners going to Mahosot will be directed to the:

- Mahosot International Clinic, tel: (021) 21 4022, which has a separate entrance on Fangum (the river road), not far from the pharmacies. It has a sign and even has a car park.
- Emergency Room: (021) 21 4023 (Mahosot Hospital)

You can telephone, but if in urgent need, go straight there. Take identification, including passport and a supply of money. You pay US$ 10 to register and should see a doctor soon thereafter. They can easily diagnose malaria, which you are unlikely to contract in Vientiane but could pick up in upcountry areas. Diagnosis of dengue is difficult and by the time you know, you are either dead or cured. Since there is no cure anyway apart from going on a drip for as long as it takes to get over it (a very popular form of treatment in Laos whatever the problem), you will be given an expensive and Spartan single room—no Thailand-style luxury facilities here—which at least keeps you from spreading whatever it is around. Chances are you will also be given a high dose of antibiotics, and maybe a few steroids thrown in.

Hepatitis

A study some time ago claimed that some 20 per cent of Lao are passive carriers of Hepatitis B. They don't know they have it, but they can infect you—unless you have survived it once, in which case you are immune but maybe you also join the carriers. Hep B can knock you out as much as cholera and have long-term effects. It is the only disease transmitted by sex or blood for which a vaccine exists. Hepatitis A and E can be infected through water. A has a vaccine, E does not. Before your diagnosis results come through, you will look more like an Asian than an Asian: yellow skin, yellow eyes and lethargy. The only cure for this is bed-rest and the drip.

The International Clinic

The International Clinic does not have that many rooms, but some always seem to be empty. You can find the Clinic easily, and find the reception desk easily, but to find a particular in-patient often requires opening all the doors of all the rooms until you find the person you want. Staff would never dream of preventing you, so before you get sick why not drop in and see the facilities? You can even visit a few hapless patients. The treatment there may be very little better than bed rest, drip and paracetamol, and the advice much the same as at any of the several cheaper private clinics around town—not surprising since all doctors come from Mahosot. But the charge will be the same as for a nice room in a more efficient Thai hospital. This is precisely why the Lao *Yellow Pages* contain far more advertisements for medical establishments in Thailand than in Laos. Have a look: there are even full colour pictures of before and after the nose job you can have at a clinic in Thailand. If you are looking for a boob-job, you will find where you can get it.

Each Province has a provincial hospital. Numbers in English are on page 375 of the current *Yellow Pages*. Do not expect a response in English. Private clinics exist in towns and foreigners may go to them. However, only Lao can open or work in such clinics, and doctors in them are doctors from one or more of the state hospitals. Tests, diagnosis and treatment are limited, as is privacy, but you get much the same standard of care as at the International Clinic, only a lot cheaper and quicker.

Australian Embassy Clinic

Foreigners for whom everything is paid, and some for whom it is not, go to the Australian Embassy Clinic. This has been called by guide books the best medical facility in Laos. It is allowed to operate for Australian and Commonwealth citizens, but I have never heard of anybody being turned away if they have the required fee. Opening times are limited to those of an embassy: 8:30 am–12:30 pm, 2:00–5:00 pm and morning only on Friday. It is expensive, and do not expect sophisticated tests or apparatus. If, however, you have an employer who pays, or international insurance, it may be reassuring to see a qualified Australian doctor. And even if told to go to Udon in Thailand, you will get a referral letter to show, not just in Udon, but to your insurance.

Call (021) 413603, or if after closing hours (020) 5511 1462 —this is a mobile that might get you straight to the doctor. There is only one doctor available, so do not expect miracles.

Hospitals in Thailand

All of the above is in Vientiane. But if you're really sick, get to Thailand as fast as you can. Nongkhai is only 25 km (15 miles) away, but you'll have to cross the bridge and go through immigration and that closes at 10:00 pm. During those opening hours, count one hour to the bridge and to get across it and into the Thai side (and take a taxi from Vientiane, not a bus from behind the Morning Market). On the Thai side you will find a few touts asking if you want to go to Udon direct. If you're really sick, you won't feel like bargaining, but fix a price and emphasise that you are going NOW.

A one way trip to the top-notch Aek Udon International Hospital, 55 km (34 miles) away should be around 500 baht. The Hospital is not pronounced A-E-K as some foreigners insist, but "ek". If "hospital" is not understood, Thai is "*rong-phaya-bahn*" but people in Nongkhai and Udon will understand the Lao "*hong-mor*".

If you are way upcountry in Laos and working with medical insurance as part of the package, ensure that it contains a medical evacuation contingency. This is ruinously expensive, but at a pinch, you might get from where you are in Laos, straight across to Thailand by helicopter. If you want to add this to your insurance, the contact is: International SOS Services—24-hour telephone in Thailand: (02) 256-7146.

Or you can go straight to the source: Aek Udon Hospital, which has an ambulance and helicopter evacuation service from Laos to Udon in Thailand. Make sure you are on their books if likely to use their services, or at least that you can quote over the phone your medical insurance policy. From Laos. the telephone number is 0066 42 342 555 or 0066 1 9540954.

Before you get to the emergency stage, check their website at: http://www/aekudon.com or email: info@aekudon.com. Local phone number (if in Thailand) is (042) 342 555.

Both Aek-Udon in Udon Thani, and Wattana Hospital (just across the bridge and turn left 400 metres towards Nongkhai) have ambulance services that should be allowed across the bridge into Vientiane and back at any time, even when the bridge gates are closed.

Wattana Hospital

Wattana advertises a 24-hour emergency service—Tel: 00 66 42 46 5201—but on the one occasion I tried it in the middle of the night, it took one hour to get a reply and three hours to get a doctor. And this was only after I had deposited a sum of money. This is just one experience which may or may not be typical.

There is another private hospital, *Ruam Phet,* on the other side of Nongkhai, a small town. This hospital is almost unused by Europeans, but the service is quick, the pharmacy well-stocked and drugs liberally dispensed (if taking a known medicine regularly, you don't want just two week's supply —*Ruam Phet* will give enough for three months or more if you say you live in Laos). Compared to expatriate-focused facilities in Bangkok, Nongkhai is third-class. But still better than anything in Laos.

You can just turn up in Nongkhai or in Udon and get seen for most problems, but the Nongkhai State Hospital, while it may be okay, is closed to outpatients at weekends except for an emergency section. Other hospitals are private, so take ATM cards or cash (not kip!) Both hospitals have reasonable dental services; Aek-Udon is very much better. Going to a dentist in Vientiane is going to cost at least as much and is not always as reliable.

VETS

If your pet needs a vet, try:
- Animal Hospital (021) 22-2195
- ABC Pet Shop (021) 41-4425 and (020) 551-1157
- Bouaphim Veterinary Clinic (021) 41-5339/(020) 224-3781
- Khamdeng Veterinary Clinic (021) 31-4575/(020) 31-4575

If worried about an expensive pedigree animal, or just one who is part of the family, there's Sri-Nakron Animal Hospital in Udon, tel: 00 66 42 32 7898. Restrictions on animal movement between countries exist, but nobody bothers much about a quiet cat or dog in the back of a car crossing the bridge.

UTILITIES

- Electricity: 220 volts. emergency number: 199
- Electricity payments and services: (021) 242 565
- Drinking water (bottle delivery): (021) 216 296, 217 130 (020) 770 5700

- Gas (cooking, bottle delivery): (021) 212 272, 219 806 (020) 55 13282, 55 16006
- Water (mains and bills): (021) 412 880-412 885
- Cable TV: (021) 452 558

INTERNATIONAL SCHOOLS

The name "International School" is used widely but not too well in Laos. The lack of good international education facilities ranks number two on the worries of expats living and working in Laos with their families. (The first is the poor medical facilities.) The problem gets greater the older your child is on entry.

The most frequent choice for parents wanting an International or English education for their English-speaking children is the:

Vientiane International School (VIS)

Located at Ban Saphantong Tai. Tel: (021) 313 606
Website: http://www.vislaopdr.com
Email: dragon@laotel.com

Most people and children say they are happy enough with this school and visits are easy to arrange with a phone call. The costs are somewhat less than the Bangkok equivalent, but are still high. The fees during 2007–8 were:

- Enrolment US$ 2,000
- Kindergarten (3 +) US$ 4,100 per year
- Primary US$ 8,400 per year
- Secondary US$ 9,200 per year
- Upper-Secondary US$ 10,206 per year

In this school, facilities exist to take the International Baccalaureate certification. It has a two-term system and semester starts from end August to June.

Panyathip Bilingual School

Website: http://.www.pbsedu.com
Tel: 413 259, 412 825, mobile: 580 3212

It features extra-curriculum language classes which includes Chinese.

Kiettisack International School

Tel/fax: 856-21-312383, mobile: 570 0308
Email: nagalao@yahoo.co.uk
Perfectly placed in Sokpaluang just across from the German Embassy, this school has around 60 per cent Lao students and is ideal if you are in the country for some time or have children of mixed parentage. It is also one of the cheapest international schools here and has one of the friendliest environments.

Their fees have not increased for ten years, but are currently around US$ 2,000 per year. The downside is that after grade 10 (at the moment) which means around 15–16 years of age, the children have to change school. The main advantage is that most of their students will turn out to be fluent in both English and Lao.

Vientiane Pattana School

Thai Airways Building, Louang Prabang Road. Tel: 219 498. This school is suitable for younger children not likely to stay in Laos beyond age 14.

Eastern Star Bilingual School

This school follows a Lao curriculum in English and team-teaches, with one foreign and one Lao teacher in each class. Classes are kept below 25 students. Most students are Lao. Tel: 261 614. Email: engine@esbs.edu.la

Ecole Hosset

If you want a good school cheap and your child speaks French, you can have the best in Vientiane at prices subsidised by France. This school is located at km3, Thadeua Road. Tel: 260 926. Website: http//www,ecolhosset.org

This large school will take in children of all nationalities—if they can follow instruction in French. English and Lao are also taught at the school (and your child may get to mix with some future important people). Admits children ages 3 to 18, and offers certification up to International Baccalaureate.

This is definitely the best value-for-money school. Francophone children from lower-income families may also be granted exceptional reductions on what are already some of the cheapest fees in Vientiane. In 2007, the cost of enrolment was US$ 200 and fees average US$ 2,440 a year, with senior secondary amounting to about US$ 3,290 per year.

Other schools often mean sending children away around age 14 or 15 if they are to continue education in English or another language with a view to attending university. The choice at the moment is limited. This is recognised by the many international schools in Bangkok and elsewhere in Thailand, which send "scouts" every year to Laos to recruit expatriate children for international schools in Thailand, often providing accommodation in a package.

HIGHER EDUCATION IN LAOS

- **National University of Laos**
  Laos has only one university. Most of its faculties and departments are at Dong Dok, some 20 km (12 miles) outside Vientiane, but some are in Vientiane town. The university has been greatly assisted in recent years by Japan, and the old-hand reference to the institution as "The Notional University of Laos" is no longer fully appropriate. For any foreigner seriously interested in the Lao language, there are comprehensive courses available.
  Tel: (021) 770 070

- **Lao-America College (LAC)**
  English-language medium. Designs special programmes of study for companies, ministries, projects. Private classes and tutoring arranged. Offers two degrees: Bachelor of Business Management, and Bachelor of Arts in English.
  Website:http://www.lac.edu.la
  Tel: 900 454-5. Email: lac@etllao.com

- **Unity School of Management**
  Nicely situated near km3. Mostly evening study. English and Lao medium. Students mostly Lao preparing for final accountancy or business external (UK) exams, which can be taken at the school or designated location.
  Tel: 314 150. Email: unity@laotel.com

- **Vientiane College**
  Located in Phonexay, with various adults and children teaching services. Distance education available, with overseas exam centres. Geared to Lao students but provides some resources of interest like consulting services which include interpreting, translation and editing.
  http://www.vientianecollege.laopdr.com
  Tel: 414 873, 414 052. Email: vtcollege@laopdr.com

EXPAT CLUBS

These have not developed to anything like the levels in Bangkok, where there is almost a club for every nationality. This is undoubtedly because the embassies in Vientiane have not developed to the level in Thailand, in fact many are represented in Laos only by the Bangkok embassy. Exceptions in Vientiane are the Australia Club, which for a couple of decades accepted just about all expats as members, but since January 2007 has closed its membership to any who are not Australian Embassy staff. There is also an International Women's Group which is largely Australian. The biggest group now catered for is the French, who may see public movies at the subsidised Alliance Francaise on Avenue Lane Xang. Many of those embassies present in Vientiane act as catalysts for social activities that usually go a bit beyond invitation of registered resident nationals to national day celebrations.

- **Vientiane Hash House Harriers**.
  Tel: (020) 7722 3867, 7721 7493.
- **Baseball or softball**. Tel: (020) 7787 3763.

LEARNING LAO AND TRANSLATION SERVICES

(See also: Higher Education). Many schools exist that are concerned with teaching English to Lao, some of these have facilities for foreigners wishing to learn Lao. These courses usually do not go far beyond beginner's level, but some schools can arrange to continue with one-to-one instruction or you make a personal arrangement with a teacher. Going to an English school for Lao means you meet many young Lao and can use them for practice. One centrally-located school regularly providing Lao language training courses for foreigners is (among others):

- **Phongsavan English Centre**.
  Opposite Parkview Hotel. Part of the Australian Centre for Languages group. Also provides translation services.
  Website:http://www.aclenglish.com
  Tel: 213 836, 215 731, 218 249
  Email: aclenglish@laopdr.com

Note: Many English-graduates from the National University provide private lessons and will come to your house. Some advertise (See: Places to Advertise). Many have no idea of teaching methods and some have difficulty with standard Lao. Try for a couple of hours before committing. Price guide: Westerners teaching English at VTE schools get US$ 5 to US$ 10 per hour; the lower end is reasonable for a good Lao teacher. While little is published in the Lao language, very basic children's books and some aids like flash cards for reading, intended to teach Lao to minorities, are useful. These are available at the Morning Market stalls.

EMBASSIES

These are listed in the *Yellow Pages* but not under the quick-find index—for some reason they are at the back of the Southern Provinces section. Some Embassies in Bangkok cover their countries' affairs in Laos by occasional visits. Where this is the case, another embassy often covers for the country regarding consular matters (getting married to a Lao, prison visits, sending passports for renewal, etc.). All ASEAN countries are represented. There is no single area of Vientiane where embassies group, although several are in the area near most Lao Ministries, between the Monument and That Luang.

- **Australia**
  Ban Phonxai (old British Embassy). Also covers consular matters for the UK, Canada and the Commonwealth countries (unless these are represented).
  Website: http://www.laos.embassy.gov.au
  Tel: 413 600, 413 805

- **France**
  Setthathirat (central). Tel: 215 258, 215 259
- **Germany**
  Sokpaluang. Tel: 312 111, 312 110
- **Japan**
  Ban Sisangvone. Tel: 414 400-3
- **Sweden**
  Wat Nak. Tel: 315 017-8
- **USA**
  That Dam (leading to Lane Xang Blvd).
  Tel: 213 966
  Website: http://www.usembassy.state.gov/laos

Government Institutions
Some useful contacts

- **National Assembly** (for its various committees)
  Tel: 413 518
- **Ethnic Affairs**
  Mr Khamphay Lathsamy, Tel: 413 539
- **Social-Cultural Affairs**
  Mr Doungdy Outhachak, Tel: 413 501
- **Law**
  Mr Thongteum Xayyasek, Tel: 413 536
- **Assurances Generales du Laos (AGL).**
  The only insurance company in Laos.
  Tel: (856-21) 215 903, 215 162
  Email: agl@aglallianz.com
- **Committee for Planning and Investment (CPI)**
  Tel: 217 020
- **Kaysone Phomvihane Museum**
  Tel: 911 215 (KM6)
- **National Museum**
  Sam Sen Thai. Near Lao Plaza Hotel.
- **Lao Chamber of Commerce and Industry**
  Tel: 219 223
- **Lao Trade Promotion Centre**
  Tel: 213 623, 216 207
- **National Library**
  Reading Room Service: Tel: 219 611

- **National Sports Committee**
  President: Dr Phoutong Sengakhom
  Tel: 217 357
- **Private Education Department**
  Tel: 212 120, 911 489

ADVERTISING

For small sales, word-of-mouth is still very much practiced. If you are looking for accommodation, a car, a language teacher, even a girlfriend, mention it to every Lao you chat with in every café you sit down in—leaving a mobile phone number. 'Wanted' notices take some time to have effect, so do not be surprised if months after you have bought a car, someone calls to offer you one. Best to take down such notices when they are no longer relevant. 'For Sale' notices should always carry a price or price range, mobile number, and if possible a picture: things for sale get far more response than things wanted. You may also pay for advertisements in:

- **Vientiane Times (English)**
  A daily paper except Sundays
  Tel: 216-364 (Ads)
  Website:http://www.vientianetimes.org.la
- **Le Renovateur (French)**
  A weekly published every Wednesday. This also contains some TV and radio programme information and what's on at the Alliance Francaise.
  Website:http://www.lerenovateur.org.la

For both of the above, go to the *Vientiane Times* office on the corner opposite Fountain Square. They can usually do things on the spot.

- **Minimarket windows.** Phimphone's, opposite the Khop Chai Deu, and her branches in Sam Sen Thai and elsewhere are still the main foreigner shopping centres. Notices are free for one week, by negotiation for long term. At the same time, place in the photo shop next door.

- **Internet Shop windows.** Particularly go for the row of shops just up from Khop Chai Deu.

BUSINESS CENTRES

There are as yet none on the Bangkok model, where you more or less rent an office and services for a temporary or longer period. The more expensive hotels (Lao Plaza, Settha Palace, Don Chan, Novotel) provide some services, often including translation, but if you just want to make photocopies, send faxes, make international calls, or use the computer or scanner, the better internet shops can often provide much cheaper services.

- **Hotel Novotel**
  The hotel has a dozen or so small business units, each with its own entrance into the car-park, one office room with a computer, telephone, desk, and attached large bedroom with ensuite. Although the prices vary and they are not cheap, there is still usually a waiting list.
- **Business Service Centre**
  This centre might be able to put you onto what you want. Tel: 263 102.

Security Services

Vientiane is a comparatively safe location, and most expatriates do not have guards on the gate. If you feel the need or have a company, try the following:
- Lao Guard Service Co. Tel: 260 586
- Lao Securicor. Tel: 351 070
- Lao Security Services. Tel: 412 592

ACCOMMODATION

Several hotels have furnished apartments to rent which may include use of swimming pool and facilities. (Count US$ 600–US$ 1,000 per month.) Apartments are useful if you are staying just a few months, but generally more expensive than a hotel room. One of the best in terms of being central and value for money is:

- **Hotel Lao**
  Heng Boun Road. Tel: 219 2801
  Email: hotellao@laotel.com

Agents
- **Peter's Rent-a-House**
  Tel: (020) 5552 6525
  Email: peter.rentahouse@gmail.com
- **Oudalee's House Renting**
  Tel: (020) 5551 2502, 5551 1791
  Email: oudalee_rangsy@yahoo.com
- **Tou Tou**
  Tel: (020) 5552 2142, 5510 0408, 7771 8417
  Email: TouTou2004@hotmail.com
- **Vientiane Property Service**
  Tel: (020) 5559 9900, 5561 9160
  Email: vientianerealtor@yahoo.com

Car Rental
- **Asia Vehicle Rental**
  Tel: 217 493, 223 687, (020) 5511070
  Website:http://www/avr.laopdr.com
  Email: avr@loxinfo.co.th

CHURCHES
- **International Church**
  English language service every Sunday, 10:00–11:00 am
  at ARDA Language Centre, near Novotel.
  Tel: 261 441
- **Catholic Centre**
  Samsenthai. Ban Kaonyot.
  Tel: 216 219
- **Lao Evangelical**
  Luang Pabang Road. Tel: 216 222
- **Seventh Day Adventist**
  Phonxay. Tel: 412 701

LIBRARIES

- **Vientiane Public Library**
  Lane Xang Avenue, on the same side as Royal Hotel, before
  the Monument. Opened every Monday to Saturday, from
  8:30 am to 6:00 pm.
- **National Library**
  Old Building facing Fountain Square.
  Opened from 9:00 am to 12:00pm and 1:30 pm to 4:30 pm
  everyday, except the 29th of each month. Reading rooms
  available.
  Tel: 219 611
- **Lao-Japan Centre Library**
  At the National University Dong Dok Campus.
  Opened every Monday to Friday, from 8:30 am to 7:30 pm,
  and Saturdays from 8:30 am to 5:00 pm.
- **French Language Centre (French books)**
  Opened every Monday to Friday 9:30 am to 6:30 pm, and
  Saturdays from 9:30 am to 4:30 pm.

BOOKSHOPS

- **Monument Books**
  Ban Mixay. A medium-sized airconditioned shop stocking
  new books. Cultural meetings and exhibitions take place
  upstairs.
  Tel: 243 708.
- **Book-Café Vientiane**
  Heng Boun Road, Ban Haysoke. Between Anou Hotel and
  Cultural Hall, next to the bank. Buys, sells and exchanges
  books in many languages. Maintains a selection of 3,000
  plus titles. English manager speaks English, French and
  Lao and knows his books. This café is well lit, organised,
  and comfortable. Opened daily, from 8:00 am to 8:00 pm.
  Tel: (020) 6689 3741.

FURTHER READING

Novels, accounts and travelogues set in Laos are very few. Some are politically charged. The following may be considered to cover the spectrum of useful background books available in English in Vientiane. To my knowledge, all are in print or in reprint and most are obtainable through the websites of Amazon, Marshall Cavendish, Asia Books, Silkworm and Borders, or obtained either directly or on order through Book-Café Vientiane and laoinsight@yahoo.com.

- Becker, Benjawan and Simmala, Buasavan, *Lao for Beginners**
- Bounyavong, Outhine, *Mother's Beloved Stories from Laos*
- Brown, Mervyn, *War in Shangri-La*
- Chamberlain, James, R. et al, *Indigenous Peoples Profile*
- Cheesman, Patricia, *Lao-Tai Textiles*
- Conroy, Paul, *Ten Months in Laos*
- Cooper, Robert, *Culture Shock! Laos**
- Cooper, Robert, *Laos Fact Book**
- Cooper, Robert, *Laos: Land of the sleeping bus**
- Cooper, Robert, *The Lao, Laos and You**
- Cooper, Robert, *The Hmong**
- Cotterill, Colin, the Dr Siri series of murder mysteries set in post revolutionary Laos. *The Coroner's Lunch, Thirty-Three Teeth, Disco for the Departed, Anarchy and Old Dogs, Curse of the Pogo Stick, The Merry Misogynist, Love Songs From a Shallow Grave**
- Dakin, Brett, *Another Quiet American*
- Danes, Kay, *Nightmare in Laos*
- Davidson, Alan, *Fish and Fish Dishes of Laos*
- Du Pont de Brie, Natasha, *Ant Egg Soup**
- Evans, Grant, *A Short History of Laos**
- Evans, Grant, *Laos: Culture and Society*
- Evans, Grant, *The Politics of Ritual and Remembrance*
- Fadiman, Anne, *The Spirit Catches You*
- Fox, Robert, *Red Flag, Blue Member*
- Halliday, John T., *Flying Through Midnight*
- Keay, John, *Mad About the Mekong**

- Kremner Christopher, *Bamboo Palace*
- Kremmer, Christopher, *Stalking the Elephant Kings**
- Lewis, Howard, *Twelve Years in Laos*
- Lewis, Norman, *A Dragon Apparent*
- Marcus, Russell, *English-Lao-English Dictionary*
- Murphy, Dervla, *One Foot in Laos*
- Nanthavongdouangsy, Viengkham, *Sinh and Lao Women*
- Ngaosyvathin, Mayoury, *Lao women: Yesterday and Today*
- Osborne, Milton, *Exploring Southeast Asia*
- Osborne, Milton, *The Mekong*
- Pholsena, Vattana, *Post-War Laos: The Politics of Culture*
- Pyle, Richard, Lost Over Laos
- Rehbein, Boike, Globalisation, Culture and Society in Laos
- Rigg, Jonathan, Living With Transition in Laos
- Robbins, Christopher, *The Ravens**
- Sing, Phia, *Traditional Recipes of Laos*
- Stuart-Fox, Martin, *A History of Laos*
- Stuart-Fox, Martin, *Buddhist Kingdom Marxist State*
- Stuart-Fox, Martin, *Historical Dictionary of Laos**
- Warner, Roger, *Shooting at the Moon*
- Yang, Sheng et al, *Cooking From The Heart: the Hmong Kitchen*

* Specially recommended to those new in Laos and those looking for readability with accuracy and objectivity within reason.

ABOUT THE AUTHOR

Robert Cooper in his WW2 jeep shortly before it caught fire and exploded in central Vientiane. After a lifetime in Laos and Thailand, researching Hmong and managing refugees, Dr Cooper, by formation an economic anthropolist, now lives in Vientiane. He currently manages the Book-Café Vientiane, the largest new and used bookshop in Laos, directs the Lao Insight Books publishing house producing books on Laos, and writes books. He is an Englishman who speaks French, Lao, Thai, Malay etc. and has been living in the area for 30 years. His other books include: *CultureShock! Thailand, Thais Mean Business, Thailand Beyond the Fringe, The Lao, Laos Fact Book, Laos: Land of the sleeping bus, The Hmong, Red Fox Goose Green* and *Red Flag.*

INDEX

Titles in the CultureShock! series:

Argentina	France	Portugal
Australia	Germany	Russia
Austria	Great Britain	San Francisco
Bahrain	Hawaii	Saudi Arabia
Beijing	Hong Kong	Scotland
Belgium	India	Shanghai
Berlin	Ireland	Singapore
Bolivia	Italy	South Africa
Borneo	Jakarta	Spain
Brazil	Japan	Sri Lanka
Bulgaria	Korea	Sweden
Cambodia	Laos	Switzerland
Canada	London	Syria
Chicago	Malaysia	Taiwan
Chile	Mauritius	Thailand
China	Morocco	Tokyo
Costa Rica	Munich	Travel Safe
Cuba	Myanmar	Turkey
Czech Republic	Netherlands	United Arab
Denmark	New Zealand	Emirates
Ecuador	Pakistan	USA
Egypt	Paris	Vancouver
Finland	Philippines	Venezuela

For more information about any of these titles, please contact any of our Marshall Cavendish offices around the world (listed on page ii) or visit our website at:

www.marshallcavendish.com/genref